THE WORKS
AND CORRESPONDENCE OF
DAVID RICARDO

VOLUME VII

PLAN OF THE EDITION

THE WORKS
AND CORRESPONDENCE OF
DAVID RICARDO

EDITED BY
PIERO SRAFFA
WITH THE COLLABORATION OF
M. H. DOBB

VOLUME VII

LETTERS 1816–1818

CAMBRIDGE
AT THE UNIVERSITY PRESS
FOR THE ROYAL ECONOMIC SOCIETY
1973

Published by the Syndics of the Cambridge University Press
Bentley House, 200 Euston Road, London NW1 2DB
American Branch: 32 East 57th Street, New York, N.Y. 10022

ISBN: 0 521 06072 9

First printed 1952
Reprinted 1962, 1973

Printed in Great Britain at the University Printing House, Cambridge
(Brooke Crutchley, University Printer)

CONTENTS OF VOLUME VII

LETTERS 1816–1818

* denotes letters not previously published

viii CONTENTS

PLATES

Gatcomb Park, Ricardo's country seat near Minchinhampton,
1814–1823 (from an engraving dated 1 Feb. 1825, in J. and
H. S. Storer's *Delineations of the County of Gloucester*)   *facing p.* 1

Autograph of Ricardo's letter to Mill, 20 Nov. 1816 (letter 189)
at the end of the volume

CALENDARS for 1816, 1817 and 1818

1816

	JAN.	FEB.	MAR.	APRIL	MAY	JUNE
S	- 7 14 21 28	- 4 11 18 25	- 3 10 17 24 31	- 7 14 21 28	5 12 19 26 -	2 9 16 23 30
M	1 8 15 22 29	- 5 12 19 26	- 4 11 18 25 -	1 8 15 22 29	6 13 20 27 -	3 10 17 24 -
Tu	2 9 16 23 30	- 6 13 20 27	- 5 12 19 26 -	2 9 16 23 30	7 14 21 28 -	4 11 18 25 -
W	3 10 17 24 31	- 7 14 21 28	- 6 13 20 27 -	3 10 17 24 -	1 8 15 22 29	5 12 19 26 -
Th	4 11 18 25 -	1 8 15 22 29	- 7 14 21 28 -	4 11 18 25 -	2 9 16 23 30	6 13 20 27 -
F	5 12 19 26 -	2 9 16 23 -	1 8 15 22 29 -	5 12 19 26 -	3 10 17 24 31	7 14 21 28 -
S	6 13 20 27 -	3 10 17 24 -	2 9 16 23 30 -	6 13 20 27 -	4 11 18 25 -	1 8 15 22 29 -

	JULY	AUG.	SEPT.	OCT.	NOV.	DEC.
S	- 7 14 21 28	4 11 18 25	1 8 15 22 29	- 6 13 20 27	- 3 10 17 24	1 8 15 22 29
M	1 8 15 22 29	5 12 19 26	2 9 16 23 30	- 7 14 21 28	- 4 11 18 25	2 9 16 23 30
Tu	2 9 16 23 30	- 6 13 20 27	3 10 17 24 -	1 8 15 22 29	- 5 12 19 26	3 10 17 24 31
W	3 10 17 24 31	- 7 14 21 28	4 11 18 25 -	2 9 16 23 30	- 6 13 20 27	4 11 18 25 -
Th	4 11 18 25 -	1 8 15 22 29	5 12 19 26 -	3 10 17 24 31	- 7 14 21 28	5 12 19 26 -
F	5 12 19 26 -	2 9 16 23 30	6 13 20 27 -	4 11 18 25 -	1 8 15 22 29	6 13 20 27 -
S	6 13 20 27 -	3 10 17 24 31	7 14 21 28 -	5 12 19 26 -	2 9 16 23 30	7 14 21 28 -

1817

	JAN.	FEB.	MAR.	APRIL	MAY	JUNE
S	- 5 12 19 26	- 2 9 16 23	- 2 9 16 23 30	- 6 13 20 21	- 4 11 18 25	1 8 15 22 29
M	- 6 13 20 27	- 3 10 17 24	- 3 10 17 24 31	- 7 14 21 28	- 5 12 19 26	2 9 16 23 30
Tu	- 7 14 21 28	- 4 11 18 25	- 4 11 18 25 -	1 8 15 22 29	- 6 13 20 27	3 10 17 24 -
W	1 8 15 22 29	- 5 12 19 26	- 5 12 19 26 -	2 9 16 23 30	- 7 14 21 28	4 11 18 25 -
Th	2 9 16 23 30	- 6 13 20 27	- 6 13 20 27 -	3 10 17 24 -	1 8 15 22 29	5 12 19 26 -
F	3 10 17 24 31	- 7 14 21 28	- 7 14 21 28 -	4 11 18 25 -	2 9 16 23 30	6 13 20 27 -
S	4 11 18 25 -	1 8 15 22 -	1 8 15 22 29 -	5 12 19 26 -	3 10 17 24 31	7 14 21 28 -

	JULY	AUG.	SEPT.	OCT.	NOV.	DEC.
S	- 6 13 20 27	- 3 10 17 24 31	- 7 14 21 28	- 5 12 19 26	- 2 9 16 23 30	- 7 14 21 28
M	- 7 14 21 28	- 4 11 18 25	1 8 15 22 29	- 6 13 20 27	- 3 10 17 24	1 8 15 22 29
Tu	1 8 15 22 29	- 5 12 19 26	2 9 16 23 30	- 7 14 21 28	- 4 11 18 25	2 9 16 23 30
W	2 9 16 23 30	- 6 13 20 27	3 10 17 24 -	1 8 15 22 29	- 5 12 19 26	3 10 17 24 31
Th	3 10 17 24 31	- 7 14 21 28	4 11 18 25 -	2 9 16 23 30	- 6 13 20 27	4 11 18 25 -
F	4 11 18 25 -	1 8 15 22 29	5 12 19 26 -	3 10 17 24 31	- 7 14 21 28	5 12 19 26 -
S	5 12 19 26 -	2 9 16 23 30	6 13 20 27 -	4 11 18 25 -	1 8 15 22 29	6 13 20 27 -

1818

	JAN.	FEB.	MAR.	APRIL	MAY	JUNE
S	- 4 11 18 25	1 8 15 22	1 8 15 22 29	- 5 12 19 26	- 3 10 17 24 31	- 7 14 21 28
M	- 5 12 19 26	2 9 16 23	2 9 16 23 30	- 6 13 20 27	- 4 11 18 25	1 8 15 22 29
Tu	- 6 13 20 27	3 10 17 24	3 10 17 24 31	- 7 14 21 28	- 5 12 19 26	2 9 16 23 30
W	- 7 14 21 28	4 11 18 25	4 11 18 25 -	1 8 15 22 29	- 6 13 20 27	3 10 17 24 -
Th	1 8 15 22 29	5 12 19 26	5 12 19 26 -	2 9 16 23 30	- 7 14 21 28	4 11 18 25 -
F	2 9 16 23 30	6 13 20 27	6 13 20 27 -	3 10 17 24 -	1 8 15 22 29	5 12 19 26 -
S	3 10 17 24 31	7 14 21 28	7 14 21 28 -	4 11 18 25 -	2 9 16 23 30	6 13 20 27 -

	JULY	AUG.	SEPT.	OCT.	NOV.	DEC.
S	- 5 12 19 26	- 2 9 16 23 30	- 6 13 20 27	4 11 18 25	1 8 15 22 29	- 6 13 20 27
M	- 6 13 20 27	- 3 10 17 24 31	- 7 14 21 28	- 5 12 19 26	2 9 16 23 30	- 7 14 21 28
Tu	- 7 14 21 28	- 4 11 18 25	1 8 15 22 29	- 6 13 20 27	3 10 17 24 -	1 8 15 22 29
W	1 8 15 22 29	- 5 12 19 26	2 9 16 23 30	- 7 14 21 28	4 11 18 25 -	2 9 16 23 30
Th	2 9 16 23 30	- 6 13 20 27	3 10 17 24 -	1 8 15 22 29	5 12 19 26 -	3 10 17 24 31
F	3 10 17 24 31	- 7 14 21 28	4 11 18 25 -	2 9 16 23 30	6 13 20 27 -	4 11 18 25 -
S	4 11 18 25 -	1 8 15 22 29	5 12 19 26 -	3 10 17 24 31	7 14 21 28 -	5 12 19 26 -

ABBREVIATIONS

R.P.   Ricardo Papers (consisting of letters received
                         by Ricardo, and other of his papers, in the
                         possession of Mr Frank Ricardo).

Mill-Ricardo papers   The letters and papers of Ricardo that belonged
                         to James Mill, and which passed into the pos-
                         session of the Cairnes family and Mr C. K. Mill.

'at Albury'   Papers in the possession of Mr Robert Malthus,
                         of The Cottage, Albury, Surrey.

The following abbreviations are used by Malthus, Mill and Bentham, respectively, in their letters:

E.I. Coll., for East India College, Haileybury.

E.I. House, for East India House, London.

Q.S.P., for Queen Square Place, Westminster.

GATCOMB PARK,

The Seat of David Ricardo Esq.ᵉ

To whom this plate is inscribed by P. & H. L. Foster.

Emery Walker Ltd ph. sc.

150. RICARDO TO MALTHUS[1]

[Reply to 146 & 148.—Answered by 152]

Gatcomb Park
2 Jan.ʸ 1816

My dear Sir

2 Jan. 1816

Your two letters have both reached me, and I am very sorry to find that I shall not have the pleasure of seeing you at Gatcomb this vacation.

I left London as you supposed the day after the Bank Court. I should have considered it fortunate if whilst I was there I had met you. My house in Brook Street is not yet in a state to receive us,[2] nor will it be this season, unless we consent to go in it with the walls unpapered and unpainted,— conditions to which we shall agree. It will be we are told in a habitable state by the latter end of the month, at which time we shall probably quit Gatcomb.

As you have not given me the pleasure of your company here, and as I wish to speak to Murray concerning my book, and to consult some Parliamentary papers which I have not got here, I intend taking a trip to town the beginning of next week. Do you think I shall have any chance of meeting you there? Remember that a letter will always find me at or follow me from the Stock Exchange.

It is exceedingly provoking that you should have been so much interrupted by College affairs as not to have made more progress with your new chapters. I shall regret your thinking it necessary to abridge or leave out any thing which

[1] Addressed: 'To / The Revᵈ T R Malthus / East India College / Hertford'.

MS at Albury.—*Letters to Malthus*, XLI.

[2] See below, p. 17.

2 Jan. 1816 you may have to say, connected with the subject,—and
particularly if you should so determine because more time
will otherwise be required before you can publish. The
question of bounties and restrictions is exceedingly important, and unless you have already given your present
opinions on that subject elsewhere, or mean to do so, it
ought to form part of the present work,—and a little delay
in the publication is not very important.

The edition which I have of your work is the first,[1] and it
is many years since I read it. When you wrote to me that
you were looking over the chapters on the Agricultural and
Manufacturing systems, with a view to make some alterations in them, I looked into those chapters and saw a great
deal in them which differed from the opinions I have formed
on that part of the subject. At your house I observed that in
a subsequent edition you had altered some of the passages to
which I particularly objected, and in the chapters as you are
now writing them it appeared to me that there was only a
slight trace of the difference we have often discussed. The
general impression which I retain of the book is excellent.
The doctrines appeared so clear and so satisfactorily laid
down that they excited an interest in me inferior only to that
produced by Adam Smith's celebrated work. I remember
mentioning to you, and I believe you told me that you had
altered it in the following editions, that I thought you argued

---

[1] As Empson points out (in
quoting this passage, *Edinburgh
Review*, Jan. 1837, p. 495), 'what
is here called the first edition is
evidently the edition of 1803',
that is to say, the second, in
which the discussion of the 'agricultural and commercial systems'
appears for the first time (Bk. III,
Chaps. VIII–IX). That Ricardo
did not possess the first edition
of the *Essay on Population* is also
shown by his having had to borrow it from Malthus for the use
of Francis Place when the latter
required it for preparing his reply
to Godwin (see Malthus to Place,
19 Feb. 1821, in *Letters to Malthus*, p. 207).

in some places as if the poor rates had no effect in increasing the quantity of food to be distributed[1]—that I thought you were bound to admit that the poor laws would increase the demand and consequently the supply. This admission does not weaken the grand point to be proved.

As for the difference between us on Profits of which you speak in your letter,[2]—you have not I think stated it correctly. You say that my opinion is "that General Profits never fall from a general fall of prices compared with labour, but from a general rise of labour compared with prices." I will not acknowledge this to be my proposition. I think that corn and labour are the variable commodities, and that other things neither rise nor fall but from difficulty or facility of production, or from some cause particularly affecting the value of money,—and that no alteration of price proceeding from these causes affect general profits;—allowing always some effect for cheapness of the raw material.

Mrs. Ricardo joins with me in kind regards to Mrs. Malthus.

Y^{rs} very truly

DAVID RICARDO

---

[1] The argument occurred in several passages of the early editions of the *Essay on Population*; some of these passages, but not all, were altered in the later editions. Cp. below, p. 202; and for references see E. Cannan, *History of the Theories of Production and Distribution*, pp. 238–40.
[2] Above, VI, 341–2.

151. MILL TO RICARDO[1]

[*Reply to* 149]

Ford Abbey Jany 3[d] 1816

My Dear Sir

3 Jan. 1816   I received your letter last night, and think it best to answer it without delay. It stands at present fixed that we shall leave this place about the 15th—But Mr. Bentham always lingers so long when he has a movement to make, that I do not expect we shall be in London much before the 1st of Febr[y.] You must not delay, therefore, till my arrival. But the time at which I think that my looking at the M.S. will stand the best chance of being useful, is when it is in the proofs; because I can then definitively take cognisance of the punctuation, which is of considerable importance—and was badly done by the printer in your last production.[2] I am satisfied that any thing else to which I should chuse to put my hand, for fear of doing more harm than good, is so trifling that it can be easily done in the proofs, with hardly any additional expence of correction, to which I shall not grudge to submit you. I am sure the matter will be all good—and that at most there will be but a few expressions in which I may fancy that I can alter a word or two for the better. In this case, the best thing for you will be to send the M.S. to the press immediately; and to tell Murray to send the proofs to me, as many at a time as the convenience of the printer will allow. Take care to send them by a coach which passes through Chard (not Ilminster or Axminster) otherwise I may be some days late in receiving them. One of the Chard coaches (perhaps both) takes parcels at the Gloucester Coffee House Piccadilly. But it is possible that before needing to send me

---

[1] Addressed: 'David Ricardo Esq / Gatcomb Park / Mincing Hampton / Gloucestershire'.—MS in *R.P.*   [2] *Essay on Profits.*

the proofs I may be in London. I am rejoiced that the whole may be published as it stands—and the only advice which I think I can offer, after what I have given, and which you have taken in so good part, is to dwell with some force upon the *moral* part of the argument against the Bank; which will not only afford a variety in the midst of the other more abstract and less familiar topics, but will really press with a more galling weight upon the parties concerned. Hold up to view unsparingly the infamy of a great and opulent body like the bank, exhibiting a wish to augment its hoards by undue gains wrested from the hands of an overburthened people.[1] Tell them, and tell them boldly, how much it would have become them,—amidst the lamentable and disgusting propensity, which distinguishes our countrymen, to prey upon the public—to exhibit to them an example which would have helped to put them to shame, (if that be a feeling of which they are capable), an example of the voluntary renunciation of all undue gettings at the expence of the public; and thus to have set their seal upon the infamy of those who follow the opposite course of making the public their prey. Do not dread the chance of any body advancing that you, as a loan contractor, and a successful one, are in the predicament which you condemn. The case is not so. You have gained nothing from the public, but under the fair laws of an open market, exposed to all the force of unrestrained competition. Your earnings are therefore your own, in the fairest and most honourable sense of the word, in the very same sense in which the gains of any man who makes rich by selling sugar or cloth to his countrymen, whether in their public or private capacity, are truly and honourably his own. Nor are your earnings greater than the superior industry and capacity which you have displayed—in a line in which capacity is

[1] Ricardo adopted this sentence almost verbatim, above, IV, 93.

3 Jan. 1816 calculated to produce more than ordinary effects—most fully entitle you to.

Nothing would be of more use, than the argument which I recommend to you to use against the bank, to lead the addle-headed public to reflect upon the essential distinction between your case and that of the men whose conduct you arraign.

You have cheered me exceedingly by your accounts of Mrs. Porter—because independently of the sufferings of so excellent a creature—I knew how impossible it was for any of you to be happy so long as she continued in so painful a state. As for that noble Esther—I know not how to express my admiration of her. She deserves something far more valuable than a crown of gold. She has it, in fact, in the recovery of that dear sister to whom she has sacrificed so much. I wish I knew a husband worthy of her—and since I cannot have her myself, that I had a son ready to become a candidate for those affections which are composed of so precious a metal. That is the true affection—the affection which shines forth in the day of adversity! How contentedly would that noble girl submit to every sacrifice and every exertion which the vicissitudes of human life can call for, in behalf of the man who by his worth and his affection should truly unite her being to his own—poverty, and rags, nay the severest labour to gain his bread, with him, would be to her a heaven, compared with canopies of state, deprived of him.

I think you will have reason by and bye, to think that I have, at any rate, no aversion to letter writing—which yet my friends, as they do complain, so they have but too much reason to complain of. However, lately, the pen runs when I sit down to write to [you]¹ and I have always made a long

¹ MS torn here and below.

letter before I can stop. As I h[ave] consumed all my other paper, too, I am forced to take a long sh[eet], for your punishment at least, if not for my own.

I am happy that you do not dislike my project of setting tasks to you. I know, from former experience, of how much use it is to one who is not hackneyed in the ways of putting his thoughts to paper, to have a limited part of a great and indefinite whole presented to him. If you approve of it, I shall take care to find you in topics, and you shall go on, from one to another, till you have gone over all the ground— and then it will be easy for you, by means of marginal contents, to take one comprehensive view of the whole, to marshal the host, and prepare it in the best possible manner for meeting the enemy—i.e.—the public eye. You were right to postpone every thing to the perfecting the M.S. of the intended publication. No doubt, you will be called upon, as you say, for the elucidation of price—because it is to tell how the events in question operate upon the relative proportions of exchangeable commodities, that is the problem to be solved. Therefore you are to set down every thing which that solution requires. Whatever the place in your ultimate work, in which it will be most convenient to distribute what you have to say on the *rationale* of price, to that place may hereafter be consigned, whatever may then be useful, of what you here bring forth.

My best regards to ladies and gentlemen of all sorts and sizes at Gatcomb. I hope Mrs. M. Ricardo has been benefited by its good air and all its other recommendations. I long to see what beautiful roses and lillies not to speak of other attractions, Miss R. is about to carry from the hills. As for Mrs. Ricardo—she will be happy, not when every body else is happy, but when it is impossible they should ever be otherwise—and as the greater part of her friends are as nearly

3 Jan. 1816 in that state as this jumble of a world permits any body's friends to be, I think I may congratulate her at this beginning of a new year.

> Believe me truly
> Yours
> J. MILL

If you leave London before I return to it, unless all the necessary communication has passed between us, it will be proper that you should give me notice, to prevent loss of time, in the possible delay of the receipt of letters. I shall let you immediately know of my arrival.[1]

152. MALTHUS TO RICARDO[2]

[*Reply to* 150.—*Answered by* 153]

E I Coll Jany 8th 1816

My dear Sir,

8 Jan. 1816   I am glad to hear you are coming to Town and hope you do not return before the beginning of next week, as I have some thoughts of being at the Club[3] next saturday, and of endeavouring to see you friday or that day. Let me have a line to say where you are likely to be, and when you leave London.

I think I shall follow your advice and take my time about the Edition I find Murray is not so impatient as I expected.

Can you give me a good reason why the money price of labour should rise because it is necessary to cultivate poorer land, and the *real* price of labour must fall.

---

[1] Bain quotes (*James Mill*, p. 153) the end-fragment of Ricardo's reply. It is dated January 1816, addressed to Mill at Ford Abbey, and reads: 'fill 8 pages in the Appendix, will that be too much?' This must refer to *Eco-* nomical and Secure Currency and not, as conjectured by Bain, to the *Principles*.

[2] Addressed: 'D. Ricardo Esqr / Stock Exchange / London'.
MS in *R.P.*

[3] The King of Clubs.

In the progress of cultivation, independently of any causes 8 Jan. 1816 but such progress, it appears to me that the money price of corn will rise, but not much, the money price of labour remain stationary nearly, and the money price of manufactured good fall from the fall of profits.

If farmers and landholders are obliged to pay more and more in parish rates for their labour, or employ more men than their farm naturally requires, will they be able to accumulate capital and purchase the other instruments necessary for cultivation.

In haste.

Ever truly Yours
T R MALTHUS.

153. RICARDO TO MALTHUS[1]

[Reply to 152]

London 10th Jany 1816—

My dear Sir

I arrived in town yesterday and found your letter at 10 Jan. 1816 the Stock Exchange. It is very uncertain whether I shall leave London to-morrow evening or monday evening. I am desirous of getting home on many accounts, but I may not be able to accomplish the business for which I came so soon as I expected and if I do not get it done by to-morrow it will in all probability detain me till monday. Thus then it is still uncertain whether we are to meet, and I do not exactly know how to make you acquainted with my movements. I will however let Mr. Murray know if I leave town to-morrow,— and if you are in the neighbourhood of Russell Square by

[1] Addressed: 'To / The Rev^d   MS at Albury.—*Letters to Mal-* T R Malthus/East India College /   *thus*, XLII. Hertford'.

sending to N.º 8 Montague Street (Mr. Basevis[1]) you will be sure to know. In the city at the Stock Exchange any of my brothers will inform you about me.

If I should not be gone will you do me the favor of dining with me on friday at Mr. Basevis,—his dinner hour is 6 oClock, and he begs me to say that he shall be much flattered by your favoring him with your company.

I was in hopes of finding you in London and of having the benefit of your opinion of my book[2] in its present state before I sent it to be printed. That advantage I must now forego, because I am desirous of getting it out before the meeting of Parliament, and have before experienced the inconvenience of too much hurry.

I cannot think it inconsistent to suppose that the money price of labour may rise when it is necessary to cultivate poorer land, whilst the real price may at the same time fall. Two opposite causes are influencing the price of labour one the enhanced price of some of the things on which wages are expended,—the other the fewer enjoyments which the labourer will have the power to command,—you think these may balance each other, or rather that the latter will prevail, I on the contrary think the former the most powerful in its effects. I must write a book to convince you.

I am glad you are not going to cut your next edition short.

Very truly Y[rs]

DAVID RICARDO

---

[1] George Basevi, sen. (1771–1851), a stockbroker, two sons of whom have been mentioned above (VI, 245, 250). In 1817, following his brother-in-law Isaac D'Israeli, he withdrew from the Jewish congregation of Bevis Marks, from which Ricardo had seceded many years before.

[2] *Economical and Secure Currency.*

154. TROWER TO RICARDO[1]

[*Reply to* 147.—*Answered by* 156]

Unsted Wood—Godalming—
Jan. 19—1816—

Dear Ricardo

Many thanks for your last kind letter. I had noticed 19 Jan. 1816
with pleasure the part you took in the discussion at the Bank
Court, and lamented the paper gave me so short an account
of what you said. Follow up your blow. I long to see that
proud presumptious city aristocracy humbled, and brought
down to its proper level; and were I not withdrawn from the
busy world I should like to fight with you, side by side, in so
good a cause—It is beyond indurance to be refused an insight
into the state of ones affairs, and to be told that duty demands
the denial. How did Mr. Bouverie acquit himself; a brother
of his is a neighbour of mine, and I was lately speaking with
him on the subject—The *inward quaking* of which you complain, be assured is experienced more or less by almost every
speaker, who addresses a public assembly; and I verily
believe, that those who have not feeling sufficient to be so
affected, are deficient in an essential requisite to public
speaking. Practice and habit will, no doubt, by degrees wear
away the impression, but its existence evinces a *sensibility*
without which no man will address an assembly to any good
purpose.—

I am rejoiced to find you are preparing to meet the public
eye in another way. Be sure to send me a copy the instant
it comes out.—You do right, I think, not to say much
on the Bullion question, as standing by itself, but, of
course you will take care not to pass it over in such a way

---

[1] Addressed: 'To/David Ricardo Esqr/Gatcomb Park/Minchinhamp-
ton / Glocestershire'. London postmark, 22 Jan. 1816.—MS in *R.P.*

19 Jan. 1816 as to lead its enemies to say you have abandoned it to its fate.—

What think you of the Savings Banks? If you can send me any information on the subject, pray do. I consider them as very important means, under good management, of improving both the condition and the morals of the poor. They would ultimately too go far to diminish the pressure of the Poors Rates, and would, I should hope, gradually supersede the Benefit Societies, to which I think there are some serious objections, although highly useful in many respects. I am collecting what information I can on the subject with a view of seeing whether on a small scale it will be practicable to establish one in this neighbourhood. But I am doubtful how far I may be able to rouse my neighbours to the exertions necessary to its successful establishment.—

I begin to look with interest to the meeting of Parliament. Many schemes are said to be in contemplation. But probably with little truth. An alteration in the Poor Laws, in the Tithes &c. &c. I trust Government will not be mad enough to touch the sinking fund. Let them have a little patience, wait for a year or two, and they may then draw upon it safely and advantageously; but to attempt it at present would be very mischievous—What think you of the probable prices of the Funds? Shall we have any more Loans? The Doctrines I preach upon the subject of the price of the produce of Land are very unpopular *here*, and occasion my neighbours to stare at me, now and then for an ass or a madman. However, I still hope no attempts will be made to bolster up the prices—The landed interest ought to look for relief not to an *encrease of prices* but to a *decrease of charges* on their estates, and this is what must eventually happen.—

Is it true, that I am to congratulate you on the marriage

of another daughter?[1] If so, I should rather condole with you, for the loss you will sustain. For how must the absence of two such daughters darken your whole house. Surely one's children are the lamps that light us to our happiness; and their separation, is as the going down of the Sun, converting day into night.—

When do you return to London—I have heard strange tidings of your house in Brook Street, tumbling about your ears. Report is a lying jade, and I hope she'll prove so in this instance, but I shall be anxious to find it contradicted by yourself, for it would be a most unpardonable neglect in your Surveyor, and a most serious inconvenience and expence to you. We shall probably go to Town for a few weeks after Easter, when I hope we shall frequently meet.

Mrs. Trower unites with me in kind remembrances to Mrs. Ricardo and your family and I remain Dear Ricardo

Yrs very Sincerely

HUTCHES TROWER.

155. RICARDO TO MURRAY[2]

Gatcomb Park, Minchinhampton
2ᵈ Febʸ 1816

Dear Sir

All the proofs have been returned by yesterday's coach to Mr. Davison,[3] so that I hope no further delay will take place in the publication of the pamphlet. For the title page I have referred him to you fearing that in my hurry I might not copy it exactly according to the advertisement.[4]

[1] Priscilla, who married Anthony Austin on 11 April 1816.
[2] Addressed: 'J. Murray Esqʳ/ Albermale Street / London'.
   MS in the possession of Sir John Murray.
[3] T. Davison, the printer.
[4] 'On the 1st of February will be published, Proposals for an Economical and Secure Currency, with Observations on the Profits of the Bank of England, as they

2 Feb. 1816   Have the goodness to enquire whether Mr. Davison has received the parcel.

It would give me great concern if you should be a loser by this publication, and you would much relieve my mind, if, in case of loss, you would allow me to bear the charge, particularly as the number of copies I shall want for my friends is, under any circumstances, unreasonably large. The deficiency will probably not be very great, but whatever it may be you must allow me to pay it. I shall be in London on tuesday. I subjoin a list of those to whom I wish copies sent.

I am Dear Sir
Your obed. Servant
DAVID RICARDO

G. Basevi	
M. Ricardo	Bow Middx
F. and R. Ricardo[1]	Stock Exchange
Francis Baily[2]	D?
Ch⁵ Laurence[3]	D?
Ch⁵ Stokes	D?
T. F. Ellis	D?
R. W. Wade[4]	D?
D. Samuda	Fountain Court, Old Bethlem
James Mill	Queen Square Westminster
J. Bentham	D?
Whishaw	

regard the Public and the Proprietors of Bank Stock. By David Ricardo, Esq. Printed for John Murray, Albemarle-street.' (Advt. in *The Times*, 22 Jan. 1816.)
[1] '38 Hatton Garden' is del. here.

[2] The astronomer and stockbroker.
[3] Chairman of the Committee of the Stock Exchange.
[4] Secretary to the Committee of the Stock Exchange.

Rev. T. R. Malthus   2 Feb. 1816
Tho.ˢ Smith   Easton Gray, Tetbury, Glostershire
Hutches Trower   Unsted Wood, Godalming Surry
C. H. Hancock, to the care of C. Nairne, Stock Exchᵍ.ᵉ
I. Keyser   Finch Lane Cornhill
Jos. Ricardo   D.º
Pascoe Grenfell   Spring Garden
C. Terry.¹   Stock Exchᵍ.ᵉ
Honb.ˡᵉ Mr. Bouverie² { I believe he is in some Banking house
                      { in the Strand.—
What an unconscionable number!

156. RICARDO TO TROWER³

[Reply to 154.—*Answered by* 159]*

                                    [Gatcomb Park, *ca.* 4 Feb. 1816]⁴
Dear Trower

    I ought to have answered your kind letter before but   4 Feb. 1816
I have been much engaged and perplexed by sundry domestic
affairs, as well as with the printing of my pamphlet⁵—besides
which I have been staying some time at Bath with my eldest
daughter.⁶

    The Bank Directors have, I fear, too much influence to
give us any hope of outvoting them in a general Court. They
would however be very much discomposed by repeated
attacks, particularly as reason and justice are so evidently

---

¹ See above, VI, 277, n. 3.
² See above, VI, 277, n. 2.
³ Addressed: 'Hutches Trower,
Esqʳ/Unsted Wood/Godalming/
Surry'.
    MS at University College, Lon-
don.—*Letters to Trower*, VII,
where it is dated 'London, February 6, 1816'.   (

⁴ Omitted in MS.—Postmarks:
Minchinhampton, undated; London, 5 Feb. 1816. Ricardo says
below that his pamphlet 'will be
out on monday'; on Saturday,
4 February, he was still at Gatcomb (cp. below, p. 18).
⁵ *Economical and Secure Currency.*
⁶ Henrietta (Mrs Clutterbuck).

4 Feb. 1816 against them. I wish some of the independent proprietors would try the question in a court of justice, for to my plain understanding the law also is against the directors. I wish you *would* fight side by side with me, and would infuse a little of your energy into some of the proprietors who think correctly; but are lukewarm from natural timidity. Mr. Bouverie is not a good speaker—he makes but little impression on his hearers from want of animation and warmth.

My pamphlet will be out on monday.[1] I have directed Mr. Murray to send you a copy immediately after it is published.

You ask my opinion of the saving Banks. I think them excellent institutions and calculated to improve the condition and morals of the poor, provided they are properly managed. My fear is that though they will at first be established by gentlemen of great respectability and fortune,—as they spread, they will at last be undertaken by speculative tradesmen, as a business from which to derive profit. The poor should have some check on the employment of the funds, or the same evils will arise as from the indefinite multiplication of country Banks.

This check should be afforded by the legislature, or there will be no security against the failure of the undertakers. The poor have no means of discovering the wealth and respectability of the parties who open these Banks.

The low price of corn is an evil to the landed gentlemen which no decrease of charges can wholly compensate—they must submit to a fall of rents and they ought to rejoice in the evidence which the low price of produce affords of the yet unexhausted state of the resources of the country. High rents are always a symptom of an approach to the stationary state

[1] 6 February.

—we are happily yet in the progressive state, and may look forward with confidence to a long course of prosperity. It is difficult to persuade the country gentlemen that the fall of rents, unaccompanied by loss of capital and population, will essentially contribute to the general welfare, and that their interest and that of the public are frequently in direct opposition.

I hope the minister will not now touch the sinking fund— I hope he will never touch it. It is the general saving bank of the Nation and should be encouraged on the same principles as encouragement is given to those institutions. I am sorry to observe that amongst those who have the power to decide on these matters there does not appear any reluctance to meddle with the sinking fund. I am told that Lord Grenville is not averse to such a measure.

It is true that I am going to lose another daughter. If she be happy I must not repine—yet both Mrs. Ricardo and myself have felt, and do still feel, that in losing the society of these dear girls we have lost a portion of our happiness.

Report has spoken truth concerning my house in Brook Street. We observed a large crack in the ceiling of the drawing room last winter. I sent for Mr. Cockerell,[1] he said it must be looked to when we left it for the summer, but that it was perfectly safe then. We have since found that we were in the utmost hazard—that Mayor of whom I bought the house was a complete knave, and from the holes in the chimnies, and the communication between them and the beams, he perhaps intended that it should be destroyed by fire, so that

---

[1] Samuel Pepys Cockerell (1754–1827), architect. He had been employed by Ricardo in altering the house in Upper Brook Street before he moved in. (Letter from Cockerell to Ricardo, 2 Dec.1811, in *R.P.*)

4 Feb. 1816 no one might ever find out the total insufficiency of the materials to support the house. What must I think of Mr. Cockerell whom I paid to examine it? What compensation can he make me for his shameful neglect? I have not seen him since the discovery. The workmen have been in it ever since July, and it will cost me several thousand Pounds. We go into it on tuesday next but are obliged to be satisfied with the newly plaistered walls, unpapered and unpainted, or we must not have gone into it this season.

I am glad to hear that you will probably pass some time in London after Easter. I hope I shall see more of you than I did last year. Mrs. Ricardo and my family unite with me in kind regards to Mrs. Trower.

Very truly yours
DAVID RICARDO

157. RICARDO TO MALTHUS[1]
[*Answered by* 158]

My dear Sir   London 7 feb.ʸ 1816

7 Feb. 1816   I arrived in town yesterday, with the whole of my numerous family. We are already as comfortably settled in Brook Street as under all circumstances we can expect, and I hasten to inform you that we have a bed ready for you, which I hope you will very soon occupy. I have forgotten on which Saturday in the month you meet at the King of Clubs, but conclude from your last meeting that it is the 2ᵈ. If so you will probably be in town to-morrow, or friday, when I shall hope that you will lodge at our house, and give

---

[1] Addressed: 'To / The Revᵈ   MS at Albury.—*Letters to Mal-*
T R Malthus / East India College /   *thus*, XLIII.
Hertford'.

us as much of your company as your numerous friends will allow you to do.—

You have probably ere this seen my book[1]—I have been reading it in its present dress, and very much lament that I make no progress in the very difficult art of composition. I believe that ought to be my study before I intrude any more of my crude notions on the public.

It is said that the Bank have made some agreement with Government, but what it is is not exactly known. They talk of the Bank advancing to Government 6 millions at 4 pc.^{t}—, besides continuing the loan of 3 millions without interest. We shall not however be long in suspence on this subject, as a general court of Proprietors is to be held to-morrow when the Directors will make some communication to the proprietors, and ask for their vote to sanction their agreement. They will ask for this without giving them any information, either respecting their savings, their profits, or the amount of public deposits.—Is not this a ridiculous piece of mockery, and an insult to our common sense? I hope there may be a few independent proprietors present who may call for information,—or who may at least demand a ballot—for which purpose 9 only are necessary.—You would be surprised at the abjectness of the city men, and the great influence which the directors have in consequence of their powers of discounting bills. I am persuaded many of the proprietors would vote very differently at a ballot, to what they would by a shew of hands.[2]—

---

[1] *Economical and Secure Currency*.

[2] At the Bank Court which was held on 8 February the Governor announced the proposed advances, which were as anticipated. Ricardo, who was present, asked a question but obtained no information. According to *The Times* of the following day 'only two or three hands' were held against the motion of the Governor—presumably those of Ricardo, Grenfell and Bouverie who were the hostile speakers. See above, V, 465 and IV, 88, n.

7 Feb. 1816   I have not thought much on our old subject,—my difficulty is in so presenting it to the minds of others as to make
them fall into the same chain of thinking as myself.—If I
could overcome the obstacles in the way of giving a clear
insight into the origin and law of relative or exchangeable
value I should have gained half the battle.—

Mrs. Ricardo joins with me in kind regards to Mrs.
Malthus.

Very truly Yours
DAVID RICARDO

158. MALTHUS TO RICARDO[1]
[Reply to 157.—Answered by 160]

My dear Sir,   E I Coll Feby 9th 1816

9 Feb. 1816   I am much obliged to you for your kind invitation,
which I should have accepted with much pleasure, if I had
been coming to Town; but probably you will have heard by
this time that the Club was last saturday, upon a new arrangement of being the first saturday in the month instead of the
last. I was not present, most of our body being unwell with
colds, and Professors not being to be spared.

I have read your pamphlet, and do not think that you have
reason to be dissatisfied with it. It seems all to be very clear
and good, and I should not wonder if it were very successful.
My only doubt with respect to the former part of it, is the one
I expressed to you, that is, whether if there were no metallic
circulation, there would not be occasionally great variations
in the value of the precious metals, from a great demand.

I was sorry to see by todays papers that so little could be

---

[1] Addressed: 'D. Ricardo Esqr / Upper Brook Street / Grosvenor
Square'.—MS in *R.P.*

done at the Bank Court. I conclude however that the business 9 Feb. 1816
is given very shortly in the Chronicle; but from the conclusion it appears that the Directors carry everything their own way without difficulty.

I have almost determined to extend my new edition[1] to another volume; but I have been doing nothing at it lately, having been compelled to be thinking of drawing up something about the College.

The Post waits. Ever truly Yours

T R MALTHUS

159. TROWER TO RICARDO[2]

[Reply to 156.—*Answered by* 161]

Dear Ricardo
Unsted Wood. Febry 20—1816.

I am much obliged to you for your Pamphlet, which 20 Feb. 1816
I have read with great interest, and the opinions of which I entirely approve. I do not flatter myself however, that the subject is yet sufficiently understood by those in authority to induce them to adopt the simple, yet important expedients you suggest. The adopting Silver as the measure of value instead of Gold, although carrying with it the advantages you state,[3] is so entirely opposed to the plan proposed by the late Earl of Liverpool that that circumstance of itself is sufficient to indispose Ministers to it. The regulation making it obligatory on the banks to receive Bullion, under the circumstances you propose, would, I am persuaded, completely keep our circulating medium at its proper level; and prevent the occasional mischievous drains upon the Bank for specie;

---

[1] Of the *Essay on Population*; see below, p. 123-4.
[2] Addressed: 'To/David Ricardo
Esqr / Upper Brook Street / Grosvenor Square'.—MS in *R.P.*
[3] Above, IV, 63.

20 Feb. 1816 which no other expedient can prevent. It carries on the face
of it however so great an innovation as no doubt to startle
those who have not well weighed its effects. The arrangement with respect to the delivery of the dividend warrants
is at once simple and efficacious for the removal of what
certainly is a very serious inconvenience;[1] but which I believe
is neither felt nor understood by those whose avocations
have not given them an opportunity of observing its practical
effects. It would however *commit* the Bank to the payment
of the Dividends before they actually receive the money from
Government, which is contrary to the general rule followed
by them. This however forms no objection of consequence
and might be obviated—Your case against the Bank is most
triumphant, and I admire much the ingenuity and dexterity
with which you have so compleatly established it. In the
debate, which has taken place in the House of Commons on
Mr. Grenfell's motion[2], not a single attempt has been made
to answer any one of your positions—And, I have no doubt,
that the arrangement between Government and the Bank has
been hurried up expressly to prevent the effect, which must
otherwise have been produced on the discussion of Grenfells
motion. But, let not the Bank imagine, that the Public will
be satisfied with this arrangement as an adequate compensation for the claims we have upon them. Our hands must be
thrust constantly into their pockets till we have taken there-
from what is honestly our due. This mode of proceeding
I should deem preferable to taking the public money out of
their hands, and disposing of it in the manner you suggest,[3]
which might expose us to dangers in the management from
which we are at present undoubtedly protected—I see no

[1] See above, IV, 74.
[2] For the appointment of a select
committee 'to enquire into the
engagements now subsisting between the public and the Bank of
England', on 13 February.
[3] Above, IV, 85–6.

fault to be found in the style of your pamphlet. The case is clearly and forcibly stated, and must carry conviction to those acquainted with the subject. Some parts perhaps might have been more dilated, and some alterations in the few first pages might have improved the construction of your sentences. Excuse the freedom with which I thus express my sentiments on your performance, and consider it I beseech you as a proof of the interest which I feel in what is of so much importance to yourself.

I am very busy arranging the plan of a Provident Fund in this neighbourhood,[1] which I have submitted to our Lord Lieutenant Lord Midleton. I have taken the Bath Institution for my model, but have made what I consider some important alterations. I propose investing the Deposits in 3 pC. in the names of Trustees making the Depositors proportional proprietors, and deducting $\frac{1}{5}$ of dividend to pay necessary expences. As it is essential to the success of these institutions that they should support themselves—

I have scarcely left room to give our united kind remembrances to Mrs. R. and family and to say I am

Ys very sincerely
HUTCHES TROWER.

160. RICARDO TO MALTHUS[2]
[Reply to 158]

London 23ᵈ feb 1816

My dear Sir

I beg to remind you that the first saturday in the next month is to-morrow sen-night, on which day, or a few days

---

[1] The Godalming Savings Bank, established 15 April 1816 (J. T. Pratt, *History of Savings Banks*, 1830, p. 189).

[2] Addressed: 'Revᵈ T R Malthus / East India College / Hertford'; on the back a list of books ('Hamilton on National debts.

23 Feb. 1816 before it, I hope to have the pleasure of seeing you in Brook Street. We have a bed always at your service, and I wish you would make the rule invariable, to take up your lodging with us whenever you visit London.

I hope you have quite determined to extend your new edition to another volume, and that you are now making great progress in it. I wish much to see a regular and connected statement of your opinions on what I deem the most difficult, and perhaps the most important topic of Political Economy, namely the progress of a country in wealth and the laws by which the increasing produce is distributed.

Have you seen Torrens' Letter to Lord Liverpool?[1]—He appears to me to have adopted all my views respecting profits and rent; and in some conversation which I had with him a few days ago, he unequivocally avowed that he was now of my opinion, that the price of labour, arising from a difficulty in procuring food, did not affect the prices of commodities. He confessed that his former view on that subject was erroneous.

I should be glad to see all the arguments in favor of my view of the question clearly and ably stated. I should not wonder if Torrens undertook it.

The sale of my last pamphlet[2] has far exceeded its merits. Murray is printing a second edition. I had no idea that the subject was of much interest to the public, but it seems that they are curious about the amount of the Bank treasure. In

Price current. Philanthropist. Stewarts lives. Arthur Young letter') and some calculations and rough notes on profits and wages are scribbled in Malthus's handwriting.

MS at Albury.—*Letters to Malthus*, XLIV.

[1] *A Letter to the Rt. Hon. the*

Earl of Liverpool on the State of the Agriculture of the United Kingdom, and on the Means of Relieving the Present Distress of the Farmer, and of securing him against the Recurrence of similar Embarrassment, by R. Torrens, London, Hatchard, 1816.

[2] *Economical and Secure Currency.*

the house of Commons the defence[1] of the contracts with 23 Feb. 1816
the Bank was very little satisfactory—they endeavored to
fix the attention of the house on what the public had got and
saved by the operations of the Bank—they seemed to think
that all the rest belonged of right to the Bank.

Will ministers be able to carry the income tax?[2]

Very truly Yours

DAVID RICARDO

161. RICARDO TO TROWER[3]

[*Reply to* 159]

London 9ᵗʰ March 1816

Dear Trower

The approbation which you express of the general 9 March 1816
subject of my pamphlet could not fail to give me much
pleasure,—but I should have been equally obliged to you for
your opinion if it had not been favourable. Truth is my
object, and if I can succeed in promoting the establishment
of right principles it cannot fail to give me satisfaction—yet
I hope I shall not be unwilling to profit from the just
criticism of those who differ from me, and to adopt more
correct views when they are fairly set before me.

I have been agreeably disappointed in the interest which
my book has excited. It has very unexpectedly to me gone
to a second edition, and is much better understood than the
more difficult subject on which I before attempted to give my
opinion. Mr. Grenfell has published his speech which I heard

[1] Against Grenfell's attack, on 13 February.
[2] The proposal to continue the Income Tax, which had originally been adopted as a war measure, was finally rejected by the House of Commons on 18 March.

[3] Addressed: 'Hutches Trower Esqʳ/ Unsted Wood/Godalming/ Surry'.
MS at University College, London.—*Letters to Trower*, VIII.

9 March 1816 him deliver.[1] It is very clear and satisfactory, but our joint efforts will I fear be of little use. The accumulated treasure of the Bank must however one day be divided, and so confident are some that a bonus, or increase of dividend, will be paid next April, that they venture to make even bets on the subject. I shall however not be satisfied without a statement of accounts,—and I can see no good reason why they should be withheld.—

I hope your efforts will succeed in establishing a saving bank in your neighbourhood. Their general diffusion in all parts of the kingdom will be of great service, if the rich and well informed will continue to bestow some attention on them. They will tend to introduce economy and forethought amongst the poor, which may in time check the propensity to a too abundant population, the great source from whence all the miseries of the poor flow in so profuse a stream. The quakers, who are a very benevolent people, are about to open a saving bank in the populous borough of Southwark, from which they anticipate the happiest effects. On my return to the country we shall attempt a similar establishment in our district.[2] I hope you will have a perfect model to offer me.

Mr. Malthus has been staying a few days with me. The disgraceful disturbances at the College,[3] have very much interfered with his leisure, which I very much regret, as he has been prevented from proceeding with the work which he has in hand. He is yet doubtful whether he shall add an additional volume to his Essay on Population, or whether he shall publish a separate and independent work, containing his present views on the interesting subjects of Agriculture and

---

[1] *The Speech of Pascoe Grenfell, Esq. in the House of Commons, on Tuesday, the 13th of February, 1816, on certain Transactions subsisting betwixt the Public & the* Bank of England. With an Appendix, London, Murray, 1816.
[2] See below, p. 220.
[3] See above, VI, 341.

Manufactures, and the encouragement which is afforded 9 March 1816
them by natural and artificial causes. Mr. Western appears
to me to hold very incorrect opinions, yet they are applauded
by many in the House of Commons.¹

I am glad to hear from Mr. Turner² that we shall soon see
you in London. I hope you will bring up a petition with you
against the property tax. It is more objectionable I think as
a 5 pc^t than as a 10 pc^t tax, yet I would willingly submit to
it if I thought that it would really end in two years. The
machinery of it is too easily worked to allow it to be at the
disposal of our extravagant ministers during a period of
peace. Mrs. Ricardo unites with me in kind remembrances
to Mrs. Trower.

Ever truly yours
DAVID RICARDO

162. RICARDO TO MALTHUS³

[*Answered by* 163]

My dear Sir

London 24th April 1816

It is not too soon to remind you that Mrs. Ricardo and 24 April 1816
I expect to have the pleasure of Mrs. Malthus' and your company at our house on your visit to London in the next week.
—I hope it will be early in the week, and that you will not
be in so great a hurry to get home as you usually are. On
the monday, after your club meeting, I shall ask a few of your
and my friends to meet you at dinner, and on sunday, or any

---

¹ C. C. Western had moved in
the House of Commons on 7
March 1816 a series of resolutions for the relief of agriculture.
² Samuel Turner, F.R.S., a Bank
Director, was Trower's brother-
in-law.

³ Addressed: 'To / The Rev^d T R
Malthus / East India College /
Hertford'.
MS at Albury.—*Letters to Mal-
thus*, XLVI.

24 April 1816 other day, perhaps Warburton and Mill will take a family meal with us.

I have just received an invitation from Mr. Blake to dine with him on friday the 3^d May, and I have taken upon myself to let you know from him that he hopes you will favor him with your company on that day. You will I trust be also agreeable to this arrangement.

I hope you have made better use of your time than I have done of mine, and that you are making rapid advances with the different works which you have in hand. I have done nothing since I saw you as I have been obliged to go very often into the city, and after leaving off for a day or two I have the greatest disinclination to commence work again. I may continue to amuse myself with my speculations, but I do not think I shall ever proceed further. Obstacles almost invincible oppose themselves to my progress, and I find the greatest difficulty to avoid confusion in the most simple of my statements.

Have you seen Torrens letters to the Earl of Lauderdale in the Sun? I think he has published 5. They are chiefly on the subject of currency and are ingenious, though I think they support some very incorrect doctrines. They are signed with his name.[1]—

Horner I understand will oppose the continuance of the restriction bill—he does not deny now the fall in the value of gold and silver since the termination of the war. There can not be a better opportunity than the present for the Bank to recommence payments in specie. Silver is actually under the

---

[1] The letters, under the heading 'National Currency', had been published in the *Sun* ('a paper that *appears* daily but never *shines*', according to the *Edinburgh Review*, May 1823, p. 368) from 18 to 23 April; a sixth and last letter appeared on 30 April. Torrens's object, as stated in the first letter, was to show 'the expediency of continuing the restriction of cash payments, and of rendering silver the standard of our currency'.

mintprice. The change is surprising [and has been] [1] brought 24 April 1816
about in a very unexpected [manner].

Mrs. Ricardo joins with me [in] kind regards to Mrs.
Malthus.

Very truly Yours

DAVID RICARDO

163. MALTHUS TO RICARDO [2]

[*Reply to* 162]

E I Coll April 28th 1816

My dear Sir,

I could not write on friday, and the intervention of 28 April 1816
saturday has delayed my answer another day. I shall have
great pleasure in being with you in Brook Street, the end of
the week, but I fear it must be for a shorter, rather than a
longer time than usual; and Mrs. Malthus is expecting her
father, and will not be able to accept Mrs. Ricardo's kind
invitation. I shall be very happy to dine with Mr. Blake on
friday if I can get to Town on that day, but it is not quite
certain; and perhaps Mr. Blake will have the goodness to
allow the engagement to remain in this state. I think it
probable that I may be obliged to return on monday. I would
not wish you therefore to ask a party on my account on that
day; but I shall be very happy to meet Mr. Mill and Mr. Warburton on sunday. With a view to any discussion on subjects
of Political Economy it is difficult to proceed with a party of
more than three or four.

You say nothing of your daughter's marriage. [3] I understand they are gone to spend a short time abroad, which I
think is a very agreeable plan. I hope they set off in good

---

[1] MS torn here and below. Square'.—MS in *R.P.*
[2] Addressed: 'D. Ricardo Esqr / [3] See above, p. 13, n. 1.
Upper Brook Street / Grosvenor

28 April 1816 spirits, and that you have had favourable accounts from them since. You and Mrs. Ricardo must necessarily feel the vacancy in your family occasioned by the separation of your two amiable and accomplished eldest daughters, so soon after each other; but they will both be settled so near you, as to make up in the best manner possible for their loss from the domestic circle.

I hardly ever meet with the *Sun*, and have not therefore seen Torrens letters. I hope the third reading of the Restriction bill will not take place tomorrow, as it will be awkward for Horner's motion to come on after the question of Restriction has been decided.[1] I really think that if we don't pay in Specie now, we shall never do it. In the present temper of the Country with regard to Currency, I should not wonder, if a fresh separation between gold and paper should take place, and the ministers should encourage it, as a preparation for an alteration in the coinage.

I have not been a bit more diligent than you. Having given up the idea of a new edition[2] this season, I suppose I have thought myself privileged to be idle. At least I can give no other account of the matter.

I cannot help thinking that the reason why with your clear head, you find a difficulty in your progress is that you are got a little into a wrong track. On the subject of determining all prices by labour, and excluding capital from the operation of the great principle of supply and demand, I think you must have swerved a little from the right course. But on this point of course you differ from me.

---

[1] On 1 May Horner moved 'that a select committee be appointed to enquire into the expediency of restoring the Cash Payments of the Bank of England'; the motion was defeated by 146 votes to 73. The third reading of the bill to continue the Bank Restriction for two years took place on 3 May.
[2] Of the *Essay on Population*.

Mrs. Malthus begs to be kindly remembered to Mrs. 28 April 1816
Ricardo.

Ever truly Yours

T R MALTHUS

164. CROMBIE TO RICARDO[1]

Sir

Major Torrens has done me a favour, by sending you 1 May 1816
a copy of my pamphlet.[2] Had I been aware, that a production
of so little value would have been acceptable, I should have
the pleasure myself of requesting your acceptance of a copy.

Nothing, Sir, believe me, would give me more uneasiness
than to misrepresent thro' inadvertence, either publicly or
privately the opinion of any gentleman, especially of one,
who treats his opponents with the candour and liberality of
Mr. Ricardo. If you admit, that there was a great demand
for guineas,—if you admit, that there was a scanty supply,
and if you affirm, that the guinea, notwithstanding, did not
rise in value, it appears to me, that I have not misrepresented
your statement.[3] But, if you deny either of the two first
positions, or do not assert the last, then I own, that I have
misunderstood, and misrepresented your sentiments. I con-

[1] Addressed: 'D. Ricardo Esq /
Upper Brook St'.
MS in *R.P.*
Alexander Crombie (1762–
1840), LL.D., Presbyterian minister, schoolmaster and writer on
many subjects. Torrens expressed
his admiration for him in the
Dedication of *Essay on Money
and Paper Currency*, 1812, and in
the Preface to *Essay on the External Corn Trade*, 1815, p. xii.

[2] *Letters on the present State of
the Agricultural Interest, addressed
to Charles Forbes, Esq. M.P.*,
London, Hunter, 1816. Ricardo's
copy, inscribed 'From Dr. Crombie by his friend Major Torrens
to David Ricardo Esq[r]', is in the
Goldsmiths' Library of the University of London.
[3] Probably refers to a long footnote in *Letters to Forbes*, pp. 20–1,
criticising Ricardo's *High Price
of Bullion*.

1 May 1816 ceive, that, if this subject were disentangled from some per-
plexities, in which it is unfortunately involved, that there
would be no diversity of opinion, respecting it: and if I can
command as much leisure, as I have inclination, I intend to
examine with attention, and analyse your pamphlet, containing, as I conceive, almost every thing of importance on
the other side.[1] If I should have time to accomplish this, the
analysis shall be submitted to your examination. There are
some points, I fear, on which we cannot agree; and it becomes a question, which of the contending parties have the
more correct notion of the points in controversy. I cannot
assent to your notion of depreciation, nor to the standard of
value, which you desire to establish—In regard to the ideas,
annexed to the expressions "cheapness" and "dearness["]
of gold, I think it evident, that we do not in fact differ so
much, as you imagine, and that, consistently with your own
theory, we must each come to the same conclusion at last.

I return you, Sir, many thanks for your friendly invitation;
but our friend Major Torrens will tell you, that I seldom or
never dine from home, except during the holidays.

Believe me respectfully

Sir

Your most obed[t]

ALEX[R] CROMBIE

Greenwich
1st May 1816

Dav. Ricardo Esq

[1] See *A Letter to D. Ricardo, Esq. containing an Analysis of his Pamphlet on the Depreciation of Bank Notes*, by the Rev. Alexander Crombie, LL.D., London, Hunter, 1817. (Reprinted, with additional notes, in *Pamphleteer*, vol. xx, 1817, pp. 529–72.) The *Letter*, which is dated 7 April 1817, opens: 'When I had the pleasure of meeting you at Woolwich, in company with our respected friend Major Torrens, I intimated my intention of analysing your pamphlet, on the depreciation of Bank Notes'.

165. TROWER TO RICARDO[1]

Unsted Wood—Godalming—
May 24—1816—

Dear Ricardo—

I conclude you have by this time become acquainted 24 May 1816
with the provisions of Mr. Rose's Bill, for the protection of
Provident Institutions,[2] I am desirous therefore of comparing
our views of that proposed Act, in order that if we see that
measure in the same light, we may exert our efforts in preventing what appears to me its mischievous tendency.

The whole Bill proceeds upon the principle, that the
Depositors whom the Bill designates *Members* shall exercise
a control over the Institution. All authority exercised by any
Committee is to *proceed from the Depositors*, by whom such
power is to be *delegated.* Now, the principle on which these
Institutions proceed and ought to proceed, is that the
Depositors shall have *no voice* or control whatever over the
management of their concerns—These Institutions are established for the express purpose of doing what the poor are
unable to do for themselves—*to take care of their money.* It
is essential therefore they should have no power of interference in its management. This Bill gives to the Depositors
the appointment of the *Officers of the Institution.* So that
those Gentlemen who have come forward to assist their
poorer neighbours are to owe their continuance in Office to
the nomination of their laborers and servants. Under such
a system we may rest assured the management of these
Institutions will not long remain in the hands of the Gentlemen with whom they originated.

[1] Addressed: 'To / David Ricardo
Esqr / Upper Brook Street / Grosvenor Square'. London postmark, 27 May 1816.
MS in *R.P.*

[2] George Rose had brought in his
bill 'for the protection and encouragement of Provident Institutions or Banks for Savings' on
15 May 1816 (*Hansard*, XXXIII,
841 ff.).

24 May 1816   The Depositors too are to have the power of *inspecting the Books*; thus laying open the concerns of every Depositor to the curiosity of his neighbour, and depriving the Institution of the benefits derived from a persuasion that the amount of Depositors Shares will be known only to the Managers. All this proceeds upon a misconception of the real object and character of the measure—It is *no joint stock purse* in which Individuals are *collectively interested*, and therefore cannot establish any pretence for the interference here proposed to be allowed—

There are many minor points open to objection which of course will not escape your notice—And it is remarkable, that the Bill is totally silent respecting the deduction for the payment of expences, which required the sanction of legislative enactment at least as much as any other part of the subject. If I have taken a correct view of the provisions of the Bill and you concur in it, do exert yourself in endeavouring to prevent the mischief, which in its present state it c[annot f]ail[1] to produce. Explanation and interfe[rence] may lead to a proper understanding and obtain the alterations necessary to make the measure useful.—How does your Institution in London proceed. I shall be desirous of hearing of its progress.[2] We go on tolerably well—and have purchased 500. Stock—the principal part of this however arising from the funds of a Benefit Society, which have been deposited with us.—

I conclude you will remain in Town for some time to come although the Country is getting into high beauty.

[1] MS torn here and below.
[2] See Joseph Hume, *An Account of the Provident Institution for Savings, established in the Western Part of the Metropolis...*, London, Stockdale, 1816 (a copy presented by Hume to Ricardo is in the Goldsmiths' Library of the University of London). Ricardo, Trower, Malthus, Hume, Torrens were amongst the managers.

Make our united Compliments to Mrs. Ricardo and family 24 May 1816 and believe me

Yours very sincerely
HUTCHES TROWER—

166. RICARDO TO MALTHUS[1]

My dear Sir   London 28 May 1816

From what you said when you left London, it is pro- 28 May 1816 bable that you will not be at the Club on saturday next. If your visit to town should be deferred till the following tuesday we have a bed at your service—it is now occupied by Mr. and Mrs. Smith, our Gloucestershire friends. In case you should come sooner I hope you will be able to pass much of your time with us. Our breakfast hour is now at so reasonable a time that I hope you will take that meal with us the first morning you are in London, and then settle how often we shall see you at dinner.

I suppose you have been too busy in official occupations, since we last met, to have made much progress in the writings which you have in hand. I hope however that you will be prepared to give the public the result of your well considered opinions in due season. We have a right to look to you for the correction of some difficulties and contradictions with which Political Economy is encumbered.

Major Torrens tells me that he shall work hard for the next few months, so that we may expect a book on the same subject from him next year.[2] He continues to hold some here-

[1] Addressed: 'To / The Rev⁴ T R Malthus/ East India College / Hertford'.

MS at Albury.—*Letters to Malthus*, XLVII.

[2] Although a forthcoming book of Torrens is mentioned from time to time in this correspondence (below, pp. 141, 251, and VIII, 22, 47), he did not publish any book, as distinct from pamphlets, till his *Essay on the Production of Wealth* in 1821.

tical opinions on money and exchange notwithstanding Mr. Mill and I have exerted all our eloquence to bring him to the right faith. We however have succeeded in removing some of the obscurity which clouds his vision on the principles of exchange.—He is I think quite a convert to *all* what you have called my peculiar opinions on profits, rent, &c^a &c^a,—so that I may now fairly say that I hold no principles on Political Economy which have not the sanction either of your or his authority, which renders it much less important that I should persevere in the task which I commenced of giving my opinions to the public.—Those principles will be much more ably supported either by you or by him than I could attempt to support them:—My labours have wholly ceased for two months;—whether in the quiet and calm of the country I shall again resume them is very doubtful. My vanity has not received sufficient stimulus to remove the temptation which is constantly offering itself to the indulgence of my idle habits.

The fine weather is come opportunely for your vacation. I suppose you will commence your travels without much delay.—I hope we shall meet at Gatcomb before you return home.—

Believe me
Ever truly Yours
DAVID RICARDO

167. RICARDO TO MᶜCULLOCH[1]

[Answered by 190]

Sir

London, Upper Brook Street
Grosvenor Square 9 June 1816

I beg to return you my thanks for the pamphlet[2] which 9 June 1816
you were so kind as to send me, and which I have read with
much pleasure. I cannot however agree with you in the
necessity of adopting the violent remedy you propose for
our present difficulties, of reducing the interest on the
National Debt, because though such a measure might be
beneficial to one class at the expence of another, it would
afford very little relief to the country, and would be a pre-
cedent of a most alarming and dangerous nature. Many
persons are of opinion, that the present agreement between
the value of paper money and bullion, has been brought
about by the fall in the value of the latter. If so the proposed
remedy would be one of positive injustice, even to those
stockholders who have lent their money to Government
during the latter years of the war, and still more so to those
who have been proprietors of stock for a longer period. My
own opinion is that there has been both a fall in the value of
the precious metals and a rise in the value of paper. Inasmuch
as the latter has taken place the stockholder has been benefited, but if it would be wise to legislate for every alteration in
the value of the currency we ought to have begun long ago,

[1] Addressed: 'J. R MCulloch Esqʳ/Edinburgh', and marked on cover: 'Opened by J. MᶜColluch Royal Hotell Edinburgh in Mistake'. On the latter (an innkeeper of Princes Street) see *Letters to MᶜCulloch*, p. 1, editor's note.
MS in British Museum.—*Letters to MᶜCulloch*, I.
[2] *An Essay on a Reduction of the Interest of the National Debt, proving, that this is the only possible Means of Relieving the Distresses of the Commercial and Agricultural Interests; and estab-lishing the Justice of that Measure on the Surest Principles of Politi-cal Economy*, London, Mawman (printed at Edinburgh), 1816, 53 pp. Cp. below, p. 93, n. 2.

9 June 1816 when the stockholders were suffering from a fall in the value of money; and such has been their situation ever since the commencement of the National Debt. No relief is ever afforded[1] to those who suffer from a fall in the value of money, but every heart sympathizes with those who are losers by its rise.

Much of our present distress arises from a fall in the value of raw produce, which would have taken place under the present circumstances if our currency had uniformly consisted of the precious metals. It is a fall totally independent of any variation in the value of money. It is confined to raw produce alone, and those who suffer by it have no more claim to relief than the West India planters, or distillers, when adverse circumstances occur in their business.—The price of raw produce cannot for any length of time keep so low as to prevent farmers from getting the general profits of stock however high they may be taxed. All taxes I apprehend fall ultimately on the consumers.—Our financial prospect is not very encouraging. The first duty of ministers, it appears to me, is to lessen our expences as much as possible, —the second is to raise the taxes till they equal our expenditure. They should I think not meddle with the sinking fund, and still less should they interfere with the dividends of the [stockhol]ders.[2] It is expenditure which will ruin u[s, not the taxes] which are necessary to pay the int[erest on that ex]penditure.—You will, I am su[re] excuse me for so freely expressing my opinion [on] matters which are interesting to us all, and on which our object can only be to discover truth, and improve the science of Political Economy.

I am Sir

Your obed[t] and humble Serv[t]

DAVID RICARDO

J. R McCulloch Esqr

[1] 'as suggested' is del. here.   [2] MS torn here and below.

168. BROADLEY TO RICARDO[1]

[*Answered by* 169]

Glasgow 3ᵈ June 1816

Mr. David Ricardo

Sir,

I have read your pamphlet upon a "Cheap Currency"   3 June 1816
with your comments upon the advantageous bargains made
by the Bank of England with the Ministers of State time
after time; the Tables of calculation you have subjoin'd
greatly elucidate your remarks and the public at large are
greatly indebted to you for them.

Your observations as to the enormous and unreasonable
advantages derived by the Bank from the public in consequence of these improvident bargains of Ministers in succession, appear to me incontrovertible; but, I am unable to
accompany you with my approbation as to the means you
suggest for obtaining a "Cheap currency".

That the Bank ought to be obliged to relinquish some of
its undue advantages as soon as opportunity offers, is what
I heartily subscribe to and fervently wish, but, that the Bank
should be ruined, or subjected to ruin, for the sake of providing the public at large a "cheap currency" is a proposition
so fully fraught with injustice to that Company and impolicy
and danger to the nation itself and the Capital in particular,
that I request permission earnestly to enter my protest
against it.

Your proposition, Sir, is utterly impracticable without
the consequence of *ruin* to the Bank be attatchd to it—
before you propose that the Bank should be compel'd to

[1] Addressed: 'Mr. David Ricardo/ London'. Postmarks, Glasgow, 7 June and London, 10 June. MS in *R.P.*

John Broadley, merchant, was the author of a pamphlet on the poor entitled *Pandora's Box, and the Evils of Britain*, London, for the Author, 1801.

3 June 1816 sell Gold Bullion at £.3.18—pʳ oz you should first provide, that it shall be enabled to *buy* Bullion at or below that price, and this is what neither you, Sir, nor all the Governments of Europe combined together can accomplish! Bullion is simply an article of *Merchandize*, and subject to rise and fall in price like other Commodities, and no power on Earth can prevent the fluctuation, and if we for a moment suppose the same prices to recur that we have of late years experienced —or, in short, if the Bank restriction Law had not fortunately taken place—that Corporation would have been ruin'd ten times over if it was even one Hundred times richer than it now is. And why Sir, wilfully ruin one useful establishment—or why should any one single *Interest* be sacrificed for an imaginary and temporary public advantage or convenience, with nothing but *utility* to merit such punishment, and without the slightest prospect of any advantage to be derived by it for so immense a risk as that of certain and utter ruin?

The Misfortune is, that you argue from an erroneous proposition or foundation, you have chosen for your standard measure of value a thing that deserves not the Name, you say Bullion at the Mint price is the Standard Measure of value, but, as the price of Bullion does and ever will *vary* it cannot deserve the denomination of *Standard*. And this, Sir, is the unfortunate condition of every Man I've yet seen write on the subject of *Currency*—nay it is in fact our Countrys misfortune that our "Standard Measure of Value" has not yet been discovered, or has been intirely overlook'd by every Writer on Political Economy &c. from the justly celebrated Adam Smith down to this day excepting none that I have met with, not even the Members of the Bullion Committee! If this standard was one understood and recognized all jarring opinions on Currency wᵈ cease and these

knotty puzzling points quite simplified. And I have a pro- 3 June 1816
posal to make to you which I hope you will comply with.

I am told you have written on *Exchanges* in an able
manner. I never saw your Book and I am faɪ off—but if
you will resolve me the following questions I will furnish
you with the only certain Standard measure of value that
great Britain possesses, as a requital for your trouble.—The
first question is—What is meant by Exchange between
Countries? that is, does it principally relate to Bills of
Exchange and their price?

2ndly will you point out distinctly an example or instance
whereby one Country gains and the other Country looses by
the rate of Exchange between them? seriously I ask for
information and your compliance will oblige

yr Hb. Sert

J. BROADLEY.

P.S. I request you to excuse this rough Scrawl—I am no
scholar but have a sort of curiosity on these subjects—so
strong indeed that I fear I may be thought a rude intruder.
however. *I mean well.*

169. RICARDO TO BROADLEY[1]

[*Reply to* 168]

Sir

London. Upper Brook Street
Grosvenor Square 14 June 1816

We differ so much on the subject of currency that there 14 June 1816
appears to be but little chance of our coming to the same

[1] Addressed: 'John Broadley Esq/
Glasgow / NB' and franked by
H. Grey Bennet, M.P.

MS in the collection of docu-
ments formed by W. F. Watson,
an Edinburgh bookseller, be-
queathed to the Scottish National
Portrait Gallery and deposited by
them in the National Library of
Scotland (MS 584, No. 975).

14 June 1816 opinion, but by a lengthened correspondence, which I should not have sufficient leisure to keep up. I must however remark on those parts of your letter where you appear to have misconceived my meaning in the pamphlet on which you have animadverted. I have no where justified the exposing of the Bank to ruin for the sake of a temporary and uncertain advantage to the public. On the contrary to the public as distinguished from the Bank, it is of no importance whether the circulation be carried on with an expensive currency, such as gold, or with a cheap one, such as paper, because in either case those who make use of money must pay for its whole nominal value. To the issuers of money, (the Bank in this case), it is of the utmost importance, for their gains are in proportion as they can substitute a cheap for a dear currency. My scheme was proposed as a measure which in my opinion would be beneficial to the Bank, without being attended with any corresponding injury to the public and therefore as of national advantage. I am still of the same opinion. You say that I have not provided for the Bank being enabled to buy gold bullion at or under the price at which they are to sell. I think I have; for as the Bank are to be the sole issuers of money, they have the power of regulating the quantity to be issued. Will you deny that a reduction of 1, 2 or 3 millions, would produce an effect on the comparative value of bank notes and gold? If you do, we are at variance on the first principles of the science. If you do not deny this proposition, then the Bank is in no danger; for they can regulate the price of gold at pleasure.

With respect to a standard measure of value, strictly so called, neither gold nor any other commodity can be such, for what is itself variable can never be an invariable measure of other things. But though it can not be an invariable measure of other things, it may be a variable measure of them,—and as we are possessed of none other than variable measures, this particular one has been by law constituted the general measure of value. It is not so variable as other things, and was therefore probably chosen; but if it were 20 times more so,—if from year to year it varied 30–40 or 50 pc^t, however inconvenient it might be; however desirable to alter the law; and change the commodity by which to estimate the value of other things; there would be no physical impossibility, as you seem to intimate, against making our paper money conform to this varying commodity. Suppose that the influence of the atmosphere were such on our measures of length, the yard for example, that it varied one fourth, being sometimes longer and sometimes shorter, than a given portion of the arc of the meridian which is supposed invariable. We might still use the yard measure and might justly call it (by law) our standard measure.

To your 1st question "What is meant by exchange between countries, that is, does it principally relate to bills of exchange and their price?["] I answer that by exchange we always mean the *price* of the currency of one country estimated in the currency of another. Thus when the exchange with Hamburgh is at 33, 33 schillings payable in Hamburgh sells in London for £1 sterling. It relates to bills and currency only and not to commodities. What may be the cause of a high or low exchange is another question. Subsidies, bad crops, unprosperous commerce may disturb the equilibrium of exports and imports, and produce powerful effects on the exchange, within its natural limits, but they do so only by affecting the relative value, or price of currency.

To your second question whether I can point out distinctly an example or instance whereby one country gains and the other country loses by the rate of exchange between

14 June 1816   them? I answer that I believe the rate of exchange quite unimportant as it affects the interests of the two countries. Inasmuch it is sometimes a symptom of subsidies being paid, of unprosperous commerce &c., it is a subject of regret when it is unfavourable. In our transactions with Hamburgh for example I believe we should neither gain nor lose by the exchange being at 28 or 33 the relative prices of commodities in the two countries being raised or lowered in proportion to the rise or fall of the exchange.—

I fear I have very imperfectly expressed my meaning on the subject of these questions,—but the Post waits and I must hastily conclude by subscribing myself

Your obed.^t Servant

DAVID RICARDO

[In his reply, dated Glasgow, 21 June 1816, Broadley, after restating his objections, agrees with Ricardo that no commodity can be a standard measure of value; but, he says, though we cannot have a *real* standard, 'we have a *nominal* standard that will be found *really true*'. 'Need I add that what I mean, is "the *Ledger pound* and its parts" all our Currency of every sort and kind is subservient to it—is expressive of it—is emblematical of it, but *itself* is the perfect measure of all and each of them and of every thing. And I beseech you to make trial of it. And altho: I wish not to intrude myself upon yet I must confess if you come into my way of thinking I should be proud to hear from you. if we differ still. farewell. do not trouble yourself for I fear I am inflexible.'—MS in *R.P.*]

170. TROWER TO RICARDO[1]

[*Answered by* 171]

Unsted Wood—July 1—1816

Dear Ricardo

1 July 1816   My reply to your kind letter[2] has been delayed longer than I intended, in consequence of my having been absent

[1] Addressed: 'To / David Ricardo Esqr / Upper Brook Street / Grosvenor Square'.—MS in *R.P.*   [2] Ricardo's letter is wanting.

on a visit to my Brother,[1] in Sussex—He has taken a very desirable place, in a very pretty Country, and is enjoying his retirement very much, as every man must do accustomed to the bustle and fatigue of *our* boisterous and——profession.—

I do not hesitate to address this to you in London, not doubting, that both you and Mrs. Ricardo will easily frame many excuses for remaining in Brook Street, even during this lovely weather. The breaking up of Parliament however must shortly shame even *you* into the Country. It is necessary too for every man to be upon the spot to protect his property from pillage or destruction, as the senseless and mischievous spirit now abroad seems to threaten danger to all. A Gentleman, a neighbour of ours, has lately had a large Barn full of Corn and a Threshing Machine burnt to the ground, although he is a very popular and highly respectable man, the brother of Mr. Gooch the Member for Suffolk.[2]— These are some of the lamentable effects of war, which I fear has made much more serious and lasting havock upon the *morals* than upon the *pockets* of the people. To repair these evils ought now to be, and I trust will be, the leading object of the Government, and of every individual of influence in the Country. In this view the School you have lately so benevolently established is a national good, and supported by your active superintendence must be of essential service in that manufacturing district.[3]

I observe by the Paper Mr. Rose's Bill for the Provident Institution will not pass this Session; what is the reason; as

[1] John Trower, a stockbroker.
[2] An account of this fire is given in the *Annual Register* for 1816, 'Chronicle', p. 91.
[3] 'A school, at Minchinhampton, on the Lancasterian system, established by Mr. Ricardo, in which about 250 boys and girls are admitted.' See 'A Digest of Parochial Returns made to the Select Committee appointed to inquire into the Education of the Poor', vol. 1, p. 304 (in *Parliamentary Papers*, 1819, vol. IX, A).

1 July 1816 the extra alteration it has undergone has made it very useful?
How goes the London Institution—what are your weekly
receipts? Ours are progressive, but uncertain, and do not
keep pace with my expectations, or perhaps I should rather
say with my wishes.—

Have you seen Mr. Waylands Book on Population and
Production, I here it is intended as a refutation of Malthus'
doctrines. I shall get it, as he is an able man, and the subject
of the highest importance. It is a fortunate circumstance,
that Mr. Malthus has not yet published the new edition of his
work, as opportunity will now be afforded him of answering
any arguments in Mr. Wayland's book that may require
observation[1]—

I hope you are prosecuting your enquiries, and that your
leisure hours in the Country will be devoted to embodying
in some substantial publication your scattered thoughts upon
the interesting question that has so long occupied your
attention—

What think you of the Funds? How long a time will
elapse before the Country recovers from its commercial
difficulties. Although as yet there is no appearance of a
change, I cannot think the gl[oom] will continue much
longer—No doubt new channels for our trade are forming
in which the current will run as strong and rapidly as formerly—

I lament the Usury Bill did not succeed.[2] The quarter in
which it originated was not sufficiently powerful, and the

---

[1] *The Principles of Population and
Production, as they are affected by
the Progress of Society; with a
view to Moral and Political Consequences*, by John Weyland, jun.,
F.R.S., London, Baldwin, 1816.
Malthus replied in *Essay on Population*, 5th ed., 1817, Appendix,
vol. III, pp. 397–424.
[2] Sergeant Onslow's bill for the
repeal of the Usury Laws; it was
withdrawn this session, but introduced again in 1817.

public prejudice is strong against it. I do not think that the 1 July 1816 general rate of interest would be much encreased if the maximum where withdrawn, but in a commercial country like this it would be highly advantageous to let it find its own level, and the restriction is a gross injustice to the capitalist. Adieu my Dear Ricardo. Mrs. Trower unites with me in kind regards to Mrs. Ricardo and family and I remain

Yrs very sincerely
Hutches Trower

171. RICARDO TO TROWER[1]
[Reply to 170.—Answered by 176]

Dear Trower London 15th July 1816

Mrs. Ricardo has already left London and I am pre- 15 July 1816 paring to follow her, so that your next letter must be directed to me at Gatcomb. You must not suppose that I have been closely confined to London since your absence from it,—for I have been to Bath for a week, and to Gatcomb for another week. Hitherto however the weather has been so unsettled that we have had no great reason to envy you country gentlemen. During my fortnight's holidays I was not only drenched to the skin by the rain, but was often precluded from leaving the house for a whole day together.

At Bath I met Mr. Elwin[2] twice at dinner, once at his own house. He is equally warm as when you saw him in the encouragement of Provident Institutions, and from the little I have seen of him I have formed a very favourable opinion

---

[1] Addressed: 'Hutches Trower Esqr/Unsted Wood/Godalming/ Surry'.
MS at University College, London.—Letters to Trower, IX.

[2] H. Elwin, one of the Managers of the Westminster Savings Bank. (See Hume's Account of the Provident Institution, mentioned above, p. 34, n. 2.)

15 July 1816 both of his head and heart. Mr. Malthus, who was also on a visit near Bath, dined with Mr. Elwin at Mr. Clutterbuck. We passed a very agreeable day, and I have reason to believe these two gentlemen were mutually pleased with each other.

When I tell you that Mr. Malthus accompanied me for a couple of days to Gatcomb, and that we were held prisoners by the weather, you will naturally conclude that we had ample opportunity to discuss our different views on some of the questions in Political Economy; and although we have approached a little in opinion, we have left ourselves sufficient matter for further controversy.

I think it very doubtful whether Mr. Malthus will notice Mr. Weyland's book, although Mr. Weyland treats him with the greatest possible courtesy. He has, I think, not in the least succeeded in establishing his own doctrines in opposition to those of Malthus on the principle of population, but he has shewn that in the early stages of society when the population presses against food, no remedy would be afforded by lessening the number of the people, because the evil they then experience proceeds from the indolence and vice of the people and not in their inability to procure necessaries. By reducing the population you reduce food in perhaps a larger proportion, and rather aggravate than remove their misery. He is singularly inconsistent in denying the truth of this principle when applied to Ireland and really recommends means by which the population of that country should be reduced,—whereas the remedy required in Ireland is a taste for other objects besides mere food. Any stimulus which should rouse the Irish to activity, which should induce them to dispose of their surplus time in procuring luxuries for themselves, instead of employing it in the most brutal pursuits, would tend more to the civilization and prosperity of their country than any other measures which could be recommended.[1]

I cannot agree with you in thinking that the war has had much effect in degrading the morals of the people. The outrages of which they are at present guilty may be sufficiently accounted for from the stagnation in trade which has never failed to produce similar consequences. I am disposed to think that the people are both improved in morals and in knowledge, and therefore that they are less outrageous under these unavoidable reverses than they formerly used to be. I am in hopes too that as they increase in knowledge they will more clearly perceive that the destruction of property aggravates and never relieves their difficulties. Surely the disastrous effects which always attend an important change in the employments of capital cannot much longer continue and we shall soon witness a renovation of commercial activity and credit. I have not in the least abated in my confidence of the real stability of the finances of the country, although I do not look with much satisfaction on the defalcation of the revenue at a time when it was already so many millions less than the expenditure. We have ample resources, but we want able ministers and a disinterested House of Commons. In our assembly the landed interest is too prevalent, and under very trying difficulties I should not have much reliance on their virtue.

If your Provident Institution is progressive you have no reason to complain, it will ultimately be productive of much good. Our receipts in Westminster are about £350— p^r week. We have realized £3000 *money* and find no difficulty in managing the business. In the City of London we shall commence business on Monday next. We have been hitherto prevented from receiving deposits from the want of a proper

[1] Weyland, *op. cit.*, pp. 25–30 and 101–103. Cp. above, I, 99, n. 2.

15 July 1816 office which has at length been supplied,—though not I think in the most eligible situation, being in Bishopsgate Church Yard. I am sorry that I cannot give my assistance at the first opening as no other manager has taken the least trouble to acquire the necessary information.[1] Pray make my kind regards to Mrs. Trower and believe me

Very truly Y^{rs}

DAVID RICARDO

I wish Mrs. Trower and you would take a trip to Gatcomb this Autumn.

---

[1] J. L. Mallet, who was one of the promoters, gives an account of the meeting at the Royal Exchange Rooms at which the foundation of the City of London Savings Bank was decided: 'The meeting was well attended, and we stated our plans, by which the money deposited in the bank was to be invested in the public Stocks, and the amount of the deposits returned to the depositors whenever called for with interest at 4 per cent. When the resolutions came to be put, a gentleman whom I did not know, and who proved to be Mr. Ricardo, expressed his entire approbation of the object for which we had met, but conceived that the Directors of the Bank should only engage to return to the depositors the value of the Stock which had been purchased with their money, because if any considerable fall in the Stocks should take place, and a great run came at the same time upon the bank, the institution would either be obliged to fail in its engagements or the Trustees to make good the deficiency. The objection was obvious and insuperable, and notwithstanding the disadvantages attending this scheme, which held out to the depositors a temptation to gamble in the stocks, without having to pay any brokerage, it was necessarily adopted for a time. Applications were immediately made to Government, who undertook to take the money of the Savings Bank at a fixed interest with certain limitations. The Bank was soon afterwards established, and led to the formation of several others in London.' (Diary entry on Ricardo's death, 1823, in *Political Economy Club, Centenary Volume*, 1921, p. 211.)

172. MALTHUS TO RICARDO[1]

[*Answered by* 174]

My dear Sir,
E I Coll August 6th [1816]

As I came through Town rather sooner than I expected, 6 Aug. 1816
I was in great hopes of catching you before you set out. I
called in Brook Street with that view but found that you had
left Town the saturday before.[2] I have been returned now
near ten days, and have been busy as usual in College
matters—indeed I am drawing up a paper relating to the
College, which is to be sent to Mr. Canning who is now
related to us in the capacity of President of the Board of
Control.[3] This, and other matters have made me lazier than
I intended to be in writing, particularly as Mr. G Eckersall
had desired me to tell you either personally, or by letter that
he had given the orders you wished respecting the Oxford
boat, but that Mrs. Hall was a very uncertain person, and
could be little depended upon for punctuality unless some
flapper were continually at her elbow, in proof of which he
had himself waited all the summer for a Canoe which he had
ordered, and which had been promised in a very short time,
but I believe has not arrived yet. You must take some
measures therefore to accelerate the order or probably it may
not be executed— perhaps the best way would be, if you are
at all in a hurry, for Mr. Hitchin[4] to call there, and chuse some
ready made boat, which she will not object to sell during the
Oxford vacation. Perhaps however the terrible weather we
have had has made you forget all these matters; but we know

[1] Addressed: 'D. Ricardo. Esqr. /
Gatcomb Park. / Minchin Hampton.' Postmark, 1816.
MS in *R.P.*
[2] 20 July.

[3] Canning had joined the Government in June 1816 as President
of the Board of Control for the
Affairs of India.
[4] James Hitchings, the tutor of
Ricardo's children.

6 Aug. 1816 you are not much afraid of rain, and we may still hope for some tolerable weather in Autumn. Mrs. Malthus and Miss L. Eckersall[1] were very much pleased with their expedition to Easton Gray and Gatcomb; and Miss E with the assistance of David's horse which she liked much, got home very safely and agreeably on the evening of the day we left you.

I had a letter from Warburton the day before yesterday. I conclude he is by this time in your neighbourhood. If you see him pray thank him for his letter for me, and say how much I regret having missed him, particularly as he is about to be absent for so long a tour as Italy.

By the by the more I think on the subject the more I feel convinced that the rate of the profits of stock depends mainly on the demand and supply of stock compared with the demand and supply of labour, and very little (directly) on facility or difficulty of production, properly so called. By facility or difficulty of production I mean the greater or less quantity of produce that can be obtained by a given quantity of labour, and by no means the quantity of any sort of produce which must be given for labour, which merely expresses the exchangeable value of that produce compared with labour, and has nothing to do with facility or difficulty of production. If a piece of land worked by 10 labourers and producing 110 quarters of corn, should afterwards produce 165 quarters with the same quantity of labour, might not the rate of profits continue the same, and the only difference be that the labourers would be paid 15 quarters instead of ten. Does not the different *rate* of profit in America and Poland in land of nearly the same quality shew that profits depend on the proportion of capital to labour, and not on facility of production.

---

[1] Lucy Eckersall (later Mrs Taunton), Mrs Malthus's sister.

I want also much to ask you what are the causes which 6 Aug. 1816
occasion an increase of demand without a diminution of
price, that is, what is the nature of that demand which increases price, and can it be general? I think it can, and that
a new value thrown into the market always tends to create
such a demand. Mrs M desires to be kindly rem^d to Mrs. R.

Ever truly Yours,

T R MALTHUS.

173. RICARDO TO MILL[1]

[*Answered by* 175]

Gatcomb Park, Minchinhampton
8 Augt 1816

My dear Sir

Ever since I have been here I have designed writing to 8 Aug. 1816
you, taking shame to myself that for the last two years, I have
always suffered you to commence the correspondence. I have
however deferred it partly out of pity to you, and partly
from the usual disinclination which I feel to exhibiting my
epistolary talents. My procrastination has not proceeded
from not having you in my thoughts, for you have often
been present to my imagination, armed with all your powers
of persuasion, when I have been inclined to renounce my
work in despair, dismayed by the difficulties which incessantly present themselves to me. Notwithstanding my fear
of your reproaches and my recollection of the encouragement you always hold out to my perseverance I am often
inclined to throw my writing aside as a task much beyond
my powers to accomplish, and I believe my sole inducement
to go on is the reflection that I am not obliged to publish,
and that the endeavor to arrange my opinions on the

[1] Addressed: 'James Mill Esqr / Ford Abbey / Chard / Somersetshire'.—MS in Mill-Ricardo papers.

8 Aug. 1816 subjects we have so often spoken, will if of no other use, afford me amusement and instruction.

I have hitherto had little temptation to desert my work for the pleasure of walking or riding, as the weather has been almost uniformly bad—yet have I not been able wholly to seclude myself from morning intruders. Those who are staying in the house with us for two or three days at a time would not I fear understand my absenting myself from them, and would regard it as a want of hospitality. What I can I will do, and when we meet in London I shall convince you that I am not equal to the task you have assigned me.

Mr. and Mrs. Austin arrived here a week ago, and are now settled in their house about 14 miles distant from us. Sylla is heartily rejoiced at being again in England, and appears to be too much of the true John Bull breed to admire the wonders of France and Italy at the expence of the comforts which must be necessarily sacrificed in viewing them. The village where she is settled is in a beautiful country, and she is luckily very little more distant from Bath, where her eldest sister lives, than from us.

Mr. Warburton, who has been on a visit to Mr. Smith, is going over the very ground from which Sylla is returned, I believe he will extend his tour to Naples. The Smiths with Mr. Binda,[1] the Italian friend of Mr. Whishaw, have been staying with us for a few days. Mr. Binda has just left them, and they (the Smith's) are going to London on monday to

[1] Giuseppe Binda, of Lucca, a refugee who had been invited to England by Lord Holland. At Holland House he met Whishaw who introduced him to the Smiths (see *The 'Pope' of Holland House*, p. 121). A letter from Thomas Smith to Ricardo of 23 March 1818 reports the fol- lowing anecdote: 'Whishaw tells me of a sad misfortune poor Binda has had who bidding at an auction for a necklace he thought was selling for 3: 10 – found when it was knocked down to him, that each pearl was this price, and had to pay 250£.' (MS in *R.P.*)

join Mr. Whishaw in a journey through Flanders and 8 Aug. 1816
Holland.

I have nothing new to tell you concerning ourselves or
our affairs. We jog on much as usual, though our family
party is so much reduced that we are rather duller than
common. Osman is at Bath, Fanny has not been long
returned from the same place, and we have no friends now
staying with us, but we expect soon to see Ralph and two of
my sisters here. Esther who has been so long a prisoner is
happily now released from her painful duty she is one of
them, and I am not a little pleased at the thoughts of seeing
her under my roof.

I hope Mrs. Mill is quite recovered from her late confine-
ment. I conclude she has by this time joined you at Ford
Abbey. You are I suppose hard at work as usual and are now
giving the last polish to the fruits of your long labours. You
will I hope find leisure this year to pay me a visit here, whether
you go further North or no. I will with pleasure meet you
at Bath and convey you from thence, and if you return to
Ford Abbey will safely deposit you at Bath again. Pray give
my best regards to Mrs. Mill and Mr. Bentham and believe me

Ever truly Y^{rs}

DAVID RICARDO

174. RICARDO TO MALTHUS[1]

[*Reply to* 172.—*Answered by* 178]

My dear Sir

Gatcomb Park
9th Aug. 1816

I am obliged to you for the interest you have taken 9 Aug. 1816
about my boat. It arrived here the latter end of last week

[1] Addressed: 'The Rev^d T R   MS at Albury.—*Letters to Mal-*
Malthus / East India College /   *thus*, XLVIII.
Hertford'.

9 Aug. 1816 and is now safely floating on Gatcomb water. I have been in it once, and found I could manage it alone; but the boat being larger, the sculls are also more bulky than Miss Eckersall's and I now quite despair of ever rivalling her in dexterity of management. It is considerably larger than the boat I had before, and will not admit of the gate being shut when she is moored in the boat-house. We are planning some contrivance to obviate that inconvenience. I am very much indebted to Mr. Geo Eckersall for the trouble he gave himself, and I should write to him to say so, if I did not fear that I should thereby rather add to his trouble. When you write pray express my kind thanks to him.

I am glad that Mrs. Malthus and Miss Eckersall were pleased with our excursion to Easton Grey[1] and Gatcomb. They and you would have better satisfied me that your visit was agreeable if you had not been in so great a hurry to put an end to it.—

Our friends at Easton Grey have been staying a few days with us, accompanied by Mr. Binda. We expected Mr. Warburton to join them here, but he wrote to delay his journey for a couple of days, and by that time the Smiths had returned home. He has however called at Gatcomb since. He must now I think have quitted Wiltshire. He appears pleased with the idea of his journey to Italy, though Mrs. Austin,[2] who is returned, did not fail to represent in the strongest colours all the disagreeables which she encountered. He I dare say is a very good traveller, and my

---

[1] On another excursion one of the guests at Easton Grey writes: 'Mr and Mrs Ricardo called here. Discussion on the moral right of deception in some cases. Mr Ricardo's opinion that the depression and commercial diffi- culties are only temporary.' (Entry of 24 July 1816 in *Diary of Benjamin Newton, Rector of Wath, 1816–1818*, ed. by C. P. Fendall and E. A. Crutchley, Cambridge, 1933, p. 10.)

[2] Ricardo's daughter Priscilla.

daughter I have always thought the very worst I ever met
with.—

The Smiths leave Easton Grey on monday for London. I suppose you have heard that they are going with Mr. Whishaw to the Netherlands and Holland:—they will I am sure be very much delighted with their excursion: They always go a journey, as indeed I think they travel through life, with a disposition to be pleased. They view every thing through a favorable medium and are not eager to spy out the defects of every object they encounter.

I have no difficulty in agreeing with you "that the rate of profits of stock depends mainly on the demand and supply of stock, compared with the demand and supply of labour" if by those words you mean the rise or fall of wages. That is my identical proposition. Now if labour rises, no matter from what cause, profits will fall;—but there are two causes which raise the wages of labour, one the demand for labourers being great in proportion to the supply—the other that the food and necessaries of the labourer are difficult of production, or require a great deal of labour to produce them. The more I reflect on the subject the more I am convinced that the latter cause has an incessant operation.

It is very seldom that the whole additional produce obtained with the same quantity of labour falls to the lot of the labourers who produce it,—but if it should, I should yet contend that the rate of profits would fall because the price of corn would fall with such an increased facility of production,—capital would be withdrawn from the land, rents would fall and profits rise. The causes you mention may operate in Poland and America—I have never denied it. The proportion between labour and capital will undoubtedly affect profits, because it will affect wages, but it is not the only element in the consideration of the

9 Aug. 1816 subject of profits;—there are other causes which also affect wages.

Whether that demand can be general which increases price must I apprehend depend on whether the precious metals can be furnished as rapidly as other commodities. If the savings or acquisitions of labour are exchanged for all commodities in the same proportion and the demand should increase in that proportion also, I can see no reason why any commodity should rise; but if the demand for cloth or gold be either great or less than the supply they may rise or fall in their exchangeable value. That is to say their market value might rise or fall but their natural[1] value would probably undergo little variation, and therefore after a time they would exchange at their usual rates. A new value thrown in the market always supposes a certain quantity of sales as well as purchases; if no part of that value consists of the precious metals I do not see how all commodities could rise. I should expect some to rise and some to fall but the general tendency would rather be to the latter.

Ever truly Y^{rs}
DAVID RICARDO

Pray give my best regards to Mrs. Malthus.

175. MILL TO RICARDO[2]
[*Reply to* 173.—*Answered by* 177]

Ford Abbey 14th August 1816
My dear Sir

14 Aug. 1816   I was much delighted with your kind letter, received a few nights ago, though it continues so much in the old desponding tone. Why should a man that is not afraid to talk

---

[1] 'natural' is ins.   / Gatcomb Park / Minchinhamp-
[2] Addressed: 'David Ricardo Esq.   ton / Gloucester Shire'.
                                       MS in *R.P.*

upon a subject before any body, be afraid to write; since writing is nothing but talking upon paper? You can not only talk before the people who are the most celebrated for their knowledge upon this subject, but you are not afraid to contest with them, and to hold your opinion in preference to theirs; and make it appear to the auditors that you are right. Well, then, just do the same thing upon paper—what more would you have?—I shall begin by and bye to think that your misgivings, and your faintness at heart, are apologies ingeniously contrived by you in defence of idleness? Or (what is a more ingenious conjecture, just come into me head) that you employ them as baits with which to fish for compliments;—as who should say,—Ah, I have not talents for the thing; my capacity is not sufficient—And then comes the kind friend, who cries, with enthusiasm, My dear Sir, allow me to correct the only mistake into which in the whole course of your life you ever fell—your talents are admirable; your capacity is immense—only do write and astonish the world! Now I, not being much practiced in the arts of pleasing, shall say quite the contrary—that no talents are wanted, but what any body possesses—you have the thoughts in your mind already and have only to put them down upon paper—after they are down, to look them over, and see that nothing is omitted which you wish to have there—that no one thing is there in more places than one—and that every thing is in the right place. Surely there is nothing in all this to frighten any body—Well, this is all you have to do. The first thing is, to go over your subject, from the beginning to the end, in any way, no matter what. If then, it don't please you, have it back, and go over the ground again, altering when you find altering to be good. If it should not please in this form, go over it again. Do you think that any man writes a good book by Divine Grace, and the favour of

14 Aug. 1816 inspiration? Rousseau declares that he never gave anything to the public, which, so far from pleasing him the first time, had not been written five times over.[1] I do not mean to let you retract your faith solemnly pledged that I am to be your School master, fully vested with all the rights belonging to that redoubtable office. Well then, in virtue of these rights, I solemnly command and ordain that you proceed, without loss of time, on the plan which you have already sketched out, till you have gone over the whole field of Political Economy, from the beginning to the end, thinking nothing of order, thinking nothing of repetitions, thinking nothing of stile—regarding nothing, in short, but to get all the thoughts blurred upon paper some how or another. We shall see what is to be done with it after that—that is the first thing. Surely you can do that—for it is only saying do what you can—and you will not pretend to say that you cannot do what you can.

Another command of mine is, that—as I know you have by this time, a pretty mass of papers, written first and last upon the subject—you put as much of them as possible, that is all except those which are absolutely necessary for you to go on with, up in a parcel, and send them here. I have a quantity of things to learn, which I known they will teach me. And perhaps they may enable me to give some directions to you which may not be useless. I mean that you should include those which you read to me in London, because hearing a thing read is very different from reading it when you have leisure by yourself. If you can put the sheets that relate to one subject up by themselves—and give some indication of what each subdivision is about, so much the better—But if not, no matter—send them higgledy-piggledy all together.

[1] 'Mes manuscrits raturés, barbouillés, mêlés, indéchiffrables, attestent la peine qu'ils m'ont coûtée. Il n'y en a pas un qu'il ne m'ait fallu transcrire quatre ou cinq fois avant de le donner à la presse.' (*Confessions*, Livre III; Genève, 1782, tome II, p. 121.)

I envy you the pleasure you have had of cross questioning the fair traveller who is just returned to you, on all the prodigies she has seen, and all the miracles she has performed. I wish I had made a part of the social circle. I kiss her beautiful hands, as the people say among whom she has been, and beg she will accept my warm felicitations on all the good things without exception which she has experienced since I had last the pleasure of seeing her.—And, after all, she likes home the best. Ay, home is home, though never so homely. I have always found that a good text.—So, Mr. Warburton, Mr. Smith, family, and Mr. Whishaw, all travellers: I am glad you can resist the mania. I suppose you are waiting to go when I go, and live where I live. A propos of travellers, I had a letter from Brougham since I came here. He was then at Geneva, which was all English, but was just going to fix in Savoy, to take the benefit of the waters.

Tell Mr. Ralph,[1] when he comes to you, that a due proportion of the cuttings of his divine elder have struck roots, and are putting forth their little white amiable buds, to the ecstasy and ravishment of Mr. Bentham. And tell also Miss Esther, that I hope she is not to be in any hurry away from Gatcomb, that if it should, by the peculiar bounty of heaven, be in my power to visit you this season, I may have an opportunity of seeing once in my life a creature something in my own shape, that is capable of preferring another human being to itself, and giving up to it the whole of its enjoyments.

I have been so much of a hermit since I came here, that I can tell you little of the actual measure of distress which is felt in this country. But does not this weather frighten you? The corn here is absolutely green, nothing whatsoever in the ear; and a perfect continuance of rain and cold. There must now be of necessity a very deficient crop, and very high

---

[1] Ricardo's brother; Esther, mentioned below, is his sister.

prices—and these with an unexampled scarcity of work will produce a degree of misery, the thought of which makes the flesh creep on ones bones—one third of the people must die—it would be a blessing to take them into the streets and high ways, and cut their throats as we do with pigs. Church-and-State, at the London tavern, where Church-and-State was nicely served, recommends subscription—a whole people to be fed by subscription![1]—I only expect my wife, and the crowd of my children tomorrow. She has had a very good convalescence—but the fatigue of such a journey would have been hazardous before.—I salute the Gatcomb family in all its ramifications, and begging them only to love me as much as I do them, am my Dear Sir

most truly Yours
J. MILL

176. TROWER TO RICARDO[2]
[Reply to 171]

Dear Ricardo

Unsted Wood—August 20—1816.

20 Aug. 1816   When I look at the date of your last kind letter I feel some degree of shame at having suffered it to remain so long unanswered. I am not disposed to admit, even in my own case, that any adequate excuse can be given for the neglect of a good correspondent; but, perhaps, I may venture to state, in palliation of the offence, that I was occupied last week by the Assizes at Guildford, in discharging the duties

---

[1] The meeting on 29 July, called by the Royal Dukes, the Archbishops, etc., to invite subscriptions for relieving the distress, had been converted by the Radicals led by Lord Cochrane into a demonstration against the 'lavish expenditure' of the Government. (*The Times*, 30 July 1816.)

[2] Addressed: 'To / David Ricardo Esqr / Gatcomb Park / Minchinhampton / Glocestershire'. MS in *R.P.*

of a grand juror. Although the Kalender was heavy, there were not many crimes of an aggravated nature—Lord Cochrane's trial excited most interest, of which you will find a full account in the papers.[1]—He was really mad enough to think, the jury would acquit him; as it was they went further than they were justified in going—Who called upon them to give an opinion whether his previous punishment had been more than adequate? And a recommendation to mercy founded upon an unauthorised opinion cannot be entitled to attention.—

I hope you are not so idle as I am, for I find I make little or no progress in my studies. I have not yet opened Wayland's Book, although I am very anxious to see his view of the subject. I intend to take that opportunity of going thoroughly into Malthus's system; for I confess, that hitherto I have felt great repugnance to the artificial checks to population he suggests. I fear the remedy would be worse than the disease—I would sooner trust to the effects of public Schools and Provident Institutions to bring about the reformation we require.

I have had a long letter from Elwin on the subject of the clause in Roses Bill relating to the great question of extending Parish Relief to Depositors.[2] He says as the original sin of its invention is mine, I am bound to foster my own begettings. I lament to find strong objections are entertained against it by the Lawyers, as I am satisfied, that the sanctioning of that measure is essential to the success of Provident Ins^{ts}. No poor man in his senses will have anything to do with them,

[1] Lord Cochrane had been arrested at a Radical meeting and was brought to trial on the charge of having escaped from jail more than a year before, while undergoing his term of imprisonment for the fraud on the Stock Exchange (see above, VI, 106).

[2] The clause allowed persons who had not more than £30 in Savings Banks to receive parish relief.

20 Aug. 1816 unless it be so provided. I merely wish a declaratory clause to be introduced stating, that a Depositor, as such, should not *necessarily* be excluded from parish relief; and leaving the discretion as to its application to particular cases, (where alone it ought to be) with the Magistrates—This question cannot be evaded. It will arise, it must be decided. And it is much wiser for the Legislature to decide it generally, than to leave it to the capricious and contradictory opinions of individuals. I am satisfied too, that there will be but few cases requiring such relief. Those whose prudent habits lead them to lay by, from time to time, a portion of their earnings are not likely to become burthensome on the parish. But unforseen accidents, or misfortunes, may drive a man to that necessity, and whenever so circumstanced he ought to share the assistance of his parish in common with his neighbors. Relief is not denied to a man having a cow, or a pig, or a cabbage garden. Why then should those who thus employ their savings be preferred to him who lays it out in a Provident Ins^t. But, even admitting the cases to be different, still I say it is *worth while* to favor the Depositor, in order to induce the poor generally to adopt those habits of prudence and economy from which we hope to derive the most important cons[equen]ces.[1] Do avail yourself of every opportunity of impressing p[ublic] men with the importance of encouraging these Ins[titutions] that we may strengthen ourselves for the hour of [need] which I fear will accompany the ensuing Session[. If the] clause is lost, farewell to Provident Institutions[.]

I am very much obliged to you for the kind wish you ex[press] that we should visit Gatcomb. It would give us great pleasure to do so, but the cares of a Nursery render it necessary for us to consider ourselves pretty much as fixtures.

---

[1] MS torn here and below.

Indeed I often lament we are removed so great a distance 20 Aug. 1816 from each other, as I doubt not we should make excellent neighbors. I should be sorry too not to think, that at some future period we may have an opportunity of peeping at Gatcomb, and of making you welcome at our small dwelling—

Adieu my Dear Ricardo. Mrs. Trower unites with me in kind regards to Mrs. Ricardo and family and I remain

Yrs very affectionately

HUTCHES TROWER

177. RICARDO TO MILL[1]

[*Reply to* 175.—*Answered by* 180]

Gatcomb Park. Minchinhampton
8th Sepr 1816

My dear Sir

Since I received your kind letter I have been in London 8 Sept. 1816 for about a week, which has been one of the causes why I have so long delayed answering it. Writing, I at least find, is something different from talking on paper. I can with some confidence maintain my opinion against my adversaries in conversation, because I know they are more intent on the matter than on the manner. Besides by a look, a remark, a sign, you know in conversation what the point of difference is, and all your efforts are directed to that point. In writing you address both those who know little, and those who know much. Every thing must be admitted, or proved, and it is difficult to know whether you will not be very obscure or very tiresome. On this subject however I mean to say no more, for I will not expose myself to the chance of your mistaking my motives. I shall proceed in my work with all due diligence, and after hastily copying what is now

[1] Addressed: 'James Mill Esqr / Ford Abbey / Chard / Somersetshire'. MS in Mill-Ricardo papers.

dispersed in various directions, I shall send it to you. In its present form I scarcely understand it myself, and I am sure you could make nothing of it. I shall not be careful to omit the repetition of the same thought, perhaps in various places, because as my fault is that of brevity and it may sometimes be proper to repeat the idea in another form, if it should be superfluous you can easily scratch your pen across it. Even when I shall have copied my dispersed papers it will be imposing a severe task on you to read them,—but you are absolute, and it is my business to obey you. They shall therefore be copied and sent, and you will then be convinced that however tractable the dispositions of your pupils may be there is a vast difference in directing the energies and talents of a young mind whose habits are not formed, and an old one whose pursuits have been in no way favourable to the object you wish to attain.

Ralph, Samson, Abigail and Esther [1] have been here sometime. I left them here whilst I went to London. We are all going for a few days to Malvern, and from thence to Worcester, where we shall take different directions, they towards their home, I towards mine. They appear very much to have enjoyed their tour, and Esther has not been the least chearful of the party.

She as well as her brothers and sister desire to be kindly remembered to you. Ralph is very much pleased that the cuttings of his elder have struck root.—Mr. and Mrs. Samuda have also been our visitors for about a week,—they leave us to day.—

The continuance of the cold and wet weather does not afford us a very good prospect for the harvest, and I am very much afraid that the poor will have much to suffer during the next winter. I cannot however relinquish my hope that they

---

[1] Ricardo's brothers and sisters.

will not long continue without work. The actual capital of the country,—the funds for the maintenance of labour cannot have been much impaired in consequence of the change from war to peace, and it appears to me that a sufficient time has elapsed to make that new distribution of employments which our altered circumstances have made necessary. The duration of the intervals between marked changes are often much longer than is generally supposed. It proceeds from the opposition which is naturally given to such change. Thus a reduction in the amount of the circulating medium should speedily operate on prices, but the resistance which is offered—the unwillingness that every man feels to sell his goods at a reduced price, induces him to borrow at a high interest and to have recourse to other shifts to postpone the necessity of selling. The effect is however certain at last, but the duration of the resistance depends on the degree of information, or the strength of the prejudices of those who offer it, and therefore it cannot be the subject of any thing like accurate calculation.

I hope you will soon be inclined to direct your footsteps towards this country. You shall devote as much of your time when here as you please to work, but I suspect that you have not more virtue than other folks, and are no more able to resist the temptations of fine weather and good humored companions than those who habitually have more idle habits. I am happy to hear that Mrs. Mill is quite recovered, pray make my kind compliments to her and accept yourself the best wishes of all the inhabitants of Gatcomb.

Yʳˢ truly

DAVID RICARDO

178. MALTHUS TO RICARDO[1]

[*Reply to* 174.—*Answered by* 179]

E I Coll Sept 8ᵗʰ 1816

My dear Sir,

8 Sept. 1816   As I know you don't much mind rain I hope you have
been enjoying yourself at Gatcomb notwithstanding the bad
weather, and that your progress on the whole has been less
impeded than that of the harvest. It has begun about us at
last and seems as if it would be pretty good if it could be got
in, but there has hardly ever been known so late a year, and
in the backward parts of the country, a late year is always a
bad one. How is the harvest about you?

I was glad to hear that you had got your Oxford boat safe
in Gatcomb water. From George's[2] account of Mrs. Hall I
did not expect that she would have been so rapid. I am a
little afraid that it is larger than you find convenient, and that
it might have been better if the original order had gone.
Should this be the case, it might be worth while to change it;
though probably from the state of the weather you have
hardly tried it sufficiently fully to determine whether it is of
the size that best suits you.

For myself I have been still a good deal engaged in College
matters, but am now beginning to think seriously of my new
edition[3], which I believe will be confined as before to 2 Vols.
I have nearly determined to leave out the questions about
bounties and restrictions, or only allude to them very shortly,
as far as they are connected with population.

If, as you say, you have no difficulty in agreeing with me
that the rate of profits depends mainly upon the demand and

[1] Addressed: 'D. Ricardo Esqr /
Gatcomb Park / Minchinhamp-
ton. / Gloucestershire.'
MS in *R.P.*

[2] George Eckersall.
[3] Of the *Essay on Population;* cp.
below, p. 123–4.

supply of stock compared with the demand and supply of
labour it is surely allowing that the profits of stock depend
upon competition, and not on facility of production; and it
will clearly follow that when land is thrown out of cultivation, the profits of stock will not necessarily rise on the
remainder, if capital and labour continue still in the same
proportion to each other. Of course I should be the very
last to deny that the difficulty of procuring food has an
incessant operation; but to shew that the mode in which it
operates is chiefly by checking food and population without
proportionately checking other sorts of commodities, I would
ask whether, if population were miraculously stopped while
the most fertile land remained uncultivated, profits would not
fall upon the supposition of an increase of capital still going
on, owing to the further accumulation of materials and
machinery and the employment of a greater *proportion* of the
stationary population in productive labour. I really think
that you have sometimes conceeded these points; but such
concessions seem quite at variance with your general doctrine respecting profits, which the longer I consider it,
appears to me more and more erroneous. The nature of every
species of capital may be illustrated by a machine the value of
which, however great its powers of production will only be
determined by the price necessary to supply it. Upon the
same principle in the most fertile soil if nothing is wanted but
to plough and sow, and the trifling advances necessary for
this purpose are in great abundance compared with the
population, is it possible to conceive that the rate of profits
should be very high? and does it not follow as I have always
said that the productiveness of industry, or the facility of
production, is totally different from the productiveness of
capital, or the rate of profits. The only reason why profits on
land are generally high in the early periods of society is, be-

8 Sept. 1816 cause labour is so well paid that population increases faster
than capital, and capital is in consequence scarce compared
with population and demand.

With regard to demand in general I cannot help thinking
that in all our discussions,—bullion, as well as corn—&c:
you have greatly underrated the effect of the wants and
tastes of mankind, on which, after all every exertion of
human industry [depends]¹; and so far is it from being true
that they may be considered as always ready for the supply,
they are really very difficult to generate. Two alternatives are
always ready to check their growth as far as the employment
of capital is concerned. Among the higher classes the luxury
of menial service, and among the lower classes the luxury of
idleness, may always be preferred to commodities, and if this
were to take place when labour and capital were thrown out of
employment in equal proportions, would not capital become
more abundant than labour, and profits fall?

Do you expect to be in Town at Xmas, or not till the
Spring? Mrs. Malthus desires to be kindly remembered to
Mrs. Ricardo. I hope Mrs. Austin is quite well after her
travels.

Ever truly Yours
T R MALTHUS.

179. RICARDO TO MALTHUS²
[Reply to 178.—Answered by 181]

Gatcomb Park
5 Oct.ʳ 1816
My dear Sir

5 Oct. 1816   Notwithstanding the bad weather I have not failed to
enjoy myself, for I have been to Cheltenham, Malvern and

¹ Omitted in MS.   Hertford'.—MS at Albury.—
² Addressed: 'To / The Revᵈ   *Letters to Malthus*, XLIX.
T. R. Malthus / East India College /

Worcester, and latterly to Bath. To be sure the continued rains make it less pleasant than it otherwise would be, but as I am not at a loss for amusement within doors, I contrive to take my walks while it is fine, and return to my library with the recommencement of rain.

I have no wish to change my Oxford boat. With very little trouble I have lengthened that part of my new boat house where she was to be kept, and I find that I can manage her tolerably well alone. Being larger she requires more labour to row than Miss Eckersall's, but considering all circumstances, and particularly my youthful family, I believe it would be unwise to change her for a smaller.

Mrs. Hall called here one morning in her gig with another woman, before I was down stairs. When I was informed of her name and business, I deputed Mr. Hitchings, as he is an Oxford man and of course is known to her, to pay her her demand. She was going a little excursion for pleasure and thought she might as well call on me in her way.

I hope your additional volume will soon follow your new edition of the old work. I shall be glad to see in a connected form your matured opinions on the progress of rent, profits, and wages, and in what manner they are affected by the increasing difficulty of procuring food, by the increase of capital, and the improvement of machinery. I fear we shall not agree on these subjects, and I should be very glad if we could fairly submit our different views to the public, that we might have some able heads engaged in considering it. Of this however I have little hope for though I feel strongly the truth of my theory I cannot succeed in stating it clearly. I have been very much impeded by the question of price and value, my former ideas on those points not being correct. My present view may be equally faulty, for it leads to conclusions at variance with all my preconceived

5 Oct. 1816 opinions.[1] I shall continue to work, if only for my own satisfaction, till I have given my theory a consistent form.

You say that you think I have sometimes conceded that if population were miraculously stopped, while the most fertile land remained uncultivated, profits would fall upon the supposition of an increase of capital still going on. I concede it now. Profits I think depend on wages,—wages depend on demand and supply of labour, and on the cost of the necessaries on which wages are expended. These two causes may be operating on profits at the same time, either in the same, or in an opposite direction. In the case you put wages would have a tendency to keep stationary as far as the supply of food was concerned, but they would have a tendency to rise in consequence of the demand for labour increasing, whilst the supply continued the same. Under such circumstances profits would of course fall. You must however allow that this is an extraordinary case, and out of the common course of events, for the tendency of the population to increase is, in our state of society, more than equal to that of the capital to increase.

I shall be in London on thursday or friday next.—Mrs. Ricardo accompanies me on a visit to her sister for a few days. I should be glad if some fortunate accident were to take you to town at the same time. If so let me know where you are to be found;—a line directed to the Stock Exchange will be certain to find me. We shall not finally leave the country till Jan.ʸ or feb.ʸ I wish you would come and see a little more of Gatcomb during your Xmas vacation. Mrs. Austin is quite well after her travels.

Ever truly Yours
DAVID RICARDO

[1] His 'present view' probably refers to 'the compatibility of a rise of wages with a fall of prices' (above, I, 63); cp. 'the curious effect' mentioned below, p. 82.

180. MILL TO RICARDO[1]

[*Reply to 177.—Answered by* 185]

Ford Abbey Oct.[r] 6th 1816

My dear Sir

I have not been without hopes that I should see the   6 Oct. 1816
parcel you promised me in your last, before I wrote to you
again. Surely it has not taken all this time to copy what you
had prepared. By the bye, on this subject of copying, let me
give you an advice. You know you have dubbed me your
master, so I am entitled to give advice, *sans façons*. Now it
is such a pity that any portion of your time should be wasted
in the mere drudgery of copying, that you should always get a
person, at any cost, to do your copying. I am obliged to copy
for myself woefully, because I cannot afford to pay for it; but
most assuredly, if I were you, I never should copy a page.

Had you only pointed out the order in which you thought
the papers should be read, I could have been well contented,
had you sent them to me, as they were. I might have saved
you some useless labour. What I want to see, in the first place,
is—all the ideas, which you think necessary for the elucidation of the subject, down upon paper—no matter in what
order—no matter how imperfectly in regard to expression.
I warrant you, we shall find the proper order for them, by
degrees, and the proper expressions too. We shall find what
has too little said about, and what has too much. And shall in
the end make such a thing as we wish to have.

In regard to your delicacy (which is so great) about giving
me trouble, let me say a word once for all. You do not doubt
that I have a *good* deal of friendship for you, and I do not
doubt that you have a *good* deal for me. But know that I
have a *great* deal for you, and wish you to have a *great*

[1] Addressed: 'David Ricardo Esq. / Gatcomb Park / Minchinhampton / Gloucestershire'.—MS in *R.P.*

6 Oct. 1816 deal for me. It follows, of course, if there is any occasion, on which I can be of any service to you, that the trouble is greatly overpaid by the pleasure. But not to lay too much stress upon this ground, lest I begin to be sentimental, I must make a bit of a confession, that I should have a pleasure in reading such papers as yours on political economy, if so it were that I hated the author as much as I like him. So your conscience may be perfectly quiet on this score. I shall be on the look-out every day, as soon, as this has had time to summon you, for the fruit of your labours. When you do send the parcel, however, you had better write to me by post; because, if left at Ilminster, with which we have no regular communication, I may not get it for some time, unless I send for it.

When you wrote to me last, you were just setting out upon a bit of a tour, which was to extend as far as Worcester. I hope it was agreeable—it must have been so, as far as the temper of those who composed the party could make it—and I wished I had been one, notwithstanding the motives I have to be industrious. My hopes of being able to visit you this year have all vanished. Our project of visiting Brougham was defeated by his absence. I had a letter from him not many days ago, dated at Milan, where he was enjoying himself greatly with the Italian literati; to whom (would you think it?) he is hugely recommended by his religious and political opinions. He was reading the Italian poets, two or three hours a day, with Monte,[1] the most celebrated poet and man of letters in Italy; and was soon to be joined by Dumont, who was to go with him to Florence. Could I have got away, I should have found infinite pleasure in spending, however, a week with you at Gatcomb; but Koe[2] upon whom I

[1] Vincenzo Monti.
[2] John Herbert Koe, a barrister who at one time was Bentham's amanuensis (see *Works of Bentham*, ed. Bowring, vol. x, p. 62).

counted to relieve me here, has been uncertain in his motions, and I could not prevail upon Mr. B. to part with me. I must content myself now with looking to another year.

Our weather has been for some time mild, or rather warm; but from the continued rains, and want of sun, I think it impossible we can have any thing but a defective crop. And as wages, at least country wages, have fallen very low, the quantity of misery for the next year will be exceedingly great. You and I, however, have always agreed, that no such loss of capital can have been sustained in this country since the last years of activity, as to have much impaired the funds for the maintenance of labour; and that we had no occasion to anticipate a permanent depression of the national industry. This year, however, will still fall heavy upon the landlords, who are the most powerful, and the most noisy party in the state; and I should not wonder if we had very absurd propositions well supported in parliament about the national debt. Cobbett, I see, is labouring the doctrine, that it is not the debt of the *nation*, as the nation, not being represented, did not contract it; that it is the debt only of the oligarchs who composed the parliament. *This* doctrine will do no harm in parliament. But the doctrine that the fundholders are drawing the rents of gentlemens estates, is one well calculated to receive attention.

Though a good deal interrupted by jobwork, of which I have always my hands a great deal too full, I am making tolerable progress in revising my poor history[1]; and hope I may at last get into the printers hands about the time I return to town. It will be a motley kind of a production, having been written at such distant times, and with so many interruptions. But I am pleased with the quantity of instruction it will convey; though I am more than doubtful as to

[1] *History of British India.*

the entertaining qualities, by which alone reputation is acquired.

I beg the acceptance of my best respects by all who care for me at Gatcomb, and around it. And am always

My Dear Sir
Very faithfully Yours
J. MILL

Should you have any disposition to purchase Ford Abbey, if it were to be sold? The rents are about £1,400 a year, besides a wood, which produces about £100 a year more.

181. MALTHUS TO RICARDO[1]

[Reply to 179.—Answered by 182]

My dear Sir   E I Coll Oct 9ᵗʰ 1816

I am sorry it so happens that I cannot contrive to be in Town the end of this week, or I should have great pleasure in meeting you. Cannot you manage to make up for the disappointment and come down to us on saturday. You will have nothing to do in Town on saturday evening and sunday at this empty time of the year, and you will give Mrs. Malthus and myself great pleasure

I am very glad to hear that you like upon the whole your Oxford boat. If you can manage it tolerably well with sculls by yourself, it is of no great importance in a *lake* that you should not be able to get on quite so fast as in a smaller boat, and its superior safety is certainly an important consideration.

I cannot guess how soon my new volume may come out after the edition of the old work. I must see first how soon the edition is completed.

---

[1] Addressed: 'D. Ricardo Esqr. / Stock Exchange. / London'.
MS in *R.P.*

I am sorry to find that you are hopeless about our agreeing 9 Oct. 1816 on the subject of labour profits &c. I had some idea that we were approaching, as it appeared to me that by allowing that profits depend upon the demand and supply of labour, you in fact allow that they depend upon competition.

Will it not be true in all cases that rent will depend upon the demand compared with the supply of good land, wages on the demand compared with the supply of labour, and profits on the demand compared with the supply of capital.

By an increased demand for capital I always mean, such prices of commodities compared with the expences of production as will yield increased profits.

If under any facility of production, an increase of capital faster than the increase of labour will lower profits, can it possibly be said that profits depend on facility of production and that the throwing poor land out of cultivation must necessarily raise them.

I am anxious to see your new ideas on the subject of price and value,—but I am interrupted by the postman.

Ever truly Yours

T R Malthus

182. RICARDO TO MALTHUS[1]

[*Reply to* 181.—*Answered by* 183]

Bow Middx 11 Oct.[r] 1816

My dear Sir

I arrived in London this morning and found your kind 11 Oct. 1816 letter, which I ought to have answered immediately, as you could not otherwise know, whether I accepted your kind invitation, before the time that you might expect me. The truth

---

[1] Addressed: 'To / The Rev.[d] MS at Albury.—*Letters to Mal-* T R Malthus / East India College / *thus*, L. Hertford –'.

11 Oct. 1816 is I forgot the day of the week, and was not aware, till I got home, that we were so near saturday. I very much regret that I shall not be able to avail myself of Mrs. Malthus' and your kindness, as I have engagements here which will prevent me from leaving town till I return to Gatcomb.

You mistake me if you suppose me to say that under no circumstances of facility of production profits could fall. What I say is that profits will rise when wages fall, and as one of the main causes of the fall of wages is cheap food and necessaries, it is *probable* that with facility of production, or cheap food and necessaries, profits would rise. At the very time that the labour of a certain number of men may produce on such land as pays no rent 1100 instead of 1000 quarters of corn, and when corn falls in consequence from £5 to £4. 10 – p.ʳ quarter, the money as well as the corn [1] wages of labour *may* rise for capital *may* have increased at a very rapid rate and labourers at a slow rate, in which case profits would fall and not rise. Under these very peculiar circumstances of higher money wages with a lower price of necessaries, the wages of labour would be in an unusual state, and would slowly revert to the old standard, when profits would feel the benefit. All I mean to contend for is that profits depend on wages, wages, under common circumstances, on the price of food, and necessaries, and the price of food and necessaries on the fertility of the last cultivated land.

In all cases it is perhaps true that rent will depend upon the demand compared with the supply of good land, and wages on the demand compared with the supply of labour, if it be allowed that the price of necessaries influence the demand and supply of labour.

I do not quite understand the expression that profits depend on the demand compared with the supply of capital.

[1] Last six words are ins.

What would you say of two countries in which there are 11 Oct. 1816
precisely equal capitals,—where wages are also equal, and
where the population is precisely in the same number.
Would the demand compared with the supply of capital be
the same in both? If you say they would I ask whether their
rate of profits would be the same under any other supposition but that of their land being exactly of the same degree of
fertility? To me it appears quite probable that the ordinary
and usual rate of profits might in one be 20 and in the other
only 15 pc.ᵗ or in any other proportions.

Pray give my kind regards to Mrs. Malthus and believe me

Ever Yours

David Ricardo

183. MALTHUS TO RICARDO[1]

[Reply to 182.—*Answered by* 184]

E I Coll Oct 13ᵗʰ [1816]

My dear Sir,

I am sorry there is no chance of our seeing you at the 13 Oct. 1816
College. Pray let me know, by return of post if you can, how
long you stay in London or its neighbourhood, as I think it
possible that I may be able to get to Town the end of this
week or beginning of next, and if you have not left it, I may
still perhaps see you before your return to Gatcomb.

To say that profits depend upon wages appears to me I
confess, a very vague proposition, as in fact they may be
extremely different with either the same money wages of
labour, or the same real wages of labour, although it is
unquestionably true, or rather a mere truism, to say that
given the production, and supposing it to consist of wages

---

[1] Addressed: 'Dᵈ. Ricardo Esqr / Stock Exchange / London'. Postmark, 1816.—MS in *R.P.*

13 Oct. 1816 and profits, the higher is the amount of one, the lower must be the amount of the other.

The real question is, what is the main cause which determines the rate of profits under all the varying degrees of productiveness? and I have no hesitation in answering distinctly that it is the proportion which capital bears to labour; or the plenty or scarcity of capital compared with the plenty or scarcity of labour; and what I mean by the demand for capital is a scarcity of capital compared with labour.

In the case you have put to me, I conceive that the profits would be the same, if the proportion of capital to labour were the same.

The chapel bell rings

Ever Yours

T R MALTHUS

184. RICARDO TO MALTHUS[1]

[*Reply to* 183]

London 14ᵗʰ Octʳ 1816

My dear Sir

14 Oct. 1816   My stay in London will not be prolonged beyond friday next.—I hope it will be convenient to you to come up before. On thursday[2] I shall be disengaged and will meet you at any place in London that may best suit you, unless you will dine with me at my brothers at Bow. His house is small, and I fear he has not, now we are with him, a spare bed to offer, and you may not like to travel so far at night. If so let us meet in the city, and get our dinner there.

The money wages of labour are I apprehend generally regulated by facility of production. With an abundant pro-

---

[1] Addressed: 'To / The Revᵈ T R Malthus / East India College / Hertford'.   MS at Albury.—*Letters to Malthus*, LI.
[2] 17 October.

duction too I think that a less proportion of the whole will be given to the landlords, and more will remain for the other two classes of capitalists and labourers,—but of this increased quantity a greater proportion will be given to Capitalists, and a less proportion to labourers. Now though what you call the real wages of labour, (but which I think a wrong term,)[1] will increase the money wages will fall. But this will not be the case with profits, what you would call real profits would increase but so would also money profits. Under the circumstances then that I have supposed the rate of profits would rise though money wages would fall. The difference between us is this. I say, that with every facility or difficulty of production, of the quantity of necessaries, that is to be divided between profits and wages, different proportions will be given to each, and that money will accurately shew those proportions. You appear to me to think that profits do not depend on the division of the produce, and that money wages may as often rise with facility of production as fall.

You state the real question fairly it is "what is the main cause which determines the rate of profits under all the varying degrees of productiveness?["] You do not appear to me [to][2] solve the question when you answer "that it is the proportion which capital bears to labour.["]

In a rich country where profits are low and where a great portion of produce is paid to the landlords for rent the proportion of labour to capital will be the greatest, and yet according to your theory it should be the least.

You will not I think deny that in a country where labour is high a manufacturer would employ more capital to produce

---

[1] Malthus calls 'real wages' (above, II, 224) what for Ricardo is the 'nominal value of wages' (above, I, 50, and cp. 274–5 n.).

[2] Omitted in MS.

14 Oct. 1816 the same commodities than what he would do in a country where wages were low, and there also would profits be low, —that is to say profits are high where capital bears a large proportion to labour and low where labour bears a large proportion to capital.

I am writing amidst the noise of the Stock Exchange and very much fear that I shall be more than usually incomprehensible

Ever Yours
DAVID RICARDO

185. RICARDO TO MILL[1]
[*Reply to* 180.—*Answered by* 186, 187 & 192]

London 14 Oct.ʳ 1816
My dear Sir

14 Oct. 1816   After the receipt of your letter I determined to bring my papers to town with me to which place I was obliged to come for a few days. I have been reading them over in the Post Chaise, and they are really so little connected, so imperfect, and altogether so very bad in their present state, that I am not doing myself common justice to expose them even to your friendly eye.

They are worse than they otherwise would be in consequence of my becoming better acquainted with the subject as I have proceeded. Much of what is said in the beginning should be left out or altered to agree with what I think the more correct views which I afterwards adopted. You will see the curious effect which the rise of wages produces on the prices of those commodities which are chiefly obtained by the aid of machinery and fixed capital. I hope you will

---

[1] Addressed: 'James Mill Esqʳ / Ford Abbey / Chard / Somersetshire'.
MS in Mill-Ricardo papers.

be able to make out what I have said on that subject, and will give me your well considered opinion on this difficult point. There are tables in which calculations are given of the present value of an annuity for any number of years to come on the supposition of money being at various rates of interest. If I had a capital of an imperishable nature which would unassisted perform work, and its value were £20000, profits being 10 pc̲t̲ the goods annually produced should be of the value of £2000—but if this capital were of a perishable nature, if for example it would last only for 10 years, the value of the goods produced should be equal to the value of an annuity which £20000 would purchase for that time, when money was at 10 pc—. Have you any doubt of the correctness of this proposition.—I believe I could not consent to send you the papers in their present state but that I am desirous of ascertaining how far your opinion coincides with mine of the correctness of the views which I have taken. A hint or two of yours will enable me to make the next copy much more perfect.

On the subject of copying I should certainly follow your suggestion and employ another person to do that drudgery for me, but I am too young a writer to proceed in that way. I never strictly copy any thing I write, but alter and try to amend every page that I rewrite. I am too much flattered with your good opinion not to be gratified with what you say respecting your regard for me. You run no risk of deceiving yourself in considering it reciprocal. You are bound to perform and I am sure will perform the duty of a friend, and tell me candidly what I am quite prepared to hear, any the most disadvantageous opinions you may form on reading my papers. You cannot think worse of them than I do.

I have been beyond measure puzzled to find out the law of price. I found on a reference to figures that my former

14 Oct. 1816 opinion could not be correct and I was full a fortnight pondering on my difficulty before I knew how to solve it. During that time I could not proceed or I should have made greater progress. I shall now consider the subject of taxation that I may have a consistent theory in the first instance on paper. When you have done with my papers be so good as to send them directed to me at T. Clutterbuck's, Widcomb, Bath.

You very much disappoint me by telling me that I shall not see you at Gatcomb this year. Perhaps a favorable opportunity may yet offer for a short absence from Ford Abbey, if so do not fail to come to us.—Our journey to Malvern was very much enjoyed by us all. I wish you had been with us. It would have been a little recreation and I know you would have been pleased with the good humor which was uniformly shewn by us all, and to which you would have contributed so good a share. I am glad to hear that Brougham is distinguished in Italy on account of his religious and political opinions as it more fully convinces me of the absurdity and malignity of the reports which are prevalent in London to his disadvantage. You will perhaps hardly believe that the scandalous story is that he has taken off the authoress of the novel which Mrs. Ricardo lately lent to you. Mrs. Ricardo who is the only one of the family now with me desires to be kindly remembered.

Ever truly Yʳˢ

DAVID RICARDO

The parcel is sent by the Bath and Exeter coach which goes from the Bolt in Tun. I return to Gatcomb on friday.

186. MILL TO RICARDO[1]
[*Reply to* 185.—*Answered by* 188]

[Ford Abbey, 23 Oct. 1816]
My Dear Sir
Your letter is dated the 14th of October; You say, "The 23 Oct. 1816
parcel is sent by the Bath and E[x]eter coach", &.c.—this is
the 23[d] of the month—no parcel has yet made its appearance
—and I am out of all patience.

In the first place, you could hardly have sent it by a
worse coach, if you had sent it by the York and Edin[r],
instead of the Bath and Exeter, which I fancy comes not
within 20 miles of this place—when (being in London) you
might have sent it by any one of two coaches, which pass
through Chard—but if it had been sent by any Exeter coach,
except the round-about one through Bath, I should have got
it either at Ilminster or Axminster. At present I know not
where it may be left; and I suspect an angry letter must be
written by you to London. If it had been carried on to
Exeter, it might have been sent back here long ago. I shall
write a line, by reason of this derangement, as soon as it
arrives.

I am grieved by a paragraph I see in the newspaper today,
that Horner is obliged to spend the winter in Italy for his
health. I dined in company with him not long before leaving
London, when he coughed in a manner that frightened me.
He will be a very great loss—even his absence this winter is
grievously to be deplored—when so many foolish, and, I
fear, some villainous schemes of finance, will be proposed and
listened to. You ought indeed to be in parliament, and you
must at any rate make arrangements for it at the general

[1] Addressed: 'David Ricardo Esq / Gatcomb Park / Minchinhampton / Gloucester Shire'. Postmark, Chard, undated. For the date, see the first sentence. MS in *R.P.*

23 Oct. 1816 election. Speak to Wakefield; or rather, without losing time, write to him. He knows a great deal about seats.

The scandal about Brougham and the lady you allude to, is not a new thing. I did not know she was abroad. But I have pretty good reason to believe she is not with Brougham.

Yours truly

J. MILL

187. MILL TO RICARDO[1]

[*Reply to* 185.—*Answered by* 188]

Ford Abbey 25th Octr 1816

My dear Sir

25 Oct. 1816   My impatience has put you to the expence of two letters, which I regret, as I do all useless expence. The parcel is here, at last, safe. It had remained, as I imagined at Taunton. I shall fall to its contents tomorrow morning, with great avidity. You may count upon my telling you exactly what I think of it. In the mean time, however, it is your business, to work as hard as you can; till you have completely accomplished what you tell me in your letter is your first object—namely, to get down upon paper a complete system of ideas upon the subject. That is right. This is exactly the proper mode of proceeding. This you are more competent to do than any body; and when this is done, it will be easy to make you see, how all the rest is to be done. I am happy to hear you are upon taxation; and shall be curious to see what comes forth, as soon as it is done. That is a point closely connected with some of the most abstruse principles of the science.

We have here had two most dreadful days—or at least we have had all yesterday and this morning very dreadful. I

[1] Addressed: 'David Ricardo Esq. / Gatcomb Park / Minchinhampton / Gloucester Shire'.—MS in *R.P.*

hardly ever saw rain fall in such torrents; and blown at the 25 Oct. 1816 same time with great violence. This day all our rivulets are rivers; and the roads overflown. We had previously a fortnight of good harvest weather—and the corn here is mostly got in. For want of sun to ripen it, a great deal of it however will not be productive—and prices will be high. Is there much suffering about you? I do not mean of the farmers, at present, whose suffering is only that of comparative poverty —but of the people who live by the daily work of their hands; and whose suffering means, starvation and death. Here the quantity is great—and our clergyman, who is also a magistrate and a good man, tells me that the decisions which as a magistrate he is obliged to make, in the case of applications for parochial aid, render his life a burthen to him—as it is giving to a man who is starving, by taking from others, the mass of the parishioners, who are but one degree removed from the starving condition.

You will now, I suppose, be partly free from visitations and from interruption. And you have two good months for exertion before the time when you will think of returning to London. I have no doubt that good fruits will be derived from them.

Believe always truly Yours
J. MILL

188. RICARDO TO MILL[1]
[Reply to 186 & 187.—Answered by 195]

Widcomb House   Bath
17 Novr 1816

My dear Sir

    I have sent you by the Coach, which leaves this place 17 Nov. 1816 this morning, the papers which I have filled since I last wrote

[1] Addressed: 'J. Mill Esqr / Ford Abbey / Chard / Somersetshire'. MS in Mill-Ricardo papers.

17 Nov. 1816 to you,—they are in the same rough state as the others, but I was desirous before you returned the first parcel that you should see these, that you might have at once under your view the whole of the principles which I hold to be correct against the great authorities which are opposed to me. On the subject of taxation you will perceive that I have altered, I hope corrected, some of the views which I had heretofore taken. I hope I shall be able to convince you of the general correctness of my principles. I have dwelt very little on the effect of those taxes on which there can be no difference of opinion, and have not mentioned many which have been ably handled by Adam Smith. His language is so clear, and his explanations so satisfactory, that I feel a reluctance to weaken the effect of it by using my words instead of his, and always feel a propensity to quote him without a word of comment. You will I hope now give me credit for having fulfilled my promise. I have actually put on paper nearly all I have to say, and if I were to do more I should be only doing badly what has already been admirably well done. I am ready however to follow any course you shall recommend, and to supply any deficiencies in my power. It must be your task to curtail.—I have an anxious desire to produce something worth publishing, but that I unaffectedly fear will not be in my power. I should however be contented if with your suggestions and corrections I could make the MS clear, so that I said every thing necessary to elucidate my opinions, and to give a consistent theory, even if it should never meet the public eye.

It is my intention to read Adam Smith once more, to take notes of all passages which very much favor, or are directly opposed to my peculiar opinions, and shall afterwards submit to you the propriety of inserting them in the proper places of my MS. In reading Adam Smith my attention may be

called to other points which I may think it important to
notice. After reading Smith I mean to read Say again,—but
as he is a living author, and a friend, I should feel some
delicacy in making my objections publicly and strongly to
his opinions, which I should not feel with Adam Smith.

I have sent the parcel from York House, and the man has
faithfully promised that it shall be immediately forwarded to
the Red Lion at Chard, to which place you will be so good
as to send for it. I hope you will have no reserve with me
but will give me your candid opinion of my performance;
be assured that however unfavourable that opinion may be
I can bear it, and notwithstanding all that has been said of
the self complacency of authors, if I know any thing of
myself, your discouragement to publish would be only a
confirmation of my own opinion, and therefore my sympathy would run with it.

Mrs. Ricardo and I have been here a week, and I know
not how much longer we shall be detained. Mrs. Ricardo's
errand is to be the first to welcome our first grandchild into
this troublesome world, and we are in hourly expectation of
the little stranger. I could have wished to remain at Gatcomb
till the anxious time was past, but Mrs. Ricardo considers
my presence as the greatest comfort to her, and she has so
often told me so that I at last begin to believe her; I am
therefore in quiet possession of a snug dressing room with
Adam Smith and Say on my table, and pass my time
with very few more interruptions than I should meet at
Gatcomb.

The absence of Horner is indeed a great loss. I meet with
no one who does not lament his illness. Whatever he has
undertaken he has done well, and has always avoided the
error into which I think Brougham is apt to fall, he never
goes beyond the mark, he never endeavors to prove too

17 Nov. 1816 much. Mr. Whishaw who corresponds with Mr. Smith our neighbour mentions Horner in every letter. I am glad to hear that he bore his journey to Paris without being much fatigued, and that Dr. Baillie has good hopes of his recovery.

I am sorry that the distresses still continue. The short crop this year was most unfortunate, it aggravated all our former ills. I am sorry to see a disposition to inflame the minds of the lower orders by persuading them that legislation can afford them any relief. The country has a right to insist, and I hope will insist, on the most rigid economy in every branch of the public expenditure, but when this is yielded nothing further can be done for us. With kind compliments to Mrs. Mill and Mr. Bentham I am My dear Sir

Ever truly yours

DAVID RICARDO

189. RICARDO TO MILL¹

[*Answered by* 195]

Widcombe House, Bath
20ᵗʰ Novʳ 1816

My dear Sir

20 Nov. 1816   On my return here from Gatcomb yesterday, where I had been to pay a visit of one evening to my bairns, I found the parcel which you had sent me. As the letter you promise will probably be directed to Gatcomb it will be some days before I shall receive it here.² I must wait therefore patiently for the further instructions which I am prepared to follow.

You would not at this moment have been again troubled with a letter from me, if I had not been anxious to correct an error in the papers which you now have.

¹ Addressed: 'James Mill Esqʳ / Ford Abbey / near / Chard /Somerset-shire'.—MS in Mill-Ricardo papers.   ² See below, p. 97, n.

I had great difficulty to reconcile to my mind, what 20 Nov. 1816 appeared to me true in argument, that a tax on the profits of stock, either by sinking the money rent of the landlord, leaving the prices of commodities as before; or by raising the prices of commodities, leaving money rent as before; would really affect the landlord. During a very restless night I discovered that I had overlooked an important fact.

I have argued as if the tax on profits would be a proportional tax on the gross produce of the land, and not on the net produce of the farmer. You will observe that in one place [1] I observe that if an equal land tax were laid on every species of land in cultivation, it would be unequal in its operation, as it would be a bounty to the landlord of the best land. It would raise the price of corn equal to the burden borne by the farmer of the worst land, but this additional price being obtained for the greater quantity of produce yielded by the better land, farmers of such land would be benefited during their leases, and after that the advantage would go to the landlord.

The cultivators of N$^{\circ}$ 1, 2, and 3 get the very same profits, the only difference is in the rent. If their land yields respectively 180, 170, and 160 quarters, and the value of 2 quarters be paid by each farmer for the tax, and the price of corn and every thing else continues unaltered after the tax, there will be no alteration in money or in corn rent, for 2 deducted from the above sums leaves 178, 168, and 158. The difference between land N$^{\circ}$ 3 and N$^{\circ}$ 1 continues 20 q^{rs}, and that between 3 and 2–10 q^{rs}. If the price be also unaltered say £4,—the rent would continue to be on N$^{\circ}$ 1 £80 on N$^{\circ}$ 2 £40.–.– and as by the supposition the price of no commodity would be raised the landlord would be untaxed. But suppose the price of corn and of every other commodity

[1] Above, I, 182.

20 Nov. 1816 raised, and raised in the same proportion by the tax; rent also would be raised in that proportion for if corn be raised 10 pc^t or from £4– to £4. 8.–, rent will be raised 10 pc^t and the land N° 1 will give £88 and N° 2 £44.– for 20 q^{rs} at £4. 8 comes to £88, and 10 q^{rs} to £44.–. If raised 25 pc^t or to £5.– rent will also rise 25 pc^t or to £50.–, so that in every case the land[lord] [1] will be unaffected by such a tax. In short a tax on the profits of stock always leaves corn rent unaltered; a tax on raw produce, tithes, &c^a, never leaves corn rent unaltered, but generally leaves money rent unaltered. [2]

This subject is now very clear to my mind, but I fear I have not succeeded in making it clear to yours for I have used a strange jumble of words. I have no doubt however but that your own reflections will lead you to the same conclusions without any explanations of mine. When I insert my amended opinion in its proper place I hope I shall be more lucid.

Mrs. Clutterbuck continues well. She and Mrs. Ricardo unite in kind regards to you.

I shall certainly remain here till tuesday next [3] on which day I must go to London. I shall not be there for more than two nights and I do not yet know whether I shall return here or go to Gatcomb.

Ever truly Yours
DAVID RICARDO

---

[1] Covered by seal.
[2] Cp. the passage in *Principles*, above, I, 211–12.

[3] 26 November.

190. M^cCULLOCH TO RICARDO[1]

[*Reply to 167.—Answered by* 194]

College Street Edinburgh
19 Novr 1816

Dear Sir

I again take the liberty of sending you a copy of my 19 Nov. 1816
Essay,[2] which you will see I have considerably enlarged—
I have attempted to obviate the objection contained in the
letter you honoured me with, viz "that the reducing of the
interest of the Public Debt, would be taking advantage of
a rise in the value of Gold and silver"; and I have endeavoured
to shew that after a reduction is made to a very considerable

---

[1] Addressed: 'David Ricardo Esq' —not passed through the post. Received by Ricardo in London on 26 November: see his reply. MS in *R.P.*

[2] *An Essay on the Question of Reducing the Interest of the National Debt; in which the Justice and Expediency of that Measure are fully established*, Edinburgh, Brown and Black, 1816, pp. viii, 213. The copy presented to Ricardo is in the library at Gatcombe. A copy in the Goldsmiths' Library of the University of London contains the autograph inscription: 'This tract I have suppressed and disavowed long ago: J. R. M^cC. Edin^r 1845'.

As in the earlier *Essay* (see above, p. 37), of which it is an enlarged version, McCulloch proposes to reduce the interest on the national debt in proportion to the fall in the price of corn since the time when the debt was contracted. McCulloch seems to have changed his views in 1821, when Mushet's *Series of Tables* (see below, VIII,

396–8) proved that the losses of the national creditor from depreciation balanced his later gains. Thereafter, he did his best to sink into oblivion his former support of what he had come to regard as 'an open and barefaced robbery' (*Edinburgh Review*, July 1821, p. 488): as Hollander (*Letters to McCulloch*, p. 9) notices, he omitted both Essays from the lists of his works prefixed to his later books and did not mention them in his *Literature of Political Economy*, 1845, or in any other of his works; also, when editing Ricardo's *Works*, he quietly omitted a footnote of the *Principles* which inconveniently referred to Mr. McCulloch's 'able publication' (see above, I, 426). In the *Literature*, however, a transparent apology for the views once entertained by certain 'well-informed persons' will be found in the comment (p. 79) on Sir James Graham's *Corn and Currency*, 1827, a pamphlet which advocated a similar proposal.

19 Nov. 1816 extent, the stockholders will still receive payment of all the *bullion* they lent—

I do not exactly understand what you mean by saying all taxes fall ultimately on the consumers. To me this seems just the same thing as to say, that all taxes fall ultimately on the public in general. The labouring class are consumers as well as producers—consumers who pay by far the greatest share of the taxes—Besides if the labouring class were to get their taxes completely reimbursed to them, the price of their products must thereby be increased, and the demand for them being consequently diminished, taxation must really bring on them the most serious of evils—

I am sorry to have to differ with you entirely on the subject of the sinking fund.—I am precisely of Says opinion—ce n'est pas qu'n veritable leurre [1]—

You will excuse the freedom of these remarks, and believe me to be with

Much respect
Dear Sir
Yours Mt ob st
J. R. M^cCULLOCH

David Ricardo Esqre

191. TROWER TO RICARDO [2]

Unsted Wood—Godalming—
Nov: 19—1816—

Dear Ricardo

19 Nov. 1816   Many thanks for your last kind letter,[3] by which I am rejoiced to find you are steadily pursuing your economical

[1] 'La caisse d'amortissement est un véritable leurre.' J.-B. Say, *De l'Angleterre et des Anglais*, Paris, Bertrand, 1815, p. 14, n.
[2] Addressed: 'To/David Ricardo Esqr / Gatcomb Park / Minchinhampton / Glocestershire'. Pro-

bably received by Ricardo on 28 November, when he passed through Gatcomb on his way from London to Bath; see below, p. 101.
MS in *R.P.*
[3] Ricardo's letter is wanting.

enquiries—The detection of error is as important as the discovery of truth; and therefore I cannot allow, that those two months were useless to you, by the labors of which you were enabled to ascertain the fallacy of the theory you were endeavouring to establish.—Superficial thinkers go blundering on from error to error, without the chance of recovery; whilst he who patiently and laboriously follows up, step by step, the consequences of his reasoning, however much he may aberrate in his progress, is sure to come safely home at last.—The subject you are engaged upon is of great interest and importance, and I do not doubt, that your enquiries will eventually produce satisfactory results.—

I have begun, but as yet have made little progress in, Wayland's Book.[1] I think however, that I can already discover great inconsistences and contradictions in his reasoning. He seems to have considered, that the moral consequences resulting from Malthus's doctrines were pernicious, and therefore was determined, at all events, to prove them false; and in his attempts to accomplish this object he has involved himself in serious difficulties. Every day's experience proves, more and more, the importance of this subject, and the necessity of having its principles firmly fixed, and properly understood. For, whatever measures may be adopted with a view to relieve the present distresses of the Country, will only have the effect of aggravating our difficulties, unless they spring from these principles and are in exact conformity to them. How are the poor fareing in your neighbourhood, what are your wages, prices of bread, meat and pork? What your stated parish relief, and your numbers out of work? We have just encreased the allowance for Parish relief, here, from 6/- to 7/- a week for a single man, 10/6 for a

[1] See above, p. 46, n. 1.

19 Nov. 1816 man and his wife, and 1/9 for each child. Our wages are 12/- week—

I have it in contemplation to act as a Magistrate, in this neighbourhood, as I see, that, by so doing, I may make myself useful, and I do not wish to be one of the drones in the hive—This makes it necessary for me to turn my attention to these subjects, and to consult Blackstone Burns and the other guides in this humble walk. But as it makes up in utility, what it wants in importance, I trust you will follow my good example; for sure I am your assistance in the great manufacturing district in which you reside must be most desireable—

Our provident fund advances slowly, indeed the times do not lead one to expect a different result. We possess £1100. Stock—The importance of having the question of extending parish relief to Depositors settled by Parliament consists in this. That unless their right to relief, under certain circumstances, should be recognised by the Legislature, Magistrates may think themselves bound, looking to the strict letter of the law with respect to paupers, to withhold it; in which case the poor would abstain from connecting themselves with a concern, which might deprive them of parish assistance. And altho' I admit, that these persons constitute a part only of those for whose benefit these institutions are established, yet they are a most important part, in as much as it is by withdrawing them from the parish funds, that we hope eventually diminish the poors rates. Besides, this question of relief *must be determined somewhere*, if by the Magistrates, without parliamentary sanction, it will most likely be settled differently in different parts of the Country, in which case the poor will be left in doubt on the subject, and will not therefore run the risk of becoming depositors; whereas the sanction of Parliament will enable the Magistrates to consider, that *by the general rule* they are authorised to grant 19 Nov. 1816 relief, and their withholding it will depend upon the circumstances of the *particular case in question*—

How are Ministers to meet the financial difficulties? What do you hear or think upon that subject? Pray do not follow my bad example but write to me soon—Make our united kind remembrances to Mrs. Ricardo and family and believe me yours very sincerely

HUTCHES TROWER

192. MILL TO RICARDO[1]

[*Reply to* 185.—*Answered by* 193]

My dear Sir

Ford Abbey Novr 18th 1816

If the length of time I have taken to read your M.S. has 18 Nov. 1816 not interrupted your progress, I shall make for it no apology. I wished to read it carefully, writing marginal contents for my own use, as I went along. And I could not conveniently bestow upon that subject more than a limited portion of each day. However I now have got through the whole, and have the contents of each paragraph, regularly numbered, before me.

Perhaps I ought to begin by speaking ill of the whole production, that I might give you confidence in my sincerity; as that seems to be your grand test. However I have time for nothing just now, but to come to the point as directly as possible. And I authorize you to believe, that I shall not even employ one word for the sake of encouraging you, as a young beginner, but shall speak the truth to you as I would have done had you been as hackneyed a stager as I am myself.

---

[1] Addressed: 'David Ricardo Esq. /Gatcomb Park/Minchinhampton / Gloucestershire' and redirected: ' T. Clutterbuck Esqre/Wedcombe House / Bath'. Received by Ricardo on 29 November; see his reply. MS in *R.P.*

18 Nov. 1816 My opinion may be given in very few words; for I think you have made out all your points. There is not a single proposition the proof of which I think is not irresistible. With the curious result pointed out in your letter with respect to the effects produced by the rise of wages, on the price of those commodities which are chiefly the return from fixed capital, I was very much struck; but have no doubt whatsoever as to the validity of your conclusions, the proof of which I think is incontrovertible.

Your explanation of the general principle that quantity of labour is the cause and measure of exchangeable value, excepting in the cases which you except, is both satisfactory, and clear.[1]

Your exposition and argumentation to shew, in opposition to A. Smith, that profits of stock do not disturb that law, are luminous.[2] So are the exposition and argumentation to shew that rent also operates no such disturbance.

And to this extent the disquisition is remarkably free of that sin which most easily besets you, of crowding too many points into one place; and summoning all the parts of the science at once to prove a particular point. The argument thus far is not only convincing, but clear, and easily understood.

At page 79[3] you begin the inquiry concerning the causes of alterations in the state of wages; and from this to p. 105, I think the topics are somewhat mixed together. I have not meditated sufficiently to be able to say how far that is avoidable; but I consider the inquiry in these pages as an inquiry not into the causes of change in the rate of wages alone, but the causes of changes in the wages, profits, and rent all together. The grounds laid down for every one of the

[1] See above, I, 12 ff.
[2] See above, I, 22, n. 3 and ff. pp.
[3] Corresponding, presumably, to I, 88, of the present ed.

opinions carry the firmest conviction to my mind; and several of the doctrines which puzzled me formerly, are now perfectly clear.

The inquiry concerning foreign trade, which commences at p. 106,[1] and continues to the end, is like the rest, original, and sound, and excellently demonstrated. That foreign trade augments not the value of a nations property: that it may be good for a country to import commodities from a country where the production of those same commodities costs more, than it would cost at home: that a change in manufacturing skill in one country, produces a new distribution of the precious metals, are new propositions of the highest importance, and which you fully prove.

You have, therefore, made great progress toward the production of a most admirable book. The stile also, is really excellent. You have improved in that respect exceedingly. There are but a few expressions in the whole which, if you had been going to print immediately, I should have recommended it to you to alter. Of these I have taken no notice at present, because they are not worth your minding. What I am anxious for is, that you should go on, exactly as you are doing, till you have got all your thoughts, in this shape, upon paper; and have gone over the whole subject. It will then be easy to give you advice about marshalling, and separating. And easy then for you to put the last hand to a work which will gain you immortal honour.

The M.S. was sent yesterday to Illminster, addressed to Mr. Clutterbuck, and is by this time at Bath. Send me the rest of what you have done. I long to hear you on tithes. I beg to hear from you without delay; and am most truly

Yours

J. MILL

[1] Above, I, 128.

193. RICARDO TO MILL[1]

[*Reply to 192.—Answered by 195*]

Widcomb, Bath
2 Dec.[r] 1816—

My dear Sir

2 Dec. 1816   I did not receive your kind letter dated the 18th ult. till friday evening,[2] which I suppose was partly owing to its being directed to Gatcomb. It arrived here four days before I returned from London, to which place I told you I was going, for a short time, in my last.

I can have no reason to doubt your sincerity, and therefore I am not a little gratified with the opinion you have given of my MS. I hope you will not think I have fallen off in the papers which you have now before you,—the subject is perhaps more difficult, and it had not previously engaged so much of my thoughts as the former. How very encouraging your letter is! You really give me hopes that my ardent wish will be attained, that I may produce something which will fairly entitle me to be considered as an improver of the science.—I shall pursue my work with increased energy, and I hope with more confidence than has hitherto accompanied my exertions. In reading Adam Smith, again, I find many opinions to question, all I believe founded on his original error respecting value. He is particularly faulty in the chapter on bounties, and is also I think wrong in some points respecting colonies, and the interest of the mother country. Would you advise me to notice every thing in his book which I think wrong? and if so would you incorporate the discussion in that part of my book where similar questions are treated, or would you refer to the appendix and let it appear there separate from the other part? Give me your

[1] Addressed: 'James Mill Esq[r] /   MS in Mill-Ricardo papers.
Ford Abbey / near / Chard /   [2] 29 November.
Somersetshire'.

advice too about noticing Say and Buchanan. In giving 2 Dec. 1816
quotations from Say, should they be in English or in French?
Buchanan amidst some important errors has some very
judicious comments on Adam Smith's text; if I notice him
at all it is right I should point out the merit of those remarks.
You perceive that I have no hesitation in applying to you in
all my difficulties. You must not however think that because
I say nothing of the trouble and time the examining and
reading my MS must take you, that I am the less sensible of
your kindness. If I am successful in my undertaking it will
be to you mainly that my success will be owing, for without
your encouragement I do not think that I should have proceeded, and it is to you that I look for assistance of the utmost
importance to me—the arranging the different parts, and
curtailing what may be superfluous.

The event, which we in our domestic circle have been so
long looking forward to with interest, has at length occurred
—Mrs. Clutterbuck has made me a grandfather. She was
brought to bed on wednesday last of a girl, during my
absence in London. I am happy to say that she and the child
are both doing well, and I hope we may now fully confide
in her safety. Mrs. Ricardo's anxiety being thus removed,
we are going home to Gatcomb this morning so that when
you write to me by the post you will direct accordingly.

As I think I told you before I arrived here on friday. I left
London on wednesday evening,[1] and after taking two of my
nieces to Gatcomb, proceeded here. Immediately on my
arrival I found an important dispatch had followed me, containing an earnest invitation to become a candidate for the
representation of Worcester, vacant by the death of Mr.
Robarts. The writer, who was introduced to my notice by
a gentleman I knew, and who appears to be well acquainted

[1] 27 November.

2 Dec. 1816 with the politics of Worcester, and to be quite au-fait in electioneering skill, expresses the utmost confidence of success, as Lord Deerhurst though having some interest, had a very bad character, and no money.[1] He assured me too that a very moderate sum would accomplish the business. A bill had been printed, and no doubt sent to Worcester, requesting the worthy electors not to promise their votes to Lord Deerhurst as an "Untitled commercial gentleman of established worth and integrity, and of well-known constitutional principles—An enemy to sinecures and other abuses, would speedily offer himself to their notice". I was requested to return an answer by return of post. Thus like Candid the most peaceable man in the world who was hurried into the commission of two murders in about as many minutes, was I, nearly as peaceable a man, to be hurried into all the horrors of a contested election. My decision was as prompt as the occasion required, and I respectfully declined the offer which was made to me.

Have you any idea yet when you shall be in London?

Very truly Y[rs]

DAVID RICARDO

194. RICARDO TO McCULLOCH[2]

[Reply to 190]

Gatcomb Park Minchinhampton
Gloucestershire 4th Dec[r] 1816

Dear Sir

4 Dec. 1816   A visit of two days[3] to London, last week, put me in possession of your book and letter, which I brought with me

[1] On 23 Dec. 1816 Viscount Deerhurst (son and heir of the Earl of Coventry) was returned as member for Worcester.
[2] Addressed: 'J. R MCullock

Esq[r]/College Street/Edinburgh'. MS in British Museum.—*Letters to McCulloch*, II.
[3] 26 and 27 November; see above, pp. 92, 101.

here on my return. Your enlarged essay has afforded me 4 Dec. 1816
both instruction and pleasure, although I cannot yet agree
in the justice of adopting the grand measure which you
propose for relieving the nation from its present difficulties.
I concur with you in all you have said on the bullion question.
—I think with you that it is too much to entrust to any
corporate body the power of raising or lowering the taxes at
pleasure, and I do not deny that for many of the loans
borrowed during the war a really greater interest will be paid
when Bank notes are at par, than what was contracted for
during the depreciation. But who depreciated the money
borrowed? what made it of less value than gold money? Was
it not the act of the legislature, and would it now be just for
the same legislature to say to a man who then lent £100,
"you must now take £3 for your interest, instead of £5,
because £3 is now as valuable as £5 was then." Will not the
lender reply "the reason why my £100 was then less valuable
than it is now was in consequence of your giving an unlimited power to a corporate body. Since 1797 I had employed my money in discounting bills and always received
£5 for every £100 for interest. By an act of yours you
reduced its value, and assured me at the time that I was
mistaken in thinking so, as my £100 was as valuable as
before. By reducing my interest now you will really pay
me only $\frac{3}{5}$ of my original £100." You may say that he
probably had not the money since 1797, that in 1812 he sold
goods to purchase stock, or to lend it to the state, and obtained an additional quantity of money because it was
depreciated, and therefore his plea is not valid; but who is to
determine this? You say that you do not propose to reduce
the interest of any part of the debt created anterior to the
depreciation of paper, but how is this part to be distinguished
from the other, how are you to distinguish the stockholder

4 Dec. 1816 of 1790 from the stockholder of 1800 or of 1810 or of 1816? It is evidently impossible, the stock is all amalgamated together—has passed through a thousand hands and can in no way be distinguished.

You say too that were the value of agricultural produce reduced, so ought the burdens of those who grow it. But would not their burdens be diminished? Would they have the same taxes to pay on an expenditure of 60/- that they now have to pay on an expenditure of 80/-. Would their tithes come to so much? Would their property tax be so great if that tax still existed? If they bought one bottle of wine would they pay the same tax as if they bought two? A part of the capital of the farmer would be removed from agriculture to manufactures,—it would be productive of value in that shape and would pay taxes equally as before. But you may say the whole will not be equally productive as before and that therefore more taxes must be raised to pay the interest of the Nat! Debt. You may repeat the quotation from Mr. Malthus [1] of which you avail yourself page 198, but Mr. Malthus does not satisfy me—I am persuaded he is wrong, though to shew his error would require more space than I now can allow myself. [2] I firmly believe that if corn fell from 80 to 60/- the ability of the people to pay taxes would be increased instead of diminished.

You say that in 1812 the state in engaging to pay an annuity of £10000 really had in view to give a power of purchasing 1600 quarters of wheat. I differ from you.— Leaving out of the question the depreciation of money it really agreed to give £10000 money, leaving it to the course of events whether £10000 should purchase in 1816—3000— or 800 quarters of wheat; it made no provision either for a

[1] *Grounds of an Opinion*, 1815,   [2] Cp. above, IV, 39-40.
pp. 38-42.

rise or fall of money, or a rise or fall of any other commodity.
If the state had any other intention your argument about
money is delusive, as neither gold nor silver is the standard
by which Bank notes should be regulated, but wheat, and
then every year or every ten years the dividend on the Nat!
Debt must be re-adjusted by the price of wheat. If the stockholder is enriched by the fall of wheat so is the mortgagee,
the discounter of bills—the manufacturer of cloth and of
every other commodity. Why not use your adjusting rule to
all these persons transactions? Your system proceeds upon
the supposition that the price of corn regulates the price of
all other things, and that when corn rises or falls, commodities also rise or fall,—but this I hold to be an erroneous
system, although you have great authorities in your favour,
no less than Adam Smith, Mr. Malthus and M. Say.[1]

If your opinion be just, when corn was at 40/-, and the
state borrowed money, it agreed to give 5000 quarters of
corn to an annuitant of £10000, but it has paid £10000
money ever since although that money would frequently
purchase no more than 2000 quarters of wheat. How will
you compensate to this man the injustice to which he has so
long been subjected?

This letter has swelled to an unconscionable length, but
I have one observation more to make and then I shall finish.

You accuse me of protesting strongly against the injustice
of encroaching on the sinking fund at the same time that
I shewed the propriety and justice of *repealing* the corn laws.[2]
In this you are mistaken I recommended no *repeal* of the
corn laws, for I wrote before they were enacted. But if I had
I should not I think have been guilty of any inconsistency—

---

[1] Cp. *Principles*, above, I, 46.

[2] McCulloch, *Essay on the Question of Reducing the Interest*, p. 210, replies to the argument in Ricardo's *Essay on Profits*, above, IV, 41.

4 Dec. 1816 laws are made for the benefit of the whole community and not for the benefit of any particular class—they may therefore be enacted or repealed as expediency may require. A parental Government however will never be unmindful of the consequences of their acts to a large class of individuals. But on the question of the sinking fund they have no choice—I consider it as a positive bargain between the nation and the stockholder, which cannot be infringed by one of the contracting parties.

I am Sir

Your obed^t Servant

DAVID RICARDO

J R MCullock Esqr

195. MILL TO RICARDO[1]

[Reply to 188, 189 *&* 193.—*Answered by* 196]

Ford Abbey 16th Decr 1816

My Dear Sir

16 Dec. 1816   I have now gone over your inquiry into the subject of Taxation,[2] with the same care as the former part of the work. I have also the pleasure to tell you that I am equally well satisfied. Now for the first time is the real operation of taxes explained; for this was a part of his subject on which Adam Smith was superficial, and added not a great deal to the knowledge of the world. Your doctrines are original, and profound, for it was by no means an easy matter to get down to them; and I have no hesitation whatsoever in saying that they are fully and completely made out. I embrace every one of them; and am ready to defend them against all the world. In this part however, there will be rather more to do in fitting

[1] Addressed:'David Ricardo Esq. / Gatcomb Park / Minchinhampton / Gloucester Shire'.

MS in *R.P.*
[2] Chapters VIII–XVIII of the *Principles.*

it for the press, than in the other. I do not mean that you do not here shew the same command of good expression as in the former; for that is a thing in which there is now not any danger of your ever failing. But in this I see you have followed the order of your own thoughts, without much studying the order which would most facilitate introduction into the minds of your readers. In preparing it for the press, that is the principal thing which you will have to study. And in that I shall perhaps be able to give you some assistance. I have marginal contents of the whole, paragraph by paragraph, and shall study them at leisure with that view.

In preparing your book, the question for you to determine is—whether you will chuse to include in it a view of the *whole* science; so as you would lay it down to a person whom you was teaching, and who knew nothing about it; so as you would state the whole from beginning to end to Miss Fanny,[1] for example, if she should entreat you, as I hope she will, to teach her the science of political economy: Or, whether you will content yourself with those parts of the science which you yourself have improved. In the first way, you would be most useful; but I rather think you will get most reputation in the last. You might, too, if you saw advantage in it, give a view of the whole science, as modeled upon your own principles, and taught to Miss Fanny (I beg her pardon, Miss Ricardo)—hereafter. In that case, what title would you give to the present work? And how would you arrange it in Chapters and Sections? Think of your Chapters and Sections; and when you have made out a list, send it to me.

With regard to those parts of Adam Smith, where his opinions are at variance with your principles, I think you are called upon to take notice of his errors. The doctrine of bounties, and prohibitions, on which there is so much error

[1] Ricardo's third daughter, then sixteen years old.

16 Dec. 1816 in the world, you should work fully—so of colonies.[1] In fact I would not have you sparing on this ground; but chiefly, nevertheless, attaching yourself to the errors which the application of your principles illustrates and exposes.

I rather think I would quote Say in English, and certainly I should not fail to point out his errors; though with that respectfulness of manner to which he is entitled. In noticing the errors of Buchanan, credit should be given him where he has seen the truth. But you are not at all called upon to go out of your way, to mention the cases in which he has avoided error. In the places where you criticize A. S., if he criticizes him in the same way, then you should allow him what credit he deserves. In regard to all these parts, when you do not think it necessary to notice A. Smith, neither would I notice the comment, right or wrong, of Mr. Buchanan. Mr. B appears to me a very feeble reasoner, and not likely to do the science much good. In his reasoning, for example, to prove that wages would not rise, in consequence of a tax, (at p. 98 of your M.S.)[2] he states four propositions, as the matter of his proof. Now of these four propositions, the two first, instead of tending to support his conclusion, refute it; the third begs the question; the fourth affirms a false fact. You have shewn completely that his conclusion is wrong. But you have not taken any notice of the extreme badness of the reasoning. This, I think, it will be necessary to do, that you may not seem not to have been aware of the degree of the badness.

You must go on putting down, upon paper, all the discussions which you think will be fitted for your work; and when we have the whole before us, we will then lay our heads together, to see how it may be sorted and shaped to the best

[1] See Chapters XXII, XXIII and   [2] Above, I, 216 ff.
XXV of the *Principles*.

advantage. As soon as you have got another cargo, you will
send it to me.—We shall be here till the time parliament
meets. You, if in the same mind as last year, will be in town
a month earlier.

Accept my sincere congratulations on the happy transit
of Mrs. Clutterbuck through the first of her trials. I was
happy to hear of her pregnancy, as a proof that her health
was getting stronger, than it has been since her marriage.

I have now another circumstance to mention, in which if
you can be of any service, I know it will give you pleasure to
be so. A little time ago, I received a letter from a lady in
Scotland, who supposed I was acquainted with Sir Benjamin
Hobhouse. She is the widow of a clergyman of the Church
of Scotland, who was a college companion, and a particular
friend of mine. The husband died a few years ago, and left
her with four children, and hardly any provision. She is an
Englishwoman, of a very good family, with a genteel education, and accustomed to very good company from her
birth. Her family, while her father lived, who died nearly
about the same time with her husband, resided at Clapham,
and in terms of intimacy with the best people there, Henry
Thorntons family, for example, and Barclay, the Brewer. At
Barclays I have visited with them. This lady, sometime ago
was advised by her friends to undertake the charge of some
daughters of gentlemen in the East Indies, sent home for
education, and who want the superintendance of a mother.
I know nobody who is better qualified for the task: and if I
needed to consign my daughters to any care but my own;
there is not a person on earth whom I would more wish them
to be with than with her. She is, indeed, a truly admirable
person, in every respect—the greatest sweetness of disposition I have almost ever known, with the gentlest manners,
and at the same time great good sense, and great firmness and

16 Dec. 1816 steadiness of character. Placed in very trying circumstances, she has gained the hearts of all who know her, people of all ranks in Edin^r, where eyes are prying, and minds not easily pleased; and respected in the highest degree. She has heard of four grand daughters of Sir Benjamin Hobhouse, the children of a Mr. Palmers in India, for whom a guardian is wanted. I see by looking at her letter that the children are not the grand daughters, though related to Sir Benjamin. She has been recommended by the family of Dr. Saunders, who was married to her aunt, to Sir Benjamin. Sir Benjamin has been spoken to from other quarter. Charles Grant, the E. India director, is a patron of Mrs. Savile (that is the ladys name) and will satisfy Sir B. as to her fitness. As she wrote to me, supposing that I knew Sir B., which I do not, I am anxious to do for her any thing that is in my power; and knowing the connection there is between the Clutterbucks and the Bar^t I resolved to request that you would get them at any rate to represent Mrs. Saviles case and pretensions; which is all I can think of that is within my power. In the mean time you will be serving a person whom you would very much like, if you knew her; and who has great need of assistance.

I coincide with your judgement, as I do in almost all things else, in your declining Worcester. If I were in your situation, the rottenest Borough I could find would be my market, with nothing to do but to part with a sum of money. I am however, very much in earnest that you should be in parliament. That, along with your book, will add to your rank, and that of your family, in a remarkable degree. You deserve it—you ought to have it—and that is the way to attain it. You will not let me add, that you may be of great use to the cause of good government, and may render important service against the cause of bad; which I know you

would value more than any rank, or any wealth. But this 16 Dec. 1816
is what you both can and will.

I send off the M.S. to day addressed to Mr. Clutterbuck.
And I shall this day finish revising the first vol. of my
history.[1] I was comforted yesterday by a declaration in a
letter I had from Sir J. Mackintosh, that he found narrative
a much more difficult species of composition than he had
any conception of; because I had found so to a painful
degree. You will be glad to hear that he is better in health
than he has been since he came to England.

Ever yours
J. MILL

196. RICARDO TO MILL[2]
[Reply to 195]

Gatcomb Park
20 Dec.ʳ 1816
My dear Sir

Your letter, and my papers, have safely come to hand, 20 Dec. 1816
and I have again the satisfaction to know that you, my
preceptor, are pleased with my performance, and are convinced by my arguments. I hope I shall be equally successful
with the public, and that you will aid me in making such an
arrangement, as will be most likely to make an impression
upon those, whose minds are not so well prepared as yours,
for the consideration of such subjects.

I now send you some observations on Adam Smith's work,
which I fear you will think only a repetition of what I have
before stated. If you should condemn it in toto, I can bear
it without any disappointment, for there is already so much

[1] *History of British India.*
[2] Addressed: 'James Mill Esqʳ /

Ford Abbey / Chard / Somersetshire'.
MS in Mill-Ricardo papers.

20 Dec. 1816 to the credit side of the account, that I am quite fortified against any small deduction. What you now receive will probably close my matter, unless in looking over Say's book, which I have not yet done, I may find any thing suggested to my mind which I have hitherto overlooked. The assistance which I shall receive from you cannot probably be given till we meet in London. I expect there will be much to take out, and as for the division into chapters, and sections, I am greatly afraid that I shall be unequal to it. You have however taught me to believe that perseverance will overcome very formidable obstacles, and I am determined that there shall be no want of exertion on my part. I am afraid that you will find the present papers more illegible than any of the former, but you know the drudgery of copying, and I was unwilling to take that trouble till I had heard your opinion of them.

It will, I think, be easier to me, to publish only those parts of the science which have particularly engaged my attention, and if my efforts should be favourably received, it may afford me a future agreeable task to take a view of the whole science.

I shall probably be in London about the 9th of January, and we shall most likely meet there early in feb.y. I will do what I can without you, and shall be quite prepared to wait till you are quite at leisure for the assistance which you will give me. I am fully aware of the great inroads I have lately made on your time, and I cannot help fearing that I have prevented you from expediting your own work as much as you otherwise would have done. I beg you however to remember that I shall not in the least suffer from delay,—my views will be as new six months hence as they are now, and therefore I hope that you will entirely put the consideration of my papers aside if they at any time interfere with your more important objects. I am glad to find that you have

gone over the first vol. of your history; I hope it will immediately go to the press, and that you may be rewarded, in
every way, for your persevering exertions.

In your letter to me you have given a good specimen of
your powers in narration, by depicting so feelingly the misfortunes, and merits, of Mrs. Savile. Sir Benjⁿ Hobhouse is
known to me, and as I have always found him very friendly
when we have met, I thought I should best serve the cause
you have at heart, by writing to him myself, and after putting
him in possession of the statement you gave me, in your own
able manner, to add the expression of my hopes and wishes.
You will probably wish to know his answer, and I shall
therefore dispatch it to you as soon as I receive it. It may
however be [delayed]¹ some days, as I shall leave home to
day [on a visi]t of two days to Sylla, and then another two
days to Henrietta, to take my leave of them before I leave
the country. I shall return here on tuesday.

I thank you for your congratulations on Mrs. Clutterbuck's safety. I am happy to tell you that she is quite well
and has the delight of seeing her infant thrive daily.—

I do not readily fall in with your suggestions respecting
a seat in Parliament; I fear I should be mere lumber there.
From the trials which I have already made I am sure I should
never be able to deliver my sentiments on any subject in
debate, and I cannot perceive in what other way I could be
in the least useful. If my book succeeds, as you promise me,
perhaps my ambition may be awakened, and I may aspire to
rank with senators, but at present I have the greatest awe
for the distinguished persons who figure in Sᵗ Stephens. If
you are indeed right in your prognostications—if I am really
to be the author of a book of merit, I shall bow to your
superior discernment. Let me however first be convinced

¹ MS torn here and below.

20 Dec. 1816 that you are not a partial judge, and do not view my performance through the medium of a too friendly bias.

Ever truly Y⸫

DAVID RICARDO

I shall forward the papers I mentioned by Saturday's, or Sunday's[1] coach from Bath.

197. RICARDO TO MALTHUS[2]

Gatcomb Park
3ᵈ Jan 1817

My dear Sir

3 Jan. 1817   A long time has elapsed since I had the pleasure of seeing you, during which time I have often intended writing as I did not hear from you, but my natural indolence prevailed, and I have procrastinated it till now. I had some faint hopes that you might be in the neighbouring county this vacation, in which case I should have hoped to prevail on you to pass a short time here, but I learnt from Mr. Binda, who is on a visit to Mr. Smith, that he had met with you at Holland house, and that it was not probable you would go far from home. I had previously enquired about you of our young neighbour George Clerk,—he, however, could only tell me you were well, he knew nothing about your intended movements.

By an advertisement in the public papers I perceive that you have been occupied in writing about your College,[3] which I regret, as I believe the task was not very agreeable to you, and as it may have prevented you from proceeding

---

[1] 21 and 22 December.
[2] Addressed: 'To / The Revᵈ T R Malthus / East India College / Hertford'.
MS at Albury.—*Letters to Malthus*, LII.

[3] Malthus's *Statements respecting the East India College, with an Appeal to Facts, in Refutation of the Charges lately brought against it, in the Court of Proprietors*, London, Murray, 1817. The Preface is dated 4 January.

with other works, in which I imagine you are more interested. I should be glad to hear that every thing you think
defective in the College was remedied, and that it was
placed on such a footing as to require only the ordinary
routine of your attention.—

I have been occasionally employed, since we met,[1] in putting my thoughts on paper, on the subjects which have often
passed under our discussion. I have encountered the usual
obstacles from difficulties of composition, but I have reso-
lutely persevered till I have committed every thing to paper
that was floating in my mind. There are a few points on
which there is a shadow of difference between my present
and my past opinions, but they are not those on which we
could not agree. I hope I shall succeed in putting my MS.
in some tolerable order, as on that will depend whether I
shall again appear before the public. What I have hitherto
done is rather a statement of my own opinions, than an attempt
at the refutation of the opinions of others. Lately, however,
I have been looking over Adam Smith, Say, and Buchanan
and where I have seen passages in their works contrary to
the principles I hold to be correct, I have noticed them, and
shall perhaps make them the subject of some comment.

I fear I shall not have the satisfaction of receiving your
acquiescence to my doctrines, particularly as I have reverted
to my former views respecting taxes on raw produce.[2]
Whatever may be correct on that subject surely Adam
Smith is wrong, as there are various passages in his book
inconsistent with each other.[3]

[1] This may refer either to their
meeting at Gatcomb early in the
summer (see p. 48), or to a
meeting suggested by Ricardo
for 17 October (see p. 80).
[2] For Ricardo's 'former views'
that such taxes are paid wholly by
the consumer, see above, III,
241–2, IV, 34, n., and VI, 173;
for their restatement at this time,
I, 156–7.
[3] See quotations above, I, 183 ff.,
and 252 ff.

3 Jan. 1817   We shall, I hope, soon meet, and renew our discussions on some of these difficult matters. I shall be in London on friday next, and hope to see you in Brook Street as our inmate, as soon after that day as business, or inclination, may draw you to London.

I want to hear your opinion of the measures lately adopted for the relief of the poor.[1] I am not one of those who think that the raising of funds for the purpose of employing the poor is a very efficacious mode of relief, as it diverts those funds from other employments which would be equally if not more productive to the community. That part of the capital which employs the poor on the roads for example cannot fail to employ men somewhere and I believe every interference is prejudicial. Pray make my kind compliments to Mrs. Malthus and believe me

Ever Y^{rs}

DAVID RICARDO

198. TROWER TO RICARDO[2]

[*Answered by* 201]

January 17—1817—
Dear Ricardo,   Unsted Wood—

17 Jan. 1817   Many thanks for your last letter,[3] by which I am happy to hear of Mrs. Clutterbuck's addition to her family.[4]

---

[1] The relief works carried on in London and various parts of the country since the autumn of 1816, with funds raised by private subscriptions; in Edinburgh 1600 men were employed in making and improving roads. Later, on 28 April 1817, the Chancellor of the Exchequer announced what has been described as 'the first experiment of the century in what are now called Relief Works': he proposed to issue Exchequer-bills to the amount of half-a-million for employing the poor on the completion of public works (W. Smart, *Economic Annals, 1801–1820*, p. 543).

[2] Addressed: 'To / David Ricardo Esqr / Upper Brook Street / Grosvenor Square'.
MS in *R.P.*

[3] Ricardo's letter is wanting.

[4] See above, p. 101.

Mrs. Trower begs to join with me in congratulations to
Mrs. Ricardo and yourself upon this joyful event. The most
effectual way I believe of adding to our happiness is to
multiply the ties by which we are bound to society.—

I am very desirous of satisfying your mind with respect to
the advantage to be derived from a clause in the Provident
Fund Bills authorising the extending of Parish relief under
certain restrictions to Depositors, who may require it.
Because, when in London, you may be of essential service
to the cause, by enforcing sound opinions upon the subject;
and by removing prejudices which seem to exist to a considerable degree respecting it.—

You say "by granting parish relief to poor Depositors you
are deferring that salutary lesson, which must, at last, be
taught them, and in so far, *prevent wages* from settling at so
high a rate as they otherwise would be."

But, surely, the great question of the support of the Poor,
is not merely a *question of Wages*; other important considerations are involved in it. Let us look more closely into
the subject of wages, and see how the matter stands. In this
point of view the poor are naturally divided into 2 classes—
1st the *single* having themselves only to support; 2^{ndly} the
married, who have their families to support also—For the 2^{d}
the present rate of wages, no doubt, is inadequate, and ought
to be encreased. But for the 1st it is *more than sufficient*. This
surplus, if prudently preserved, would form a *fund* for the
supply of future extra demands, but it is all idly spent—as
long, therefore, as this want of foresight exists any further
encrease of wages to the *single man* would be productive of
mischief instead of *good*. But you cannot encrease the wages
of the *married*, without also encreasing those of the *single*,
it is not practicable to make any distinction between them.
You must therefore endeavour to encourage habits of pru-

17 Jan. 1817 dence and economy in the single, and such is the object of the Provident Funds. But, no person will belong to these Institutions if they perceive, that they are saving, *not for their own benefit*, but for the benefit of *their neighbours*. And they must perceive this, when they find themselves denied that relief, which is extended to the extravagant. An alteration in the *habits* of the lower classes must be the foundation upon which any measure is built, calculated for their permanent benefit.—It is obvious, that it would be *impossible* to establish the rate of wages at such a sum as will be adequate to the support of *a man and his family*. Nor would it be expedient if it were—for it would be tantamount to giving a Bonus to the extravagance and profligacy of the *single*. For instance 16/- in this part of the Country are necessary for the support of a man his wife and 2 children, whilst 8/- are considered sufficient for a single man. The rate of wages is now 12/- If then on account of the *married* they were raised to 16/- see what would be the situation of the single. He would be receiving *double* what was requisite for his necessities and this, without habits of economy, would be productive of most mischievous effects. The grand object therefore appears to me to *entice* the single and the young into *habits of prudence*, and in order to obtain this object, it is well worth while to make *some sacrifice*, even *admitting* the clause in question to be one. But, I believe, that however important in principle, and by way of example, it would be rarely necessary *to act upon it*; because the prudent Depositor is not likely to become chargeable, except through sickness or misfortune, in which case he would have a strong claim on his Parish. Many other considerations are connected with this very interesting question, but no doubt you will think you have had enough and more than enough in one letter, therefore I shall conclude.

Greenough has been staying a few days with me. He is

as enthusiastic as ever in his favorite pursuit. His map is not   17 Jan. 1817
yet published, nor does it appear likely to be. In the mean-
time, inferior works are daily depriving him of that merit of
originality to which his Map is entitled[1]—

Our united kind remembrances to Mrs. Ricardo and family
and believe me My Dear Ricardo—

Yrs very truly

HUTCHES TROWER

199. RICARDO TO MALTHUS[2]

[*Answered by* 200]

Upper Brook Street London

My dear Sir   24 Jan.ʸ 1817

I have read your pamphlet[3] with great pleasure, and am   24 Jan. 1817
very much satisfied with your arguments in favour of a
college in preference to a school for the education of the
young men destined to manage the complicated affairs of our
Indian Empire. The testimonies from India in favour of the
young men sent from the College, as compared with those
who went out to India before the establishment of the college
make powerfully for you, and do not appear to have been
answered by your opponents.—

I observe by the papers that the discussion on this subject
will be renewed at the India house on the 6ᵗʰ feb.ʸ at which
time I conclude that you will be in London. If so I hope you
will make my house your head quarters.—

[1] G. B. Greenough's Geological
Map of England, presented to the
Geological Society in 1812, was
not published till 1820; mean-
while, in 1815, William Smith had
published a similar map. (See
H. B. Woodward, *History of the
Geological Society of London*, 1907,
pp. 56–9.)

[2] Addressed: 'To / The Revᵈ
T. R Malthus / East India College /
Hertford'.
    MS at Albury.—*Letters to Mal-
thus*, LIII.
[3] *Statements respecting the East
India College.*

9-2

24 Jan. 1817   Mr. Murray promised to send copies of your book to the gentlemen you directed me to mention to him.

It appears to me that one great cause of our difference in opinion, on the subjects which we have so often discussed, is that you have always in your mind the immediate and temporary effects of particular changes—whereas I put these immediate and temporary effects quite aside, and fix my whole attention on the permanent state of things which will result from them. Perhaps you estimate these temporary effects too highly, whilst I am too much disposed to undervalue them. To manage the subject quite right they should be carefully distinguished and mentioned, and the due effects ascribed to each.

I have been reading again your 3 last pamphlets on rent and corn and cannot help thinking there is some ambiguity in the language. The word "high price of raw produce" is calculated to produce a different impression on your reader from what you mean.[1] Your first and third causes of high price appear to me to be directly at variance with each other. The first is the fertility of land, the third the scarcity of fertile land. The 2^{d} cause too I think never operates.[2] There is one passage in particular which expresses fully my opinions—I have not the book by me and cannot refer you to the page, but it begins "I have no hesitation in stating that independently of irregularities in the currency &c^{a}." it is in the essay on rent.[3]

Surely Buchanan is right and your comment wrong; rent is not a creation but a transfer of wealth. It is the necessary consequence of rent being the effect and not the cause of high price.[4]—

---

[1] Cp. above, I, 401.
[2] See above, I, 400 ff.

[3] *Inquiry into...Rent*, p. 40. Quoted in full above, I, 410.
[4] See above, I, 398–9.

Say and I would say that by turning revenue into Capital 24 Jan. 1817 we shall obtain both an increased supply and an increased demand,—but if the same capital be so created I do not approve of its present application,—taking it out of the hands of those who know best how to employ it, to encourage industry of a different kind and under the superintendence of those who know nothing of the wants and demands of mankind and blindly produce cloth or stockings of which we have already too much, or improve roads which nobody wishes to travel.[1]

Mrs. Ricardo joins me in kind regards to Mrs. Malthus.

Very truly Yours

DAVID RICARDO

200. MALTHUS TO RICARDO[2]

[Reply to 199]

E I Coll Jany 26 [1817]

My Dear Sir,

I fear I shall not be able to leave College at the time of 26 Jan. 1817 the meeting of the Court of Proprietors, or it would give me great pleasure to accept your kind invitation. I am glad you are satisfied with the arguments of the pamphlet. I should not indeed have much fear of its effects, if there were not so strong a body of persons to contend with, who only think of sending out their sons, as soon, and with as little expense of education, as they can.

I agree with you that one cause of our difference in opinion is that which you mention. I certainly am disposed to refer

---

[1] This refers to Malthus's reply (which is wanting) to Ricardo's question about relief works, on p. 116 above. [But see below, XI, x–xi.]

[2] Addressed: 'D. Ricardo Esqr / 56. Upper Brook Street / Grosvenor Square / London'. Postmark, 1817.—MS in *R.P.*

26 Jan. 1817 frequently to things as they are, as the only way of making one's writings practically useful to society, and I think also the only way of being secure from falling into the errors of the taylors of Laputa, and by a slight mistake at the outset arrive at conclusions the most distant from the truth. Besides I really think that the progress of society consists of irregular movements, and that to omit the consideration of causes which for eight or ten years will give a great *stimulus* to production and population, or a great *check* to them, is to omit the causes of the wealth and poverty of nations—the grand object of all enquiries in Political Economy. A writer may, to be sure, make any hypothesis he pleases; but if he supposes what is not at all true practically, he precludes himself from drawing any practical inferences from his hypothesis. In your essay on profits you suppose the real wages of labour constant; but as they vary with every alteration in the prices of commodities, (while they remain nominally the same) and are in reality as variable as profits, there is no chance of your inferences being just as applied to the actual state of things. We see in all the countries around us, and in our own particularly, periods of greater and less prosperity, and sometimes of adversity, but *never* the uniform progress which you seem alone to contemplate.

But to come to a still more specific and fundamental cause of our difference, I think it is this. You seem to think that the wants and tastes of mankind are always ready for the supply; while I am most decidedly of opinion that few things are more difficult, than to inspire new tastes and wants, particularly out of old materials; that one of the great elements of demand is the value that people set upon commodities, and that the more completely the supply is suited to the demand the higher will this value be, and the more day's labour will it exchange for, or give the power of commanding.

The advantage of foreign commerce consists in a great degree in its tendency to increase this value [and]¹ the disadvantage of a fall in the money price of [any] class of commodity which is not made up by a proportionate increase of their quantity, arises from the diminution of the sum of values thus occasioned, or the smaller quantity of labour that these values can command. I am quite of opinion that *practically* the actual check to produce and population arises more from want of stimulus than want of power to produce.

I think as you say there may be some ambiguity in some parts of the language of my inquiry into rent; but I cannot see the contradiction you allude to, in my first and third causes; nor do I understand at all what you mean by saying that the second never operates. Has the production of food which tends to give the labourer a greater command of it, (provided it be properly distributed) no tendency to increase population? Or are not the fertility of land, and the scarcity of fertile land, both absolutely necessary to produce high rents, or a great excess of the price of corn above the cost of production? Is it possible that high rent can exist without *fertility* whatever may be the *scarcity* of land? or is it possible that high *rents* can exist without *scarcity* whatever may be the fertility?

The sentence you so much approve of is I think not sufficiently limited. I believe that the *bullion* price of corn in this country is higher than in Sweden although the last land taken into cultivation in Sweden is less fertile than ours, and I do not think that the reason of this can properly be attributed to *irregularity* of currency. The points relating to the causes of high money price are those which I most wish to alter.

I am busy about my new edition which is after all to be

¹ MS torn here and below.

26 Jan. 1817 three volumes.¹ There are some points I want to consult you about, but I am much hurried. Perhaps I shall be able to leave College and will let you know.

Mrs. M desires to be kindly remembered to Mrs. Ricardo.

Ever Yours

T R MALTHUS

201. RICARDO TO TROWER²

[*Reply to* 198.—*Answered by* 203]

Dear Trower

London 27 Jany 1817

27 Jan. 1817 Is it not desirable that the poor laws should be done away, and the labouring classes should receive the recompence for their labour rather in the shape of wages than in that of bounty? If you answer in the affirmative then there is no way of preventing the single man from receiving more than is sufficient for his support, and I can see no reason to regret it. When the wages of a married man with a family are barely adequate to his own and his family's maintenance, the wages of the single man may be ample. All this I admit, but if it is a necessary consequence of the abolition of the poor laws it must be acquiesced in under the circumstances of an abolition. Even if it were an evil, which I think it is not, it must be endured for the sake of the good which would accompany it.

The ill effects of the poor laws then I suppose to be admitted and their abolition to be desirable the question then is how is it to be effected? Can it be by any other means than

¹ *An Essay on the Principle of Population*, 'The Fifth Edition, with Important Additions', 3 vols., London, Murray, 1817.

² Addressed: 'Hutches Trower Esqʳ / Unsted Wood / Godalming / Surry'.
MS at University College, London.—*Letters to Trower*, X.

by gradually limiting their application, by encouraging the poor man to depend on his own exertions only? Is not this to be done by refusing all relief in the first instance to any but those whose necessities absolutely require it—to administer it to them in the most sparing manner, and lastly to abolish the poor laws altogether? If the poor rates are to be resorted to not only by those who have no other means of subsisting, but by those who are possessed of property, instead of limiting their application you would extend it; instead of repressing population you would still further encourage it, and would place at a greater distance the ultimate effect which we have in view. It is a painful reflection but not less true on that account that we can never get into a good system, after so long persevering in a bad one but by much previous suffering of the poor. The population can only be repressed by diminishing the encouragement to its *excessive* increase,—by leaving contracts between the poor and their employers perfectly free, which would limit the quantity of labour in the market to the effective demand for it. By engaging to feed all who may require food you in some measure create an unlimited demand for human beings, and if it were not for the bad administration of the poor laws —for the occasional hard heartedness of overseers and the avarice of parishes which in a degree checks their evil effects, the population and the rates would go on increasing in a regular progression till the rich were reduced to poverty, and till there would no longer be any distinction of ranks. The particular clause then in the Savings Bank Bill must be examined in reference to its effects on the poor rates. By omitting the clause you narrow the application of the rates— you encourage a part of the population to maintain themselves and to afford a good moral example to others, and you gradually prepare the way for the adoption of a better system.

27 Jan. 1817 The only argument of weight in favour of the clause is that without it saving will be discouraged. I cannot believe that this would be found to be the case; no man saves with the poor house in perspective. Poor and rich all have confidence in their good fortune and whilst their affairs are prosperous never dream of a reverse.

I have scarcely left myself room to thank you and Mrs. Trower for your kind congratulations to Mrs. Ricardo and me, on the birth of our grandchild. I hope you are right and that these numerous ties are calculated to increase our happiness.

I suppose I must not expect you in London for 2 or 3 months; you generally come in the gayest time. I am sorry to see our finances in so bad a state, and so turbulent a spirit abroad. We want an energetic minister possessing and meriting the confidence of the people in his talents and integrity.

I am Dear Trower, very truly Y^{rs},

DAVID RICARDO

202. RICARDO TO MALTHUS[1]

My dear Sir

8 Feb. 1817   I am not in the least acquainted with the subject on which your papers[2] treat, but that is no reason why I should not mention what appears to me defective. In page 8 you add $\frac{1}{6}$ to the births for probable omissions and $\frac{1}{12}$ for deaths,

[1] Addressed: 'For/The Rev⁴ T.R Malthus'—not passed through the post, being probably enclosed with Malthus's papers.
  MS at Albury.—*Letters to Malthus*, LIV.
[2] The MS or a proof of *Additions to the Fourth and Former Editions*

of *An Essay on the Principle of Population, &c. &c.*, London, Murray, 1817. Ricardo's page-references do not agree with the pagination either of the separately published *Additions* or of vol. II of the *Essay*, 5th ed., 1817.

but you do not tell your reader why these proportions are 8 Feb. 1817
taken rather than $\frac{1}{4}$ or $\frac{1}{3}$, nor can I discover on what grounds
those numbers are chosen.[1]

You sometimes take averages from the known facts of
certain years, but your averages are formed on an arithmetical ratio while your application is to a geometrical series.
I submit whether this is correct.

If as you say in page 14 births are to burials as 47 to 30
and the mortality as 1 to 47 the addition to the population
would be little more than $\frac{1}{83}$ instead of $\frac{1}{82}$ for out of every
1410 persons 30 would die and 47 be born and consequently
there would be an increase of 17, but 1410 divided by 17 is
82.94 or 83 nearly, and therefore if 1410 gives an increase of 17
—9,287,000 will give an increase of 111,970 or 1,119,700 in
ten years which will raise the population

$$\left.\begin{array}{r} 9,287,000 \\ 1\ 119\ 700 \\ \hline 10,406,700 \end{array}\right\} \quad \text{instead of } 10,483,000.\text{—}$$

In Page 16 the mortality is supposed to be as before 1 in
47 and the births to the population as 1 to $29\frac{1}{2}$, and the
population to be 9,287,000.—This latter sum divided by $29\frac{1}{2}$
gives 314,813 the annual number of births, and divided by
47 gives 197595 the annual number of deaths, deduct one

from the other $\dfrac{\begin{array}{r}314813\\197595\end{array}}{117218}$ gives 117218 for the annual in-

crease which in 10 years would be 1 172 180 which
added to the former population of— 9 287 000

gives— 10,459,180 instead
of 10,531,000[2]

[1] On p. 17 of *Additions*, Malthus
gives reason for these estimates.
[2] In *Additions* (p. 21), the latter

figure is obtained by taking
9,887,000 (the mean between the
population of 1800 and that of

8 Feb. 1817   I have marked in pages 35 and 36 some very trifling errors. These are all I can discover with the facts which are before me.—

Ever truly Y^{rs}

DAVID RICARDO

8 Feb 1817

203. TROWER TO RICARDO[1]
[Reply to 201.—Answered by 205]

Unsted Wood—Godalming
Feb. 9—1817.

Dear Ricardo

9 Feb. 1817   I observe Mr. Rose has moved for leave to bring in his Bill for the protection of Provident Institutions.[2] I shall therefore be *very much obliged* to you to ascertain and let me know, whether this Bill is the *same* as that he introduced last year; if not the same, in *what respect it differs*, and *particularly* with regard to the *clause touching Parish Relief*—You, and I do not differ *at all* with respect to the grievous tendency of the poor laws, and to the necessity of making them give way to a better system. The only question is how can this important alteration be most easily and effectually accomplished? I am one, who looks to the Institution of Provident Funds as facilitating in a *very considerable degree* this great object; as calculated to diminish to no small extent, the quantum of evil which it is to be feared must accompany this alteration— I am therefore anxious to extend these Institutions throughout the Country. This can only be achieved by holding out *inducements* to the poor to become depositors therein. And

1810) instead of 9,287,000 (the population of 1800) as the basis for calculating the annual numbers of births and deaths during the interval.

[1] Addressed: 'To / David Ricardo Esqr / Upper Brook Street / Grosvenor Square'.
MS in *R.P.*
[2] See above, p. 33, n. 2.

the only reason why I am anxious for the clause enab'ing 9 Feb. 1817 relief to be granted to depositors, *if required* and *under certain restrictions*, is that I consider it *calculated to afford great encouragement* to the poor, to save their money, and so dispose of it.

I contend, that not *one shilling* will be *added* thereby to the *poor rates*; but, on the contrary, that it will tend *considerably to their diminution*—*Without it*, your Institutions will do *nothing*, as far as the *poor are concerned*; they may go on receiving the savings of *servants*, and of people not coming within the scope of the poor laws, but they will rank among their numbers *few*, if *any* of the laboring classes. If these latter become depositors the rates *must* be diminished, to a certain extent; if they do not, these rates will go on encreasing in spite of your provident Institutions. But this is not all— I contend further, that in point of fact you are giving up *nothing*. For it is not probable, that Depositors will be reduced to the necessity of asking the proffered relief. The thrifty man is not likely to become burthensome to his Country—and none but thrifty men will belong to these Institutions. It is however one of the strongest arguments in favor of these Institutions, that if properly regulated, and encouraged, they are calculated to *make thrifty men*, to *convert* the *thoughtless spendthrift* into the cautious and prudent *economist*. In my last letter I never intended to object to the single man's receiving more than sufficient for his immediate necessities; quite the contrary—his so doing is the *foundation* upon which these Institutions are built for it is from *that class of people only*, that we can expect to derive Depositors—I only wish therefore to give these men an assurance that they are accumulating, not for the purpose of saving the money of their richer neighbours, but for their own benefit. For the former object you will never succeed

9 Feb. 1817 in urging them to do any thing, for the latter you may induce to perform every thing—
Have you seen Dr. Haygarths and Mr. Bowles pamphlets on Provident Institutions.[1] Is there any thing new in them. I was very sorry I could not contrive to pass a few hours with you whilst I was in London but Mrs. Trower was then far from well, and I hurried home, now I am happy to say she is much better.—
Pray make our kind compliments to Mrs. Ricardo and family and believe me

Yrs very truly
HUTCHES TROWER

204. RICARDO TO MALTHUS[2]

London 21 Feb.ʸ 1817

My dear Sir

21 Feb. 1817   I am very sorry that you were prevented from being in London yesterday.—I fully expected to see you as I thought the subject of debate at the India House[3] was of too much interest not to make you desirous of hearing it.—
Mr. Grant[4] was I assure you a warm advocate in the cause

[1] John Haygarth, M.D., *An Explanation of the Principles and Proceedings of the Provident Institution at Bath, for Savings*, London, Longman, 1816.
John Bowles, *Reasons for the Establishment of Provident Institutions, called Savings' Banks; with a word of Caution respecting their formation...*, 3rd ed., London, J. M. Richardson, 1817.
[2] Addressed: 'To / The Revᵈ T R Malthus/East India College/ Hertford'.
MS at Albury.—*Letters to Malthus*, LV.

[3] The meeting of the Court of Proprietors of the East India Company to consider Randle Jackson's motion for an inquiry into the state of the College at Haileybury, with a view to either transforming it into an institution 'more in the nature of a school' or abolishing it altogether.
[4] Robert Grant, an ex-director; he was the son of Charles Grant, sen., a former chairman of the Company and originator of the scheme for the foundation of the College.

of the College. He spoke admirably, and with great effect, improving in energy and eloquence as he proceeded. He did justice to the various qualifications of the professors for the responsible situations which they filled, and I believe left nothing unsaid which might assist the cause which he so ably defended. I thought him very severe on Randle Jackson, who will find it difficult to answer some parts of his speech. In the Times the report of what he said is very correct, as far as it goes, but it is necessarily a very abbreviated statement.—

Mr. Kinnaird[1] began by speaking in the most respectful manner of you, and indeed in terms of great eulogy—but afterwards I think absurdly dwelt on your being an interested party, and an advocate for the college, and imitated Mr. Jackson in his irony on those whom he first declared were highly deserving of respect. In what manner could we have any correct account of the college and its concerns but from an interested party? Who could speak of its management, attainments and discipline but those who were acquainted with it? He however gave up the only strong grounds they had, (if they had been true) for inquiring into the affairs of the college, for he said that he had no idea that there was more immorality and profligacy in the East India College than in any other seminary—neither did he say any thing of a want of proficiency in the students, but his main argument was built on the general principle that a supply of intellectual attainments will as surely follow an effectual demand for it, as the supply of any material commodity will follow effectual demand.

Mr. Grant I should mention supported a directly contrary principle.—Mr. Kinnaird dwelt very much on the compulsion under which parents were of sending their children to this particular institution. He seemed to me to adopt Mr.

[1] Douglas Kinnaird, friend of Byron and Hobhouse.

21 Feb. 1817 Mill's view of the subject and his argument would have been quite as applicable to all colleges if parents were compelled to send their children to them. He passed over the compulsion under which parents were to send their children to college who wished to bring them up to the church &c.ª. In a few minutes conversation which I had with him after the debate I urged this objection and he answered that they had a choice among a large number of colleges whereas in your case they were confined to this one.

He finished by assuring me that my friend had a bad cause—that it could not be defended, and must fall.

Mr. Impey's speech was badly timed,—he should not have immediately followed Mr. Grant,—for he could not then say any thing new, nor could he repeat any thing that had been said half as well as Mr. Grant had said it before.—

The debate will be renewed on tuesday.¹ If you should come up I shall expect you in Brook Street. If I do not see you and you are disengaged on the saturday evening following, I shall be glad to pass a day with you, commencing my visit at that time.—

Mrs. Ricardo is obliged to Mrs. Malthus for her invitation but she could not conveniently quit home.

Very truly Y^{rs}

DAVID RICARDO

25 February.

205. RICARDO TO TROWER[1]

[Reply to 203.—Answered by 209]

London 24 Feb 1817

Dear Trower

Mr. Rose you will have seen has himself answered your 24 Feb. 1817
questions concerning his proposed measures for regulating
Provident Institutions, by the introduction of his bill into
the House of Commons, which I believe does not in any
material point, differ from that of last year. It retains the
clause respecting giving parish relief to contributors, notwithstanding they may have funds in the Bank, which I
apprehend will not be suffered to pass without opposition.
I am glad to find that we do not differ with respect to the
pernicious tendency of the poor laws.—we both wish to see
them amended or abolished, but I believe are not quite
agreed on the means of obtaining so salutary an end. If
I thought with you that the clause in question was calculated
to afford great encouragement to the poor to become depositors in these Institutions, I should be friendly to it. My
apprehension from its continuing is more that it will not
diminish the poor rates than that it will cause any addition to
them. There are as you observe two classes of labourers, the
single and the married. Notwithstanding that the tendency
of the poor laws is to reduce the wages of these classes to[2] the
least possible amount on which single men can live, yet this
effect is not probably fully accomplished. If it were, neither
the single man, who receives no relief from the parish, nor
the married man who does, could possibly become depositors,
for they would have nothing to deposit. We must suppose
then that the single men receive more than their wants

---

[1] Addressed: 'Hutches Trower
Esq[r]/ Unsted Wood / Godalming /
Surry'.

MS at University College, London.—*Letters to Trower*, XI.
[2] 'a perfect' is del. here.

24 Feb. 1817 require. Our object is to encourage them to accumulate what they can save from their wages, and the question is what effect the insertion or omission of this clause will have on their minds. You think that the chances of poverty are so constantly before their eyes, and that it appears so probable that they may themselves fall into that state, that they would have no motive to acquire property if the possession of property precluded them from receiving relief. I on the contrary maintain that after expending on their own wants the property they had acquired they would be in no worse situation for having acquired it. This of course you would allow, but I am of opinion that the chances of a reverse of fortune are always considerably undervalued by all of us, and therefore that the fear of falling into poverty can have very little influence on the mind of any man whose wages are such as to enable him to save a part of his earnings. The only good that the most sanguine can expect from these Institutions is the withdrawing of this class from the influence of the poor rates and thus by diminishing the number of paupers introduce [more]¹ independent feelings. You will accomplish this object most surely if you take security for the permanence of a man's good habits. Exclude the clause he will know that to preserve his treasure he must be saving and prudent; insert it he will as surely know that he may indulge in a week or month's dissipation without infringing on it. I am not so sanguine as many as to the excellent effects which are to follow from these Banks unless we at the same time raise the general rate of wages by confining the operation of the poor laws to cases of extreme necessity. We are I think beginning at the wrong end. Every thing would go on well if we could rescue the lowest labourers with families from an habitual reliance on the rates. By so doing we should better

¹ MS torn.

the condition of all above that class and then these Institu- 24 Feb. 1817 tions would become powerful auxiliaries. As it is they may introduce better habits amongst a few who now lavish their money away in idleness and extravagance, but in the other case the field would be extended, and the result gratifying to every friend of the poor and to the cause of good government. These rates are a yawning gulph in which all that is valuable will be ultimately swallowed. I hope Mrs. Trower continues in good health. Pray make Mrs. Ricardos and my compl^{ts} to her.

Ever yours
DAVID RICARDO[1]

206. RICARDO TO MALTHUS[2]

[Answered by 207]

My dear Sir London 5 March [1817][3]

The public papers have ere this informed you of the 5 March 1817 result of yesterday's ballot at the India House; Mr. Jackson's motion[4] was lost by a majority of 21 or 22.

Mr. Jackson, in his reply, said every thing of you that your most partial friends could wish, and indeed the general tone of his speech, yesterday, was much more moderate than that by which he introduced his motion.

Mr. Bosanquet's[5] comments on some passages in your

---

[1] On the last sheet of the letter Trower writes: 'The answer to this argument is that the poor man is liable to difficulties independent of his own foresight and prudence and that he ought to be secured against them by relief if distress should come upon him.'
[2] Addressed: 'To / The Rev^d

T. R Malthus / East India College / Hertford'.
MS at Albury.—*Letters to Malthus*, XLV (where it is dated 1816).
[3] Actually written '1816'; postmark, 1817.
[4] See above, p. 130, n. 3.
[5] Jacob Bosanquet, an East India Director.

5 March 1817   pamphlet,[1] leads me to think that he must have misunderstood you, as I conceive that it was not your intention by recommending the Directors to appoint more young men than there were vacant writerships, that the unsuccessful candidates should be finally and irrecoverably dismissed from all chance of going out to India. I imagine that it was your intention to let them be again competitors for one of the prizes of the following year, and therefore that the punishment of their neglect would rather be a delay in their appointment than an absolute dismission. Mr. Bosanquet appeared to me to argue on the latter supposition.

Mr. Elphinstone[2] spoke very kindly, and very handsomely of the professors, yet I thought that he was by far the most formidable opponent of the College, as at present constituted, and the one that I should have been least able to answer. His speech was short, but from the moderation of his language, it produced, I think, a considerable effect, and gave great courage to Mr. Jackson's party.

I hope this subject will not be again revived, or rather I hope that the proficiency of the young men, and the absence of all turbulence, will satisfy every one of the impolicy of interfering with the establishment.—

I am sorry to be under the necessity of putting off my visit to you, but I shall not be able to be with you on saturday. We have, before we expected it, received an account of Mrs. Austin's accouchement, and her mother is so very desirous of seeing her, and Mrs. Clutterbuck, who is with her, that we are going very early on Monday morning, accompanied by Fanny, into Gloucestershire, so that I must defer my visit to you to some more favourable opportunity.—

Perhaps you may be in London to the King of Clubs. If

[1] *Statements respecting the East India College.*

[2] William Elphinstone, an East India Director.

so pray come to us. I wanted to shew you my observations[1] 5 March 1817
on your pamphlets before they go to the printers. If I do
not see you on friday I shall send them by the coach in a
few days. As they are the last article in my very poor performance the printer will probably not want them till my
return. When you have read them pray send them with
your observations to Brook Street by the coach.

Mrs. Ricardo joins with me in kind regards to Mrs.
Malthus

Very truly Y^{rs}

DAVID RICARDO

207. MALTHUS TO RICARDO[2]

[Reply to 206.—Answered by 208]

My dear Sir,   E I Coll March 7th 1817

I am much obliged to you for your letter, and the 7 March 1817
account of the proceedings of the Court, but am sorry to
hear that we shall not see you on saturday. I beg leave however to congratulate you on the cause; and hope to hear of
Mrs. Austins rapid convalescence.

The effect produced on the Court by Mr. Elphinstons
speech was on account of its containing accusations against
the Professors, which were probably believed to be true, but
which are in reality quite without foundation. The official
records will shew that in every case where there was a power
of addressing the Students, the Professors *did* address them;
but in general the great aim of the Students has been conceal-
ment, and they have run to their own rooms the moment the

---

[1] The last chapter of the *Prin-*
ciples ('Mr. Malthus's Opinions
on Rent').

[2] Addressed: 'D. Ricardo Esqr. /
56. Upper Brook Street / Grosvenor Square / London.'
MS in *R.P.*

7 March 1817 Professors came near them. On the last occasion in particular, the one to which I believe Mr. Jackson made some particular allusion, the assault was completely over, and every student retired to his rooms, before the alarm could be given to the Professors; and it is to be sure a most gross absurdity to suppose that young men who thought it necessary to put on masks for an attack upon the servants would stay in the Quadrangle to be harangued by the Professors. The affair took place late at night; when the Principal and most of the Professors were in bed, and before any body could get to the spot there was the most perfect quiet throughout the College.

With regard to conciliation, I really believe that more has been attempted in that way, than at any school or College with which I am acquainted; and if the Students do not like the place, I am quite persuaded, that it is not from want of conciliation, but from the discipline, and the situation of the place not being favourable to amusement. Riding driving and excursions, at the repeated instigations of the Directors, have not only been rendered more difficult than at the Universities (where they are in a manner allowed) but more difficult perhaps than among the head classes of Eaton Westminster and Harrow, and the situation of the place, at a distance from any Town does not certainly afford a field for much entertainment.

With regard to the first of these two charges, it is so directly contrary to the fact, that I believe we shall think it necessary distinctly to deny it in some way or other. The latter does not admit of an appeal to facts, but is nevertheless essentially unfounded.

The King of Clubs was *last* saturday, and I received an admonition from Sharp for not being present. I shall endeavour to behave better the next time.

I shall be happy to receive your manuscript and tell you 7 March 1817 what I think of it.

By the by Bosanquet did not mistake my meaning. Mrs. M joins with me in kind regards to Mrs. Ricardo.

Ever truly Yours

T R MALTHUS.

208. RICARDO TO MALTHUS[1]

[Reply to 207]

London 9th March 1817

My dear Sir

I leave London to-morrow morning very early for 9 March 1817 Gloucestershire from whence I shall return some time before your next meeting at the King of Clubs, so that I hope you will do me the favour to come to Brook Street when you visit town on that occasion.

The accounts which we daily receive of Mrs. Austin's health are highly satisfactory,—she is now I hope entirely out of all danger, and is already sufficiently recovered to enjoy the company of her affectionate visitors. Mr. Warburton and Mr. Binda have but just preceded us, for they left town for Easton Grey on friday last,—we shall probably meet them there before our return.

This letter will accompany that part of my MS. which refers to you. I hope I have not in any respect misapprehended you; and however we may differ in opinion on the subjects that we have so often discussed, I trust you will not think that I have exceeded the bounds of fair criticism, in

[1] Addressed: 'To / The Revd T. R Malthus / East India College / Hertford'—not passed through the post, being enclosed with the MSS in a parcel.—MS at Albury. *Letters to Malthus*, LVI.

9 March 1817 my remarks on the passages of your pamphlets which I have selected for animadversion.

The printing goes on briskly. We have had a sheet a day since the commencement, and eleven sheets are now corrected.[1] In their printed form they appear worse, in my eyes, than before, and I need all the encouragement of my partial correctors to keep alive a spark of hope respecting their reception. I wish it were fairly out of my hands and that it may not be delayed I have taken every precaution that it shall proceed uninterruptedly in my absence. As yet I have no misgivings about the doctrines themselves, all my fears are for the language and arrangement and above all that I may not have succeeded in clearly shewing what the opinions are which I am desirous of submitting to fair investigation.

I hope that College affairs will no longer occupy an undue proportion of your attention, but that you will be able to give a finishing hand to the works which you are about to publish. Mrs. Marcet will immediately publish a second addition[2]: I have given her my opinion on some passages of her book, and have pointed out those which I know you would dispute with me. If she begins to listen to our controversy the printing of her book will be long delayed,—she had better avoid it and keep her course on neutral ground. I believe we should sadly puzzle Miss Caroline and I doubt whether Mrs. B[3] herself could clear up the difficulty.—

[1] Corresponding to I, 1–145 in the present edition.
[2] The second edition of *Conversations on Political Economy; in which the Elements of that Science are Familiarly Explained*, By the author of *Conversations on Chemistry*, London, Longman, 1817. The 'Advertisement', or Preface, dated 11 July, says 'the Author has availed herself of a few useful hints from her friends, and of some recent valuable publications on Political Economy'; the additions include a new chapter on foreign trade.
[3] 'Mrs. B.' and 'Caroline' are the interlocutors in the *Conversations*.

From some conversation which I had yesterday morning 9 March 1817 with Mr. Murray it appears that Torrens has been offering his book[1] to him, but Murray is very lukewarm in the negociation, and really very much underrates Torrens' talents. He thinks that the sale of Torrens best work, that on corn, was very limited, he talked of its not having exceeded 150 copies.

Since writing the above I have seen Mr. Hume, he tells me that he has heard that the Directors are about to institute an inquiry into the state of the College themselves.—

Mrs. Ricardo joins with me in kind regards to Mrs. Malthus.

Very truly Y^{rs}
DAVID RICARDO

209. TROWER TO RICARDO[2]
[Reply to 205]

Unsted Wood—Godalming
March 18. 1817.

Dear Ricardo—

On the disputed subject of the relief clause in Rose's 18 March 1817 Bill I beg to refer you to two letters I have sent to the times newspaper signed a Manager of a Provident Fund, one appeared on the 21. February and the other on the 18 march —They pretend to nothing but a plain statement of the argument; and it would give me pleasure to think they will meet with your approbation—You will see, that I rest the importance of the clause in question upon its being essential to the success of our Institutions—These are so connected with the subject of the Poor Laws, that it was impossible not to touch upon it, yet it is so fearful a one, that I forbear from

---

[1] Cp. above, p. 35, n. 2.   Esq / Brook Street / Grosvenor
[2] Addressed: 'To / David Ricardo   Square'.—MS in R.P.

18 March 1817 pursuing it. In recommending to begin by *encreasing wages*, I do not mean to suggest any direct interference in the prices of labor, but the adoption of such collateral measures as must materially contribute to quicken the demand for labor. Such for instance as encouraging emigration, reducing, or repealing those taxes which affect most heavily our aggricultural and commercial interests. I am aware, that the Revenue forbids this to any extent unless the taxes are imposed, and I should not hesitate to recommend a new Income tax; a tax which ought never to have been repealed.

An enemy as I am to all interference I ask with *fear and trembling*, least you should deem me a supporter of vicious and exploded doctrines, what you think would be the effect, *under existing circumstances*, of regulating the *minimum of wages*. I see myself many objections to it, yet I wish to hear what you have to say upon the subject. It would diminish the amount of the poor rates, and put a stop to a most mischievous and unjust abuse arising out of the present system—Farmers, and even Gentlemen are getting their work done at the Parish allowance of 7/ or 8/ a week whilst the rate of wages is generally 12/. They do this by turning off their laborers in the first instance, and then engaging men of the Parish at the reduced rate I have mentioned.—

I have been looking in the paper to see if your new publication is announced, pray let me know when it is to make its appearance, I am impatient to see it.

Have you read Armata?[1] I like it very much, tho' I differ in the view taken of the politics of the last 25 years. I am rejoiced to see the violent reformers thus falling off from the cause, one after another. Lord Grey, Lord Lauderdale, Lord Erskine &. &. This is delightful!

[1] *Armata: A fragment* [Anon.], London, Murray, 1817. A political satire by Lord Erskine in the manner of *Gulliver's Travels*.

We do not intend visiting Town this spring which I lament, 18 March 1817 only in as much as it prevents me the pleasure of seeing my particular friends, among which number I have very sincere pleasure in considering you my Dear Ricardo, so pray believe me to be yrs very sincerely

HUTCHES TROWER

Mrs. Trower unites with me in kind regards to Mrs. R. and family.

210. RICARDO TO MALTHUS[1]

My dear Sir   London 22 March 1817

I have been expecting you, both yesterday, and to day, 22 March 1817 and it is only after a most laborious calculation that I am led to suspect that the meeting of your Club is not till next saturday. Next friday then, or any earlier day, I hope, we shall see you in Brook Street, and I am desired by Mrs. Ricardo to say that if Mrs. Malthus will also favour us with her company, she will be very happy to see her.

If you should come on or before friday,[2] the printer will not before that day want that part of my MS which I sent to you, but if he uses due diligence he will certainly be ready for it about that time. If you have any remarks to make on it which will require much consideration on my part, be so good as to send it me before, for as the time approaches that I am to appear in print, I seem to become more dissatisfied with my work, and less capable to give any proposition contained in it a patient investigation.

It is now 5 oClock, and notwithstanding my doubts have been gathering strength since the morning, I am but just

[1] Addressed: 'The Revᵈ T R   MS at Albury.—*Letters to Mal-*
Malthus / East India College /   *thus,* LVII.
Hertford'.   [2] 28 March.

22 March 1817 convinced, after tracing back with Mr. Hitchings the day you were last here, that I shall not see you this day.

In great haste

Y^{rs} very truly

DAVID RICARDO

We returned from Gloucestershire on tuesday last.

211. RICARDO TO MALTHUS[1]

My dear Sir

London 26 March 1817

26 March 1817 This morning I intended that my letter to you to day should inform you that I would have the pleasure of passing next saturday and sunday with you at Haileybury, but a circumstance has taken place which will make it necessary for me to go to Bath on friday next,[2] from which place I shall again return to London early in the next week.

As you say you will not be in town till after Easter perhaps it will be convenient to you to see me at Haileybury on

[1] Addressed: 'Rev^d T R Malthus / East India College / Hertford'. MS at Albury.—*Letters to Malthus*, LVIII.

[2] Ricardo's departure for Bath was delayed till Monday, 31 March, as is shown by the following extracts from two letters written by Whishaw, in London, to Thomas Smith, at Easton Grey: 2 April 1817, 'I accompanied Ricardo on Saturday [29 March] to Holland House. He seemed pleased with his visit. His book is coming out immediately.' 4 April 1817, 'I write only to say that Mr. Ricardo has just concluded a treaty for the marriage of his son Osman with some lady whom the young man met at Bath, and who, I believe, is of a Warwickshire family. I have not heard her name, but Binda says they are highly pleased with the connection. Mr. Ricardo went down on this business to Bath on Monday [31 March], and returned yesterday morning. To-morrow [Easter-eve], I believe, he will join our party at the College. It cannot be said that Ricardo has been improperly influenced, as to the principles of population, by his intimacy with Malthus. He will enjoy the blessing of Abraham, and may expect to see a tribe of grandchildren and great-grandchildren round his table' (*The 'Pope' of Holland House*, pp. 180–81). Osman Ricardo was married to Harriet Mallory on 22 May 1817.

saturday sen'night. If so I shall be with you on that day, at 26 March 1817 your dinner hour, and if I do not hear from you before, I shall conclude that you have no engagement which will render my visit inconvenient.—

I mean this day to put the last of my papers in the printers hands, and hope he will be able to finish the printing before my visit to you, but of this I have some doubt, as he does not proceed regularly at the same even pace.

I agree with you that after having so often heard your opinions, in contradiction to mine, it would not be of much use just now when my book is actually in the press to enter again on your reasons for differing with me. I did not send you the manuscripts with any such intention, I merely wished you to see that part which related to you before I published, that I might not inadvertently misrepresent your[1] statement. I cannot have the least objection to insert the note you mention,[2] although I cannot but regret that we should differ so much as to the just and fair import of the words *real price*. When you see my book altogether you will not perhaps differ from me so much as you now think you do. You may, and I believe will, object to the correctness of many of my terms, as they will appear to you fanciful, and not always properly applied, but making allowance for such deviations you will I am sure agree with much of the matter. On some points indeed there is no difference between us, and on others our chief disagreement would be in the mode of representing them.

I have written this letter at intervals between other engagements as I have been repeatedly interrupted. I now hear the post man's bell and must hasten to conclude

Very truly Y^{rs}

DAVID RICARDO

[1] 'opinions' is del. here.   [2] See above, I, 415.

212. RICARDO TO TROWER[1]

[Answered by 214]

Dear Trower   London 30 March 1817

30 March 1817   Before I leave London, for a very few days, I am
desirous that you should know that I applied the morning
after I saw you to the proper officer in the Vote Office of the
House of Commons, to get you a set of Parliamentary papers,
but I am sorry to say without success. It seems that a very
limited number of copies are printed besides those distributed
to the members: these are the perquisite of two gentlemen
in the office, but they are all disposed of, and at no price can
a single copy now be obtained there. To console you under
your disappointment, I can assure you that it will give me
great pleasure to lend you, whenever you may want them,
any of my papers or reports. The report of last year respecting
the employment of children in Manufactures[2] should have
been sent to you in town the other day, but I did not know
your direction. I heard you say something about Montague
Place, but I knew not at whose house you were to be found
there. This year there have been very few reports,—the only
one of importance is a very thick one containing the laws in
reference to Roman catholics in the different protestant
countries of Europe.[3] If you would like to have this, as well

---

[1] Addressed: 'Hutches Trower Esq[r]/Unsted Wood/Godalming/Surry'. MS at University College, London.—*Letters to Trower*, XII.

[2] 'Report of the Minutes of Evidence taken before the Select Committee on the State of the Children employed in the Manufactories of The United Kingdom, 25 April–18 June 1816', *Parliamentary Papers*, 1816, vol. III.

[3] 'Report from the Select Committee appointed to report the nature and substance of the Laws and Ordinances existing in Foreign States, respecting the Regulation of their Roman Catholic Subjects, in Ecclesiastical matters, and their intercourse with the See of Rome, or any other Foreign Ecclesiastical Jurisdiction', *Parliamentary Papers*, 1816, vol. VII A.

as the one before named, I will send them to you by the 30 March 1817
coach, and you may keep them for a twelvemonth if you
please.

I called yesterday on my printer, and he appeared more
inclined, than on the day you were with me, to promise that
my book should be out on the Monday following the next.[1]
When you read it remember that I want from you the candid
opinion of a friend, both respecting the matter and manner.
Independently of the desire which I have to form a correct
judgement of the merits and demerits of the work, the
opinions of those, whose opinions are worth having, will
enable me to make such alterations in it as may render it
more fit for the public eye if a second edition should be
required—therefore I request you not [to be][2] sparing in
your criticism.

I hope that on your return home you found Mrs. Trower
and your children well, and that the former approved of the
manner in which you executed your various commissions in
London. If any were omitted I fear I must share the blame:
the incessant talk which I kept up during our walk was well
calculated to drive more important matters from your mind.
I hope too that you will reconsider your resolution of not
visiting London this spring. Living so near town it is a duty
which you owe to yourself and to your friends to meet them
at least once in the year.

With best wishes to Mrs. Trower in which Mrs. Ricardo
most cordially unites, I am

Dear Trower
Very sincerely Y^{rs}
DAVID RICARDO

'Supplementary Papers' to ditto, ordered to be printed 28 March 1817, *ib.* 1817, vol. xv.

[1] 7 April. Publication of the *Principles* was delayed till 19 April.
[2] MS torn.

213. RICARDO TO MALTHUS[1]

My dear Sir

3 April 1817   I came up to London last night by the Mail from Salisbury and have just seen your letter. Mr. Whishaw told me when we last met, that he was going to your house on saturday, and I feared that my projected visit might, on account of numbers, be inconvenient to you, and I expected to hear from you to that effect. You have however suggested the getting me a bed out of your house, with which I shall be well satisfied, let it be hard or soft, narrow or roomy. I shall therefore be with you on saturday at dinner, unless I have a letter from you, by return of post, to say that you find a difficulty in the proposed arrangement. I need not I hope say that I shall be very willing to defer my visit for a week or fortnight if it should be more convenient to you. Pray make no ceremony with me, and do not receive me if there be the least difficulty about the bed.

Y[rs] very truly
DAVID RICARDO

London 3 [April][2] 1817

214. TROWER TO RICARDO[3]

[*Reply to* 212]

Unsted Wood—Godalming
April 28—1817—

Dear Ricardo,

28 April 1817   Many thanks for the "Principles of Political Economy" which arrived a few days ago; and to the serious consideration

[1] Addressed: 'Rev[d] T. R Malthus / East India College / Hertford'.
MS at Albury.—*Letters to Malthus*, LIX, where it is dated 3 June 1817.
[2] In MS 'June'; postmark 3 April 1817, which date agrees

with Whishaw's letters quoted above, p. 144, n. 2.
[3] Addressed: 'To / David Ricardo Esq[r] / Upper Brook S[t] / Grosvenor Sq[re]'.
MS in *R.P.*

of which I shall proceed with great eagerness and interest, 28 April 1817 and without delay. I see by your table of contents, that your enquiry embraces all the important questions connected with this great subject. I have not a doubt your Book will be very generally read by all those who take an interest in these discussions, and I beg of you to let me know what you hear is said of your performance by those whose opinions are worth attending to.—I see advertised in the paper a letter addressed to you by a Dr. Crombie,[1] is it worth my reading? I do not know anything of the character of the writer. Is his object to explain and enforce; or to refute the doctrines laid down by you in the pamphlet he reviews?—

You have probably seen a 3^d letter on Provident Institutions in the Times of the 10 April. I thought it necessary to compleat the arguments in the 2^d letter[2]—But, the Editor after having delayed for some time its publication, whilst he infused into his leading paragraphs the substance of what he approved, at length gives a *garbled* account of it, leaving out all that part which recommended a *modified Income Tax* to supply the deficiency in the revenue, occasioned by taking off certain commercial taxes; and thus makes me appear guilty of the *absurdity* of recommending the abolition of millions of taxes, without suggesting how their place might be supplied! Upon my remonstrating with the Editor upon this most unwarrantable liberty, he has written me a letter appologizing, and stating his reasons, with which he hopes I shall be satisfied. But still my apparent absurdity remains, and therefore to those friends, who know the letters to be mine, I am desirous of rescuing myself from the charge of such obvious folly.—

I am much obliged to you for the trouble you took about the parliamentary Papers. In consequence of the new regula-

[1] See above, p. 32, n. 1.   [2] See above, p. 141.

28 April 1817 tion respecting the printing the Votes, I have written to the
Deputy Serjeant at Arms, with whom I am acquainted to see
if he can put me in the way of getting the Reports and Votes
together.—

I thank you for your offer to lend me some of the Reports;
and I am disposed to trouble you so far as to beg the use of
the Police Report,[1] that on education,[2] and on the employment of Children in Manufactures.[3]

Mr. Owen's plan appears to me to be very absurd as well
as objectionable—The evil is *want of demand for laborers*, that
is for manufactures or produce of some sort or other—But,
whilst that demand remains the same, what good do you do
by setting up new manufactures to be made by children,
when the necessary effect of any such measure, if it succeed,
is to take such manufactures out of the hands of some other
persons, who previously were engaged in it? As a remedy
therefore for any of the existing evils it must be perfectly
inoperative; and as a system for the education of the lower
classes highly objectionable, by collecting together, in large
masses, those, who, on every account, (except that of expence) ought to be broken down into small parcels, if I may
so express myself.[4] Mrs. T. unites in kind remembrances to
Mrs. R. and believe me

Yours very truly

HUTCHES TROWER

[1] 'Report from the Committee on
the State of the Police of The
Metropolis; with the Minutes of
Evidence', *Parliamentary Papers*,
1816, vol. v.
[2] 'Report from Select Committee
on the Education of the Lower
Orders in The Metropolis; with
the Minutes of Evidence',
[Brougham's Report], *Parliamentary Papers*, 1816, vol. IV.

[3] See above, p. 146, n. 2.
[4] Robert Owen's plan for the
regeneration of the world was
first put forward in the *Report to
the Committee of the Association
for the Relief of the Manufacturing
and Labouring Poor, laid before
the Committee of the House of
Commons on the Poor Laws*; the
Report was printed in full in *The
Times* of 9 April 1817.

215. RICARDO TO SINCLAIR[1]

Upper Brook Street, 4th May 1817.

Sir,

I thank you for your pamphlet,[2] which I have read with
attention. I agree with you, that a part of our distress has
been occasioned by the reduction of the circulation; but I
consider it as a necessary price for the establishment of a
better system, than that of encouraging an indefinite amount
of paper circulation. I cannot think that any but a very small
further reduction will be necessary, to enable the Bank to
meet any demands that may be made on them for specie.
The remedy, grievous as it is, is the necessary consequence of
former error. I hope we shall never try an unchecked paper
circulation again, though I have no objection to a paper
circulation, and nothing but a paper circulation. It is obvious that, if we have forty millions, or any other given
amount of taxes to pay, they will fall heavier on those who
are to pay them, if money, by the diminution of its quantity,
is raised in value. I have not seen Mr. Attwood's publication.[3]
I am, Sir, your obedient and humble servant,

DAVID RICARDO.

4 May 1817

---

[1] *Correspondence of Sir John Sinclair*, vol. I, p. 321; *Letters to Trower*, XIV.
[2] *On the Means of Arresting the Progress of the National Calamity*, London, Nicol, 1817 (Preface dated 31 March 1817); reprinted in *Pamphleteer*, vol. X, 1817, No. XX.
[3] *Prosperity Restored; or Reflections on the Cause of the Public Distresses and on the only Means of Relieving them*, by Thomas Attwood, Esq. of Birmingham, London, Baldwin, 1817. Sinclair often quotes it in his pamphlet and, referring to it and to *The Remedy, or Thoughts on our Present Distresses*, by the same author, says: 'These pamphlets should be read by every one, who wishes to be thoroughly master of those important discussions' (p. 10).

216. TROWER TO RICARDO[1]

[Answered by 217]

Unsted Wood—Godalming
May 7—1817—

Dear Ricardo—

7 May 1817   The object of this letter is to request you will inform me in what light the new clause in Rose's bill, respecting the investment of the Funds of Provident Institutions in the Commissions of the Sinking Fund, is viewed by the Institutions in London; and whether they feel disposed so to model their plans as to come within the provisions of the Bill should they be adopted by Parliament. It is a very important consideration—No doubt it is highly desirable to secure the Depositors from the probability of loss; and especially as the so doing will be the means of extending more widely the influence of these Institutions. That security, which it was not in the power of the Trustees of Institutions prudently to offer, may, no doubt, be safely afforded by Government. The objection seems to be, that, by so doing, Depositors will not equally feel that they have a stake in the Country the safety of which, in a great degree, depends upon their own good conduct. Upon this moral influence I calculated in our Institutions—It is liable also to abuse, to obviate which it is enacted, that no Institution shall be able to avail itself of the benefits of the Government Investment, the annual payments of whose individual Depositors are allowed to exceed £50. Here comes the question then how far it is worth the while of Institutions framed as ours are, to qualify their Regulations so as to come within the prescribed limitations—I am disposed to think it is—But as I only received the Bill this morning, I have not yet sufficiently considered it. Pray let

[1] Addressed: 'To / David Ricardo Esq[r] / Upper Brook Street / Grosvenor Square'.—MS in *R.P.*

me know your opinion, what steps your Institutions think 7 May 1817
of taking, and also our parent Institution at Bath? Is Elwin
still in London; if he is pray beg him to write to me on the
subject.

The adoption of this measure by Rose is a compleat
confession, that he felt the security of repayment of full
money offered by his, and similar institutions, could not be
complied with; or if not so, where the necessity of calling in
the aid of Government? Looking to the universality of these
Institutions I am rather disposed to admit the propriety of
submitting them, whilst in their infancy, to one general
national system—

Huskisson's clause I entirely disapprove of. It is unnecessary and unadviseable—

Yrs very truly—
HUTCHES TROWER.

NB. Many thanks for your Reports.

217. RICARDO TO TROWER[1]
[Reply to 216]

Dear Trower
London 9 May 1817

I write although I can give you little information on the 9 May 1817
subject of your inquiry. I understand it is proposed that the
managers of the three Provident Institutions in London, shall
meet for the purpose of agreeing on some general regulations,
at which it will no doubt be discussed whether it will be
expedient to alter the rules, to enable us to avail ourselves
of the privelege about to be granted of obtaining debentures
at a fixed rate of interest, with a return of the money at the

---

[1] Addressed: 'Hutches Trower   MS at University College, Lon-
Esqʳ/Unsted Wood/Godalming/   don.—Letters to Trower, XIII.
Surry'.

9 May 1817 will of the trustees. It appears to me so desireable that the depositor should be secured in the receipt of the precise sum of money which he may originally deposit that notwithstanding there are great objections against the limiting each man's deposit to £50, it should be agreed to, if on no other condition this advantage is to be obtained. This point has not yet been discussed, nor offered for discussion in our particular establishment,[1] and probably will not be till the clause has been approved by Parliament.

I am very much surprised at Ministers sanctioning such a clause, for it cannot be doubted that if the amount of deposits should become very large, it will not only subject the country to a considerable tax, but may on the breaking out of a war very much embarrass the financial operations. Suppose that a sum as large as 3 millions of debentures should be issued by the Bank in return for deposits made by trustees, when 3 pc^{ts} are at 85, Government would by purchasing 3 pc^{ts} obtain only $3\frac{1}{2}$ pc. on 3 millions for which they would be paying to the holders of debentures more than $4\frac{1}{2}$ pc, thus losing £30,000 p^r ann., and when 3 pc^{ts} fell to 60 they would be called upon for the payment of this sum of 3 millions at a very inconvenient time, as to obtain it they would lose the difference between 85 at which they bought, and 60 at which they would be forced to sell or £750,000. Now though I am a friend to these Institutions I do not think that they are deserving of these extraordinary bonuses, particularly as I am persuaded that this loss to the public would not act as any great encouragement to savings. The depositors whether they received 5, 4 or 3 pc. for their money would be of little importance in determining them to economical habits.

With respect to the moral influence of[2] these Institutions do you think that a depositor will feel that he has an equal

---

[1] See above, p. 50, n.   [2] Replaces 'on'.

stake in the country and is therefore interested in its peace 9 May 1817 and good government whether he have £5 in the funds or in a government debenture? In that respect I can see no difference.

Mr. Elwin is engaged to dine with me on monday next when I shall give him your message. I shall not I think see him before.

Mrs. Ricardo joins with me in kind regards to Mrs. Trower

Very truly y^{rs}

DAVID RICARDO

218. RICARDO TO BARTON[1]

Sir

In the letter with which you have favoured me, you 20 May 1817 have stated your reasons for differing with my theory of profits very clearly and concisely, but it appears to me that you have not succeeded in shewing it to be defective.

My proposition is as you have stated it; "that the rate of

[1] Addressed: 'Jn⁰ Barton Esqr at / Mrs: Woodrouffe Smith's / Clapham / Surry.'
    MS in the possession of Prof. J. H. Hollander, Baltimore. (See Maggs Bros., Autographs Cat. No. 352, Xmas 1916).—Published in a note to the reprint of John Barton's *Condition of the Labouring Classes of Society*, ed. by J. H. Hollander, Baltimore, 1934, pp. 67-9, from which it is reprinted here (with a correction in the address from a photostat supplied by Prof. Hollander).
    John Barton (1789–1852) was a Quaker, and one of the promoters of the Savings Bank, the Lancasterian School, and the Mechanics' Institution at Chiches-ter, where he lived. See *Gentleman's Magazine*, April 1852, and the biography of his son and namesake *John Barton, A Memoir*, by C. E. Barton, London, 1910.
    When this letter was written Ricardo's *Principles* had been out for a month. Barton's *Observations on the Circumstances which influence the Condition of the Labouring Classes of Society*, London, Arch, 1817, was written in June (as the author says, p. 46) and published later in the year (cp. *Monthly Literary Advertiser*, 10 Nov. 1817). In that pamphlet Barton seems to have accepted Ricardo's explanation on the first point of this letter, but he persists in his second objection.

20 May 1817 profit is regulated in all cases by the rate of wages, one being inversely as the other." The supposition which you have made does not invalidate its truth for if there should be "a general and progressive decrease of the value of money which should diminish the real income of the fundholder, and of persons living on fixed salaries" still the rate of profit would not rise. The supposition infers[1] that all things rise in price, as it is by this operation that the fundholders income is reduced,—he will receive the same nominal sum as before, but in expending such sum he will obtain fewer commodities in return.

The farmer and the manufacturer on the contrary, will, in consequence of the rise in the price of commodities, have a larger nominal income, but not a larger real income, as though they will receive more money for their goods, they will also have to pay more money for the goods which they themselves consume. The farmer indeed will be benefited during the existence of his lease, for one of his outgoings, namely, his rent, will not even nominally increase,—but the general rate of agricultural profits is not to be measured by the particular profits of one, or of a hundred farmers who are peculiarly favourably situated, but by the gains which a farmer commencing business can obtain who is obliged to pay a rent regulated by the current value of money.

But if the fundholder's power of consuming commodities is diminished will not the farmer's and manufacturer's be increased? Undoubtedly it will, but their profits will not therefore be increased. The fundholder derives his income from the taxes which are paid, partly by himself, and partly by the other classes: now if a part of the taxes be remitted the fundholder will receive less, and the other classes will be really gainers in their expenditure, but not in their profits.

[1] Replaces 'supposes'.

Suppose I paid £1000 p^r Ann. for income tax, my profits being £10000 p^r Ann^m; when the tax is remitted I am £1000 p^r Ann^m richer, but my profits are still only £10,000, and bear the same proportion as before to the money value of the capital, from which this profit was derived. I am benefited then not by my increased gains, not by any alteration in the rate of profits, but by my power of expending a larger proportion of those profits on myself, and a less proportion on the public, or stockholder.

Your second objection may be rather more difficult to answer but it does not appear to me to be more defensible.[1]

It is undoubtedly true that in proportion as the accumulations of capital are realised in fixed capital, such as machinery, buildings, &c. they will give less permanent employment to labour, and therefore there will be a less demand for men, and a less necessity for an increase of population, than if the accumulated capital had been employed as circulating capital. But the quantity of goods produced, over and above the necessary consumption, would be precisely the same in both cases, or rather the balance would be in favour of the fixed capital, and not of the circulating capital, as you suppose. You say "Additions to circulating capital increase the supply of commodities in a like proportion; double the circulating capital and twice as much goods will be produced. But the same amount added to fixed capital, increases the supply of goods in a much smaller degree. A man lays out £1000 in hiring workmen to produce cloth thus the quantity of cloth at market is increased by £1100 worth.

But if he lay out the £1000 in building a steam engine for the same purpose the quantity of cloth at market is increased only by the £100 worth, yet in either case the capitalist gains

[1] For Ricardo's subsequent change of opinion on this point, see the chapter 'On Machinery' in ed. 3 of the *Principles*.

20 May 1817 the same profit, viz. 10 p^{ct}" If the labourers hired by the circulating capital were themselves machines and could be made to work without consuming food and necessaries, your argument would be correct, but in fact the master who employs them gets only £100 worth of cloth, the remaining £1000 worth is devoted to their maintenance, and it is clear that instead of producing £1100 worth of cloth they would be obliged to employ their labour in producing food and necessaries for themselves of the value of £1000 if they could not prevail on those who before manufactured cloth to allow them to produce the cloth whilst these others produced the food and necessaries which the new workmen would subsequently require in exchange for the cloth. By the terms of your supposition the men to be employed are in addition to the number before employed, and therefore neither food nor necessaries can be provided for them but by devoting their own labour to such an object, or by prevailing on the society to consent to a different distribution of employments. Ten elevenths of the labour which the additional £1000 can command will be really employed in providing for the maintenance &c. of the labourers, although these particular labourers may in no way immediately contribute to it. This proportion of the capital will be expended in supporting a rapidly perishable machine, and the real net income of the country will be increased by £100 worth of cloth, and not by £1100 worth. £1000 worth of goods will be actually consumed by those who reproduce a value equal to £1100 and £100 only will be clear gain to the society. In the case of the fixed capital £1000 worth of goods less will be produced, but at the same time £1000 worth less will be consumed, and the clear¹ income of the society will be equally of the value of £100. The case is evidently put for

¹ Replaces 'net'.

the sake of the argument, and could not really take place, for there is no new creation of machinery which entirely supersedes the use of the labour of man. A steam engine requires the constant labour of man—he must regulate its motion and velocity—he must procure coals for the fire necessary to work it—he must attend to its annual repairs, and by degrees in a rich country the employment of men for these purposes becomes on an average as nearly a fixed quantity, as the number of men devoted to any other occupation. Although steam engines should last for a hundred years the average demand for them might vary very little.

In your conclusion on this subject you make I think the same mistake as before, you suppose that because the stockholder and those having fixed salaries have less command over the comforts and necessaries of life, and the manufacturers and farmers[1] more, that therefore the rate of profits of the latter will increase, which is by no means a necessary consequence, as a man may be benefited by his income becoming more efficient in expenditure than before, although it bears no greater proportion to his capital.

On this subject I have completely satisfied myself but as your previous thoughts may not have run in the same channel as mine have done, I may have made use of language which will fail to bring conviction to your mind. At any rate I request you to read from page 44[2] to the end of the chapter in my late publication and to consider also the passage in Page 131[3]

I am Sir

Your obed: Serv:

DAVID RICARDO

Upper Brook Street
20 May 1817

---

[1] 'and farmers' is ins.   [2] Above, I, 64.   [3] Above, I, 119.

219. RICARDO TO TROWER[1]

[Answered by 224]

Dear Trower   Antwerp 15 June 1817

You will be very much surprised at receiving an answer
to your letter[2] dated from this place, but here I am, enjoying
in the most delightful weather, one of the most agreeable
journeys I have ever taken. My Brother Ralph only is with
me. We landed on tuesday last[3] at Calais, and have already
been through the towns of Cassel, Lisle, and Ghent. Each
place appears to improve on the last, and Antwerp, where
we now are, is certainly the grandest. I am quite astonished
at the magnificence and splendour of the Cathedrals and
Churches in this country,—they far surpass any thing that
I have seen in our own country, and the pictures which are
to be found in them are the chefs d'œuvres of the masters by
whom they are painted. To see the descent from the Cross
by Rubens, which is in the Cathedral here, is alone worth
all the trouble of a journey from London. There are others
nearly as good in this and in the other churches, besides
innumerable beautiful specimens of the delightful art of
painting in the public and private collections. We intend
leaving this place to morrow for Brussells from which place
we propose going by Namur to Liege and thence to Cologne.
From Cologne we shall proceed up the Rhine to Franckfort
and Heidelberg and then we shall make the best of our way
to Paris, and after seeing the beauties of that luxurious capital
we shall return home. I have long had a desire to make a tour
on the continent, but one week before setting out I had not
any idea that it was so near its accomplishment. Our
pleasure is damped by witnessing every where the greatest

[1] Addressed: 'Hutches Trower   MS at University College, Lon-
Esq[r] / Godalming / Surrey / Eng-   don.—*Letters to Trower*, XV.
land'. English postmark, 20 June.   [2] Trower's letter is wanting.
                                     [3] 10 June.

distress and poverty, proceeding in a great degree from the last bad harvest. We are told that bread is more than 3 times its ordinary price, and would be higher if other causes did not abridge the ability of the purchasers to pay for it. The poor are obliged to have recourse to food which is never eaten by human beings but on the greatest emergencies. It is some consolation however to see every where around us in this fertile country abundant fields of corn, looking beautifully, and holding out the fairest prospects of an abundant harvest. Besides the evils resulting from dear food the people have to struggle as well as ourselves with a stagnation in trade. At the table d'hote yesterday in conversation with an intelligent man he ascribed much of this to the disadvantage of their trade with England, although he was abundantly inconsistent on this subject. First he complained of the goods which were imported from England, they were totally unlike what were formerly obtained from that country, and were made only to please the eye. Secondly he insisted on the necessity of rigourous enactments against the introduction of British manufactures on the continent while England continued her prohibitory system—they were now obliged, he said, to buy every thing, and were not allowed to sell any thing, and therefore were under the necessity of paying the balance in gold and silver. As well as I could, in my bad French, I endeavoured to set him right, and to correct his erroneous theory, but I fear I have not satisfied him that retaliation in such a case only aggravates the evil sought to be removed.—I cannot but lament however that England who ought to be the example to other nations for liberal and correct principles, should be justly accused of being the foremost in departing from the maxims of free trade, and shackling the most advantageous distribution of the general commerce of the world.

15 June 1817 You will conceive my surprise when I tell you that while I was present at the celebration of Mass to day, in the great Cathedral, with all my attention fixed on the mummery by which I was surrounded, I was tapped on the shoulder by our friend Elwin, who had the evening before arrived from Bruxelles, in his way to Douay, where he is going to see a nephew whom he had a week before left at that place, after which he will immediately return to England. I experienced from him his usual kindness, for he insisted on our dining with him and his companion, Mr. Oxley[1] I believe his name, at his hotel. We accepted his invitation and after very much enjoying his company we went together to the Play, from which we are just returned. He will I have no doubt soon write to you himself.

I have scarcely left myself room to say how very much pleased I was with your observations on my book.—I shall take it very kind of you indeed to furnish me with every observation which you may think of importance to enable me either to explain what is obscure, or to correct what is faulty, previously to my publishing a second edition. Murray tells me that a second edition will most assuredly be required and you will of course conclude that I shall be most anxious to give it every improvement in my power,—you cannot therefore oblige me more than freely to animadvert on every part of it.

Pray make my compliments to Mrs. Trower. I hope that she and your children are well,—and believe me with the greatest regard,

Y^{rs} very sincerely

DAVID RICARDO

[1] Probably Charles Oxley, of Ripon, Yorks.

220. RICARDO TO MILL[1]

Carlsruhe 2ᵈ July 1817

My dear Sir

Here we are at the most distant point of our journey, 2 July 1817
after having seen an abundance of capital towns, beautiful
pictures, splendid palaces, and magnificent cathedrals. We
have also been delighted with some of the finest prospects in
nature, have clambered hills—looked at the stratification of
rocks—examined the craters of extinct volcanoes, and have
swum on the rapid stream of the Rhine. If I could but
acquire the language of the initiated, I should pass for a great
traveller on my return, and might speak of the works of
Rubens, Vandyk and Teniers in a way to give an impression
that I was a first rate judge of the beauties displayed by those
eminent artists. Without however making any pretensions
I have had great pleasure in seeing the chef d'œuvres of the
Flemish school, but I cannot repress my astonishment at the
immense number of pictures which are shewn on the continent as those of Rubens particularly. Making every
allowance for the assistance which he may have had, it
appears incredible that he could have given the finishing
touches only to the pictures which bear his name.

We are not inactive travellers. We rise generally at six and
are never in bed till 11. We take very little time at our meals,
and are incessantly walking, or travelling. We are very much
delayed by the dilatoriness of the German Post, which being
a monopoly, is of course very much mismanaged, and I
suspect great advantages are taken of our ignorance. French
is of no use to us excepting at the Inns—neither Post masters,
Postillions nor Barrier keepers know one word of the language. This morning we were detained one hour in changing

[1] Addressed: 'James Mill Ésqʳ / Queen Square / Westminster /
London'.—MS in Mill-Ricardo papers.

2 July 1817 horses, and we seldom lose less than half an hour when this operation is necessary. Our treatment at the Inns is on the whole very good, though my stomach does not readily reconcile itself to their dishes, nor to the Rhenish Wine which is sold under the name of the best old Hock.

You have often heard of the beauties of Heidelberg, and of the charming scenery by which the ruins of the old Chateau is surrounded. They have not, I think, been in the least exaggerated. We passed the greater part of yesterday in wandering about the hills and gardens in its neighbourhood, and there is not a spot which we did not find highly interesting. It was one of the loveliest days that I ever beheld, neither too warm nor too cold, and I do not think that it was possible to enjoy the combined beauties of nature in greater perfection. Having now gone through all the most delightful country we shall make the best of our way to Paris, at which place we shall arrive several days later than we originally intended, and yet, as I told you before, we have been active citizens.

It is delightful, and consolatory, to see the corn-fields, and vineyards, looking every where so well. The rye which is an essential part of the food of the poor on the continent is carrying in all directions, and the wheat and barley crops have every appearance of being abundant. In Flanders our pleasure was very much damped by witnessing the extreme distress of the starving wretched looking people with which every street was filled. Their petitions for relief were clamorous and importunate, and we never stirred without having a dozen of these beggars constantly at our heels. Bread is universally 3 times as high in price as it was 2 years ago, and great complaints are made of the stagnation of trade, and the want of employment. As we left Flanders the appearances of distress diminished. At Frankfort, a town with which I was particularly pleased, there was no greater portion of beggars than might be expected in a populous city, and the same observation is true of Coblentz, Mayence &c.ª &c.ª.—I have literally only seen the country, and have had no opportunity of making myself acquainted with many things of which I should like to have been informed—but our's is much too rapid a course to enable me to know much of the inhabitants and their customs, particularly here, where even good French is not understood by one in a hundred thousand, and where my bad French is almost unintelligible to a much less proportion. I do not know whether you expected a letter from me, but I should not have had an easy conscience if I had not written one. If my power equalled my wishes it should have been an entertaining one, but I now fear that you will find it terribly dull.

I hope that your printing goes on rapidly and that I shall find you ready to accompany me to Gatcomb the latter end of this month.

We have been this evening walking in the gardens of the Grand Duke, after doing him the honour of inspecting his palace and furniture. An immense treasure must have been expended by this family, here, at Manheim and Baden, in building, furnishing and decorating palaces. They are very splendid but one cannot help regretting that the labour of the people was not more usefully directed as however indulgent we may be to luxury it appears here disproportioned to the resources of the state. My companion[1] has been sometime in bed and it is now time that I should follow his example. With the greatest regard I am

My dear Sir Very truly Yrs

DAVID RICARDO

May I request you to give my kind regards to Mrs. Mill and to John.

[1] Ralph Ricardo.

221. SAY TO RICARDO[1]

21 July 1817   Voici, mon cher Monsieur, un exemplaire de ma 3ᵉ edition,[2] où vous trouverez plusieurs corrections dont quelques unes m'ont été suggerées par mes conversations avec vous. Les editions suivantes en offriront bien d'autres encore que je devrai à vos ouvrages. Ma théorie des valeurs vaut deja mieux que celle que vous avez critiquée; il vous suffira de comparer le chap. 1 du Liv. II avec celui de la seconde edition, et diverses parties de l'Epitome.

Voici de plus une lettre et un petit paquet pour Mr. Malthus que je recommande à vos soins.[3]

J'attends de votre delicatesse que vous ne parlerez pas de mes idées de spéculation sur la farine de pommes de terre.[4] Si vous aviez quelqu'envie de placer des fonds de cette manière en france, j'aimerais que ce fût de compte-à-demi avec moi. Je regarde cet emploi comme très sûr. Vous feriez constater par un tiers ami, l'existence en magazin des quantités achetées. La marchandise est inaltérable. Son prix ne peut pas tomber au dessous de celui de la belle farine puisqu'on a la faculté de l'y mêler sans alterer son prix; et les frais de transport, de garde &c. sont faciles à calculer. Je peux vous donner des renseignemens plus précis sur tout cela.

Je vous souhaite un heureux retour chez vous. Donnez moi votre adresse à Londres.

Votre constamment devoué

J. B. SAY

Lundi matin 21 juillet [1817][5]

[1] Addressed: 'David Ricardo Esqᵉ'—not passed through the post. (Ricardo was still in Paris.) MS in *R.P.*

[2] *Traité d'Économie politique, ou simple exposition de la manière dont se forment, se distribuent et se consomment les richesses; Troi-*sième édition, à laquelle se trouve joint un épitome des principes fondamentaux de l'Économie politique, 2 vols., Paris, Deterville, 1817.

[3] See below, p. 168.

[4] Cp. letter 241.

[5] Omitted in MS; for dating, see preceding footnotes.

L'ami de Bentham avec qui vous avez diné est le Docteur 21 July 1817
Swediaur, medecin, suedois d'origine.[1]
Mes amitiés à M. votre frere.[2]

222. RICARDO TO MALTHUS[3]
[*Answered by* 225]

My dear Sir

London 25 July 1817

I am just returned from my six weeks excursion highly 25 July 1817
pleased with every thing I have seen. I very much regretted
that you were not with me, as I am sure you would have
been gratified with the towns of Flanders, and the scenery
about Namur, the Rhine and the castle of Heidelberg. I met
Mr. Hamilton[4] at Luneville, he was going through the
country that I had just quitted, and I hope he was as much
pleased with it as I was. I fear that his engagements at the
College made him devote less time to it than was required to
enjoy all its beauties. We found that we were obliged to
hurry over it with more expedition than we wished. Mrs.
Ricardo has been at Gatcomb rather more than a week and
to morrow I shall quit town and join her there. Since tuesday[5] morning when I left Paris I have been incessantly
travelling in the day and have not devoted many hours to
sleep. I shall not be sorry to have a few days rest. Your
college was liberal to France for I not only met Mr. Hamilton

---

[1] Francis Xavier Schwediaur; 'a
German physician in Paris,...
Gallicè Swediar', 'a pleasing man,
of a great deal of knowledge in
his way', wrote Bentham (*Works*,
ed. by Bowring, 1843, vol. x,
pp. 88, 382).
[2] Ralph; cp. above, p. 160.
[3] Addressed: 'Rev.d T. R Malthus/
East India College / Hertford'

—not passed through the post,
apparently being enclosed with
Say's book and letter for Malthus.
MS at Albury.—*Letters to Malthus*, LX.
[4] Alexander Hamilton, Professor
of Hindu Literature and History
of Asia at the East India College.
[5] 22 July.

25 July 1817 there, but Mr. le Bas,[1] and the gentleman, whose name I forget, who teaches the French language at that Institution.[2]

I hope you have been enjoying your excursion and that you found less distress in Ireland than has been represented as existing there. The prospect of a good harvest is some consolation for the sufferings which the poor have been forced to endure;—in every country of Europe they have endured much, and in every one they are anticipating a return of plenty

M Say was very much gratified with your present,[3] and requested me to forward a letter and a small duodecimo volume which he has just published.[4] The letter I send you, but the book as well as his work on Political Economy, the third edition of which he gave to me, has been detained at the Custom House at Dover that they may have sufficient time to calculate the duty on them. As I did not wish to stay at Dover till the next day I requested the master of the Inn to pay the duty and to forward them by Osman who will be on his return from France in a few days. The book is an interesting little work in the manner of Rochefoucauld, and appears to me to be ably done. M. Say was very agreeable and friendly—he dined with me one day and I with him another. He is engaged in a commercial concern to which I believe he gives great attention.—

I fear that it will be a long time before you and I meet, tho' I shall probably be in London once or twice in the next 3 months. I hope you will be disposed to bend your steps westerly in your winter vacation, and that you will not fail

[1] Rev. C. W. Le Bas, Professor of Mathematics and Natural Philosophy, and Dean of the College.

[2] M. de Foligny.

[3] Probably the *Additions*, 1817, to the *Essay on Population*.

[4] *Petit volume contenant quelques apperçus des hommes et de la société*, Paris, Deterville, 1817. See letter 221.

to pay us a visit at Gatcomb; but not such a visit as the last, 25 July 1817
—I shall not be satisfied with a flying excursion. Perhaps
Mr. Whishaw will favour me with his company at the same
time, if so, with the assistance of my friend Smith we should
I hope contrive to make the time pass agreeably to both of
you.—

   Being very tired and very sleepy I hasten to conclude.

Very truly Y^{rs}

DAVID RICARDO

223. RICARDO TO MILL[1]

[Answered by 227]

Gatcomb Park   Minchinhampton
7 Aug. 1817

My dear Sir

   I conclude that by this time you are comfortably settled 7 Aug. 1817
in your summer habitation, and are regularly seated every
day, and for many hours of the day, at your table in the large
general room, in the spot where I saw it near the stove of
which the management is devoted to your skill when the
weather requires that the temperature of your room should
be raised. The correction of the press and the arrangement
of some minor points in your last volume must still engage
a large portion of your time, but when these are finished you
will be puzzled in your choice of a subject for a new occupation. I hope you will be happy in your selection, and that
when you sink in the grave loaded with years you may be
entitled to the never fading laurel awarded to the benefactors
of mankind. My wish would be incomplete if I did not also
claim for you some more solid proofs of the gratitude of
your contemporaries. I hope then that your purse may at

[1] Addressed: 'J. Mill Esqr / Ford Abbey / Chard / Somersetshire'.
MS in Mill-Ricardo papers.

least be as well lined as mine is, provided it does not inflect upon you the cares and anxious responsibility of wealth. If it would have that effect then I wish your wealth to be limited to that point at which it will be most productive of happiness.

I was very much obliged both to you and to Mr. Bentham for the loan of the month's newspapers—I have read them with very great interest and will return them when we meet in London.

I had the satisfaction of receiving a very warm welcome on reaching my home after my extended travels, and of finding all the inhabitants of Gatcomb in the best health and spirits,—and although I had so lately seen a variety of beautiful country, my own fields and the views from them had lost none of their attractions, but on the contrary were regarded with increased interest and attachment. Our happiness is made up of an infinite number of particulars, which to me exist no where in such great abundance as at home. Novelty has its charms, but an isolated being in a foreign country will very soon exhaust its pleasures, and will naturally turn his eyes towards the scene of all his agreeable associations.

Our country is at present in its best dress and I am anxious that you should see it so attired. With the rest of the country we are looking forward to abundant crops. The wheat is beginning to turn to the proper colour for the sickle, and as we shall this day carry the last portion of our hay, I suppose that we shall without much delay commence our corn harvest. An abundant crop will soon make the people forget all their past misfortunes, and we may I hope consider the present period as one from which we shall commence a long course of prosperity. Once settled in the new occupations which a state of peace renders it expedient should be undertaken by us, I know of nothing to impede our progress, but the relative situation of other countries. A state of peace will inspire us with a confidence in the security of property entrusted to their management which will inevitably draw capital from this country where interest is low, to others where it is high. The immense burthen of taxation which the residents of this country will have to sustain compared with the residents of others will have its natural effects, and will further tend to impede the employment of capital in England,—but perhaps these will have the effect of making our progress more slow, they will not wholly arrest it. We have happily some natural advantages which cannot be exported.—

I have not yet seen my three eldest girls, they have been altogether at Bognor for a month and will be coming home in little more than a week. Osman too will be returning about the same time and will hear with great pleasure that we have heard of a house excellently well calculated for him at about a mile from Gatcomb. The situation in respect of beauty of country is every thing he could wish.

We are going in a few hours to Easton Grey the place where Mr. Smith resides,—we shall stay with him a couple of nights. Mr. Belsham[1] is on a visit to him. Mr. Whishaw I suppose you have heard is either gone or is going into Italy, he will be absent about two months, and is without a companion in his journey. Mr. Binda expected some employment with a foreign ambassador here, but was disappointed in obtaining it in consequence of his connection with the late Government of Murat. He was then offered a situation in

[1] Thomas Belsham (1750–1829), the Unitarian minister of Essex Street Chapel. Thomas Smith had been his pupil at the Dissent-ing Academy at Daventry in 1784 (see John Williams, *Memoirs of T. Belsham*, 1833, p. 734).

7 Aug. 1817 the Brazils if he could set off immediately,—in less than 4 days he was at Plymouth expecting to sail every minute. I have not heard whether he has actually quitted England. He was very desirous of remaining here and even now flatters himself that his absence will be but short. Pray make my kind regards to Mrs. Mill and to Mr. Bentham and believe me

Ever Y^{rs}

DAVID RICARDO

224. TROWER TO RICARDO[1]
[Reply to 219.—Answered by 226]

Unsted Wood—
August 8. [1817]

My Dear Ricardo

8 Aug. 1817   Your last welcome letter should not have remained so long unanswered had I not concluded, that some time would elapse before you returned from your travels.—

I was indeed much surprised at remarking the date of your letter, and not less gratified by your devoting to me a portion of your time whilst you must have had so many calls upon it.—You have done perfectly right in making this excursion —it will afford you many pleasing recollections.—When I hear my friends expatiating upon the various interests excited by these foreign rambles I am impatient to spread my wings and be off; but when these impressions begin to fade, I magnify the difficulties and inconveniences of quitting family and pursuits, and determine to remain where I am.—

These claims encrease upon me, and I now have to announce to you the birth of another daughter. Whilst *you*, though not

[1] Addressed: 'To / David Ricardo Esqr / Gatcomb Park / Minchinhampton'. Postmark, 1817.—MS in *R.P.*

a much *older man* and yet a much *older parent* are already
living over again in the lives of your Grand Children!

I hope in your next you will be able to give me some accounts of the criticisms you have heard made upon your work—will it figure away in the next Numbers of the Edinburgh and Quarterly? I asked Lord King the other day if he had seen it, he said, that he had not, but he intended to get it.—

What time I have been able to catch, lately, for reading, has been devoted to the attainment of that smattering of law which is necessary for a Country Justice; and which is not to be attained without some application. I am interesting myself too in an attempt to improve the wretched state of our County Gaols, and I am not without hope we shall succeed in procuring one upon a scale suited to the necessities of the County.

Have you read the second part of Armata?[1] it is more amusing than the first; with the exception of the latter part which, however just, but ill accords with the playful sportive character of the remainder of the Volume.—

That *shabby* fellow Elwin has not written to me; but if nothing else will animate his pen I expect at least to hear from him on the subject of Provident Institutions! We have not yet done anything to accommodate our Institutions to the provisions of Rose's Bill, as I am anxious to learn what has been determined upon by the leading Institutions. My own opinion is, that it would be better to pay 4 pC^t on debentures, calculated for successive periods of *months* and upon successive sums of $12/6$—which would amount exactly to $\frac{1}{2}[d.]$ p^r month. This would lower the amount of our fund for expences, but it would simplify our accounts. Do you

---

[1] *The Second Part of Armata*, [Anon.], London, Murray, 1817. Cp. above, p. 142, n. 1.

8 Aug. 1817 know what Malthus has done in Hertfordshire in this subject? I rejoice to see our political machine getting gradually into order—funds rising—commerce reviving, land recovering its value—these are good symptoms, and I trust an abundant harvest will quicken the progress of this good work. How are the crops in your neighborhood. Here they are most promising. Nor ought we to complain of the fall of land in this neighborhood, as I have been obliged to give at the rate of 30 years purchase for a few acres—and other land here has been sold at the same rate.—Adieu my Dear Ricardo remember us both very kindly to Mrs. R. and family and believe me

Yrs very sincerely
HUTCHES TROWER

225. MALTHUS TO RICARDO[1]
[*Reply to 222.—Answered by 228*]

My dear Sir,   E I Coll August 17th 1817

17 Aug. 1817   I returned later from my Tour in Ireland than I expected; and the accumulated business I found on my return, together with an accidental interruption last friday, and the want of a post the following day, have delayed my answer to your kind letter longer than I intended.

I arrived in Town on the fourth of August, and was in great hopes of finding you in Brook Street as I understood that you had been much pleased with your tour, and thought it probable therefore, that you might have delayed your return longer than you intended. I just caught Whishaw however before he started, and he told me that you had left

[1] Addressed: 'D. Ricardo Esqr / Gatcomb / Minchinhampton /Glocestershire'.—MS in *R.P.*

London for Gatcomb above a week. I was quite glad to hear
from Whishaw both while I was in Ireland and after my
return, that you were much pleased with your tour in
Flanders. I should certainly have liked much to be with you,
though I have been both gratified and instructed by my tour
in Ireland. Though the distress was certainly great, it was I
think on the whole less than I expected, and though it
necessarily increased the number of beggars it did not essentially interfere with the comfort or safety of our travels, which
answered extremely well. Our head quarters were at Mr.
Wynne's in Westmeath,[1] but we made a tour in the South,
through Kings County, Queens County, Tipperary, Water-
ford, Kerry, and back by Limerick. Through most of this
country, great marks of improvement were observable,
though its progress had received a severe check during the
last two years, the effect of which was peculiarly to aggravate
the predominant evil of Ireland, namely a population greatly
in excess above the demand for labour, though in general
not much in excess above the means of subsistence on account
of the rapidity with which potatoes have increased under a
system of cultivating them on very small properties rather
with a view to support than sale. The *Land* in Ireland is
infinitely more peopled than in England; and to give full
effect to the natural resources of the country, a great part of
this population should be swept from the soil into large
manufacturing and commercial Towns.

The face of the country is in many parts very uninteresting
from the want of hedges and trees in the inclosures; but other
parts are not deficient in trees, and often present grand and
fine features. Nothing indeed can be more beautiful than
Killarney, and Glengariff, a part of Bantry bay. The county

---

[1] Henry Wynne, rector of Killucan, Westmeath, who had married a
sister of Mrs. Malthus.

17 Aug. 1817 of Wicklow also which I saw afterwards by myself is extremely picturesque and beautiful. On the whole our Tour answered extremely partly from its peculiar beauties, and partly from its peculiar deformities. The crops were looking remarkably well, and so many more potatoes than usual were planted last year, that I almost fear there will be a glut.

If you come to Town at any time to stay at all, you may as well let me [know]¹ to take the chance of our meeting. It would give me great pleasure to make you a visit at Gatcomb at Xmas; and I should want little inducement with regard to company; but I rather doubt whether I shall be able to accomplish it.

I have read over your book again with much gratification. There is much collateral matter in which I quite agree with you. I also quite agree with you that the difficulty of procuring subsistence is the necessarily limiting cause with regard to profits, but I still cannot agree with you that labour alone in the sense you understand it is either in theory or fact the best measure of exchangeable value; or that the state of the land practically determines the existing rate of profits in different countries. Pray do you allow that in different countries, where profits are different, your theory of value does not hold good. I dont feel quite sure.

Mrs. M joins me in kind regards to Mrs. Ricardo.

Ever truly Yours

T R Malthus.

¹ Omitted in MS.

226. RICARDO TO TROWER[1]

[*Reply to 224.—Answered by 235*]

Gatcomb Park Minchinhampton
23^{d} Aug 1817

My dear Trower

I congratulate Mrs. Trower and you on the birth of 23 Aug. 1817
(I believe) your third daughter, and sincerely wish that she
may grow up to be all that fond parents can wish, and that
she may long add to the happiness of your domestic circle.
True I am a much older parent than you, and now that I am
a grandfather I should be puzzled, even with the assistance
of Mr. Malthus, and Major Torrens, to calculate the accelerated
ratio at which my progeny is increasing. I am sure that it is
neither arithmetical nor geometrical. I have some notion of
consulting with Mr. Owen on the best plan of establishing
one of his villages for me and my descendants, admitting
only in addition a sufficient number of families to prevent
the necessity of celibacy. Now that the poor man is deserted
by the world, and even by the editor of the Times, who had
so ridiculously puffed him forward,[2] he will be at leisure to
devote all his talents, and all his enthusiasm to so hopeful
a scheme.

[1] Addressed: 'Hutches Trower Esqr/ Unsted Wood / Godalming / Surrey'.
MS at University College, London.—*Letters to Trower*, XVI.
[2] *The Times'* breach with Owen was caused by his speech on 21 Aug. 1817, unexpectedly denouncing all religions that had hitherto been taught to man: 'by the errors of these systems [man] has been made a weak, imbecile animal; a furious bigot and fanatic; or a miserable hypocrite; and should these qualities be carried, not only into the projected villages, but *into Paradise itself, a Paradise would be no longer found!*' The next day *The Times* opened its leading article: 'The curtain dropt yesterday upon Mr. Owen's drama, not soon, it is probable, to be lifted up again....Mr. Owen promised a Paradise to mankind, but, as far as we can understand, not such a Paradise as a sane mind would enjoy, or a disciple of Christianity could meditate without terror'. (See F. Podmore, *Robert Owen, A Biography*, 1907, p. 249.)

23 Aug. 1817   I have been returned from the Continent about a month, after an absence from home of little more than 6 weeks. I assure you that they were six weeks of active exertion, which was amply rewarded by the gratification which I had; in viewing the different objects which came under my notice. The towns, Cathedrals and pictures of Flanders,—the country about the Rhine and Hiedelberg,—Frankfort, Coblents and some other towns in Germany have all afforded me very great pleasure, and my fortnight's stay in Paris was not the least agreeable of my journey. An excursion to Paris merely, is so very easily accomplished, that I shall be tempted to go there again with my family. Every body should see the Louvre and Versailles who lives within a week's journey of them.

I can give you but little information respecting the criticisms on my book,—indeed I have heard of none but from M. Say, and Mr. Malthus for some months past. The former I saw several times at Paris,—he was very friendly and agreeable—spoke favourably of my book—was quite sure that in a very few years there would not be a shadow of difference between us, but he complained that I had made demands too great on the continued exercise of thought on the part of my reader, and had not sufficiently relieved him or assisted him by a few occasional examples, and illustrations, in support of my theory. He said that he was reading me with a pen in his hand, making notes to be employed in the next edition of his work, and he found it required all his attention to follow me. In the last edition of his work, published before my book appeared, he has spoken of me in very flattering terms, far exceeding my deserts.[1]

[1] *Traité d'Économie politique*, 3rd ed., 1817; Say refers to Ricardo as 'l'homme de l'Europe qui entend le mieux la théorie et la pratique des Monnaies', vol. II, p. 29, n.

In a letter which I lately received from Mr. Malthus[1] he 23 Aug. 1817
mentions my book in the following manner: "I have read
your book again with much gratification. There is much
collateral matter in which I quite agree with you. I also quite
agree with you that the difficulty of procuring subsistence is
the necessarily limiting cause with regard to profits, but still
I cannot agree with you that labour done in the sense you
understand it is either in theory or fact the best measure of
exchangeable value; or that the state of the land practically
determines the existing rate of profits in different countries.
Pray do you allow that in different countries where profits
are different your theory of value does not hold good?
I don't feel quite sure." On the whole I have reason to be
satisfied with the opinions of these distinguished professors.
I was told by Mill that Major Torrens had applied to the
editor of the Edinburgh Review for permission to review my
book in that journal, and the answer returned was that they
must first know from Malthus whether he meant to undertake
it. As I have every reason to believe that Malthus will not
do it, it is probable that Torrens' offer may be accepted.[2]
I presented Torrens with one of the first copies of my book:
—he was disappointed that I had not mentioned his name in
it, and wrote to me to that effect, claiming some merit as the

[1] Letter 225.
[2] In a letter to Francis Place,
dated London, 11 Sept. 1817,
Torrens writes: 'I called upon
Brougham the day before yesterday to say that my review of
Ricardo's Work was ready and to
know whether Malthus was engaged by the Edinburgh on that
work. He could not give me any
answer but s.d he w.d write to
Jeffrey on the subject. I hope you
are making notes on Ricardo as
I shall be very anxious to compare

your observations and conclusions with my own. On many
points I do not agree with
Ricardo but of the general merit
and originality of his work I have
a very high opinion.' (MS in
British Museum, Add. 37,949,
fol. 52.) Ricardo's *Principles* were
reviewed in the *Edinburgh Review*
by McCulloch (see below, p. 280,
n. 2) and Torrens criticised them
in the *Edinburgh Magazine* (see
below, p. 315, n. 1). On Place's
Notes, see below, p. 183, n. 3.

23 Aug. 1817 original discoverer of some of the principles which I endeavoured to establish. I had no design of neglecting his merits, and omitted to mention him because none of his doctrines appeared to me strikingly new and did not particularly come with[in the]¹ scope of the subject I was treating. There were so[me things] in his bo[ok about] which I pointedly differed from him but refrained from [noticing] them because I knew he was sensible they were wrong, and had adopted, and was going soon to publish, more correct views to the public. In the correspondence which ensued between him and me I endeavoured to shew, and according to Mill's opinion I did shew, that on all those points which I had as I thought for the first time brought forward, his published opinions were in fact in opposition to mine, and on those which he said we agreed upon and for which he claimed the merit of originality they were all to be found in Adam Smith or Malthus, and therefore neither of us could be called discoverers. Our altercation was carried on without the least acrimony, and ended by a complete restoration of cordiality, though accompanied with rather more reserve than before. He has dined with me twice since, and the last time he met Mr. Malthus for the first time, and stoutly defended my doctrines, to which he is quite a convert, against Mr. Malthus opposition to them. You will oblige me not to mention his application to the Editor of the Review unless you hear it from some other quarter.

I only staid one day in town on my journey from Paris to Gatcomb, so that I am ignorant of the proceedings of the savings Bank Institution. Your plan² is a good one if it do not too much encroach on the fund for expences. I fear that our reduced treasure can bear no further diminution.

Our crops are abundant but we are in bad spirits at the

¹ MS torn here and below.　　² See above, p. 173.

appearance of the weather. We hardly pass a day without 23 Aug. 1817
heavy rain, and the atmosphere is so cold that we are never
without a fire. An abundant harvest is at the present moment
of the first importance—it is at all times a great ingredient
towards the happiness of the mass of the people, however it
may on some occasions affect the interest of a particular class
of individuals.

Do you not think the funds enormously high[1] with a
revenue so deficient.

Mrs. Ricardo joins with me in kind regards to Mrs. Trower.

Y^{rs} truly

DAVID RICARDO

227. MILL TO RICARDO[2]

[Reply to 223.—Answered by 229]

Ford Abbey Augt 24th 1817

My Dear Sir

I have deferred writing in hopes of being able to send 24 Aug. 1817
you a long letter; but if I wait for time to do that, it seems to
me, that I may wait long enough. You shall, therefore, get
a few hurried lines for the present; and something better,
when it pleases God.

In the first place, many thanks for your good wishes. If
I had all the good things you would like to see me have,
I should be pretty well off. Oh, yes—I should like vastly
well, to have a purse as full as yours. But yet the difference
between a very moderate supply, and that weight of fortune
which would enable me to produce important effects, I should
not value very much. Give me £20,000 a year, and I will
shew you a parliament radically reformed, in one half of

---

[1] Consols had risen from 62 in
January 1817 to 81 in August.
[2] Addressed: 'David Ricardo Esq.
/ Gatcomb Park / Minchinhamp-
ton / Gloucestershire.'
MS in *R.P.*

24 Aug. 1817   20 years. In the absence of this, all I want is, such a provision, as would exempt me from all the vexation of thinking about the subject, and from the necessity of turning my pen from subjects of great importance, which would bring no money, to write on subjects of no importance at all, because the money is wanted. This, I confess, annoys me oftener than perhaps it ought.

Nothing more true, than what you have experienced—that home is the source of the sweetest sensations. Even here, though I have all my family about me, and though by consenting to come here, I am conferring an obligation, not receiving it, yet I am less happy than at home, and could enjoy the country more in a very poor cottage of my own.[1]

I can well conceive you received a warm reception; for I know how well you are beloved by all who belong to you. And yours is a family that seem to have the knack of loving one another. I am very happy to hear that you have been so lucky in a residence for Mr. Osman,[2] and I am truly sorry that I have not had the pleasure of making the acquaintance of a person so amiable and deserving as I hear on all hands is the partner of whom he has had the wisdom to make choice, but hope one time or another to meet with his pardon and hers, for allowing a quantity of things to keep me from waiting upon them, till, lo! they were gone.

Two of my three volumes[3] are printed, and nearly 100

[1] The residence of the Mills at Ford Abbey as the guests of Bentham, which continued for the greater part of each year from 1814 to 1818, was looked upon with misgivings by Mill's friends: 'I am deeply interested about Mill —for with all my admiration of Mr Bentham—he is too good a man to become a dependant of any individual—and I fear that the in-creasing expences of his young family must render him so, unless we can place him at the head of this new school.' (Wakefield to Place, 17 Aug. 1814, MS in British Museum, Add. 35152.)
[2] Osman Ricardo and his wife had returned from the Continent and were living at Hyde near Gatcomb Park.
[3] *History of British India.*

pages of the last. But Col. Wilks, who was resident in
Mysore, and had peculiar advantages in regard to materials,
has written a history of that country, of which two volumes
have just come out.[1] They put me under the necessity of a
very careful comparison of what I have said with what he has
said upon the same ground—and the facts which he has
added to those got from my former authorities, have even
made me write several passages, a-fresh. This, with the
speed at which my printers go, has kept me very closely
engaged. And now the Editor of the Encyclop. Brit. is
pressing me for an article on *Colonies*.

I have no news whatsoever. We expect the Romillys[2] here
toward the end of September. Place has been here for a
fortnight. He has become a huge favourite with Mr. Bentham. He has indeed laid him under no small obligations by
managing for him very well some business which before was
managed very ill. And this was the only mode of rewarding
him. He is studying your book, with great care. And
declares that he is getting conviction, in spite of himself, in
every point as he goes along. He is a very surprising man.[3]

You are not to take this specimen of me in maintaining
our correspondence, as the pattern you are to follow, but
rather as an example you are to shun. The fact is, I am truly
desirous of knowing what occupation you are setting about.
Your mind is capable of too much—and mind I say so without the smallest intention to flatter you, and wish I could
have found words importing blame rather than praise, to

---

[1] Mark Wilks, *Historical Sketches of the South of India, in an Attempt to trace the History of Mysoor...*, London, Longman, vol. I, 1810, vols. II–III, 1817.
[2] Sir Samuel and Lady Romilly.
[3] On Place's two months' re-sidence at Ford Abbey, see Gra-

ham Wallas, *Life of Francis Place*, pp. 73–7. Wallas says (*ib.*, p. 162) that the Notes which Place wrote when reading Ricardo's *Principles* are nearly as long as the book itself; they are not in the Place Papers in the British Museum.

24 Aug. 1817 have said the same thing with—to let it lie idle—therefore
you must hold it a religious duty to work—to work hard
and perseveringly—If I had a cottage within a couple of
miles of you, how I would keep you to it! However, in the
mean time, let me know what you are doing or thinking to
do—because I may be able to give you good advice.

I am glad you are likely to become the master of the
ground in Leicester Square—because on reasonable terms it
is a desirable property, come of the school what may.[1]

J. MILL

228. RICARDO TO MALTHUS[2]

[*Reply to 225*]

Gatcomb Park, Minchinhampton
4 Sep.[r] 1817

My dear Sir

4 Sept. 1817   I thank you very much for your kind letter of the 17th
Aug.[t]. I am pleased to hear that your journey to Ireland
turned out so well. The account you give of the improvements before the check which they received during the last
two years, as well as of the situation of the people, agrees
exactly with what I should expect to find. Humbold in his
account of New Spain points out the very same evils as you
do in Ireland, proceeding too from the same cause.[3] The
land there yields a great abundance of Bananas, Manioc,
Potatoes and Wheat with very little labour, and the people
having no taste for luxuries, and having abundance of food,
have the privilege of being idle. No other advantage would

[1] See below, p. 198, n. 1.
[2] Addressed: 'To / The Rev[d]
T. R Malthus / East India College /
Hertford'—not passed through
the post.
MS at Albury.—*Letters to Malthus*, LXI.

[3] See the quotations from Humboldt given by Malthus (above
II, 337 ff.) and Malthus's comparison of New Spain with Ireland
(*ib.*, 344).

I think result from the disposable [1] labour being employed in manufactures than in preventing its being turned to profligate and mischievous pursuits, dangerous to the public peace. Happiness is the object to be desired, and we cannot be quite sure that provided he is equally well fed, a man may not be happier in the enjoyment of the luxury of idleness than in the enjoyment of the luxuries of a neat cottage, and good clothes. And after all we do not know if these would fall to his share. His labour might only increase the enjoyments of his employer.[2]

Mr. Smith has heard from Mr. Whishaw,—he was at Paris when he wrote, on the eve of recommencing his journey.[3] I hope he may enjoy his tour. It is a pity that he is without an agreeable companion—he is of so sociable a disposition that he would have had pleasure in communicating his feelings, and comparing them with those of another intelligent person. Mr. Smith has also heard from Mr. Warburton, who has set out on the very same tour that I have been taking, with the addition of Holland, through which country he means to pass. He has a very intelligent companion in Dr. Woolaston.[4]—

At the very moment that we were beginning to despair of the weather it has changed and is now beautiful. Our hopes will I trust not be disappointed, and we shall be enabled safely to house the abundant crops with which our lands in every county[5] are loaded. I doubt whether we have even during the late distresses ceased to advance as a nation in wealth, but at present I think no one can doubt that we are again

---

[1] Replaces 'idle'.
[2] The last two sentences are ins.
[3] See Whishaw's letter to Smith in *The 'Pope' of Holland House*, p. 190.

[4] W. H. Wollaston, M.D., F.R.S., the chemist and mineralogist, at this time Vice-President of the Geological Society.
[5] Printed 'country (*sic*)' in *Letters to Malthus*; but MS reads 'county'.

4 Sept. 1817 making forward strides in prosperity,—a bad harvest does
not perhaps very much check the progress of wealth but it
materially interferes with the general happiness.—

You flatter me very much by your second perusal of my
book, and I am happy to find that there are but a very few
important points on which we materially differ. I certainly
allow that my theory of value does not hold good in different
countries when profits are different. If you look to Page 156[1]
and the following pages you will see my ideas on that subject.

It is only yesterday that I received the book from Dover
which M. Say entrusted me with for you; I send that and
this letter together by Mrs. Ricardo who is going to London
for a few days—she has undertaken to send my parcel to the
Hertford Coach.

Osman who is very desirous of residing near us has met
with a house in a delightful situation within $1\frac{1}{2}$ miles of us,
and it is to oblige him that his mother undertakes the long
journey to town for the purpose of exercising her skill, and
of giving him the benefit of her experience in the choice of
furniture.—[2]

I still hope that Mrs. Malthus and you will be able to visit
us at your next vacation,—if you go to Bath and do not
come over to us I shall not know how to forgive you.—

I have heard lately from Mill[3]—he is still hard at work in
correcting the press and finishing his book—he tells me that
Sir Sam! and Lady Romilly are expected at Ford Abbey.—
I fully expect that I shall see him here before he returns to
London.

[1] Above, I, 133.
[2] 'I rode to Hyde on Monday and
had an hour tête a tête with Mrs
Osman. She shewd me her house,
beautifully situated, and in its em-
bellishments doing great credit

to Mrs Ricardo's taste.' (Letter of
Thomas Smith to Ricardo, dated
Easton Grey, 4 Feb. 1818.—MS
in R.P.)
[3] Letter 227.

I do not know when I shall be obliged to go to town but 4 Sept. 1817 whenever it may happen I will let you know as I would not willingly forego any chance of meeting you.—

Mr. Smith's house is the centre of attraction for all his able London friends and he is kind enough always to allow me to participate in the pleasure which their company affords him. We have already had Mr. Warburton and Mr. Belsham, and in a few days he expects to see Mr. Mallet.[1] Mr. Smith continues to reign pre-eminent in the goodwill of all his neighbours and indeed I do not know any one who is entitled to dispute the palm with him. Mrs. Ricardo joins with me in kind regards to Mrs. Malthus.

Ever truly Y^{rs}

DAVID RICARDO

This is a sad blundering letter,—bad even from me, but you must excuse it, and will I am sure when I tell you that

---

[1] J. L. Mallet mentions this visit in his diary when writing in Sept. 1823 on Ricardo's death: 'When I was in Gloucestershire in September 1817 on a visit to a mutual friend, Mr. Smith of Easton Grey, he [Ricardo] came there for a couple of days, and drove me to his own place, and also to Wooton under Edge, where one of his daughters, Mrs. Austin, resided. I remember his then saying that he did not conceive how any man who could get his 3½ per cent. by land could leave his money in the funds; which shows the distrust great dealers in public stocks entertain of that sort of property: and yet the 3 per cents. which were then at 61 [Mallet's memory was at fault—in September 1817 they were at 81; cp. above, p. 181,

n. 1] are now at 83. We went together with our friend Mr. Smith, to a meeting of country gentlemen held at Tetbury for the purpose of establishing a savings bank...The Duke of Beaufort was in the chair, and I was much pleased with the intelligence and attention of the persons present (among whom was Lord Ducie), and by the marked deference and respect shewn to Mr. Ricardo, whom they all knew as a neighbour, and who was so good as to introduce me to them, as one of the founders of the London Savings Banks.' (*Political Economy Club, Centenary Volume*, 1921, pp. 210–11.) The Tetbury Savings Bank was established on 8 Sept. 1817. (J. T. Pratt, *History of Savings Banks*, 1830, p. 66.) Cp. below, p. 220.

4 Sept. 1817 I am just recovering from the languor and weakness caused by the powerful medicines which I have been obliged to take in consequence of something of a bilious attack, accompanied by fever. The night before last I was very ill,—yesterday I was better, and to day I have no complaint left but weakness.

229. RICARDO TO MILL[1]

[Reply to 227.—Answered by 232]

Gatcomb Park
12 Sep[r] 1817

My dear Sir

12 Sept. 1817   When you breakfasted with me the morning I quitted London I ought to have secured you—to have had you tied neck and heels, put into a post chaise, and have brought you with me. All my other chances of seeing you here are I fear but slight. You say not a word of coming, in your letter, and Dumont, on whose visit at Ford Abbey your visit here in some measure depended, is I understand doing the honours of his country towards Mr. Whishaw, whom he is hospitably entertaining. Let me request you to take this matter into your serious consideration, or you may be exposed to some other scheme of violence when you least expect it.

My wishes for good fortune to you shall in future be limited to that smaller amount which you I think wisely have determined best secures happiness. After your avowal of the manner in which you would employ the larger sum if you had it, I am not desirous of entrusting you with it. Such mighty things are not to be accomplished with such comparatively insignificant means—you would meet with disappointment at every step, because you would fail in your object, and if you succeeded it would in all probability still

[1] Addressed: 'James Mill Esq[r] / Ford Abbey / Chard / Somersetshire'. MS in Mill-Ricardo papers.

produce disappointment. You shall have only a small independent fortune.

I am glad to hear that so much of your work is printed as 2 volumes and part of the third. I shall be more glad when it is fairly launched, and you are free from the anxiety which the period of publication inevitably brings.

Sir Sam! and Lady Romilly have been on a very short visit to a neighbour of mine a Mr. Phelps.[1] He lives about 4 miles from here in a curious ancient house and is I believe a barrister —he has not been here more than a few months, he came from another part of Gloucestershire. Mr. and Mrs. Smith, with Mr. Mallet, who is their visitor, met Sir Sam! and Lady Romilly. They are probably now on their way to Ford Abbey.

I shall be very proud of having Mr. Place a convert to my doctrines, I am sure he reads without prejudice, and with an earnest wish to discover truth—he will not continue to hold opinions merely because he held them before, and I shall be sure to have at his hands, all I want, impartial justice.— I hear from Mr. Grenfell that Lord Grenville has written to him that he also is not reading but is studying my book; I should like to have such a Lord amongst my disciples.[2]

I am employing my time very badly, I am reading without plan or order. I have got through Humbold's New Spain,[3] Mackenzie voyage in North America[4]—part of the travels of Ali Bey[5] and have been looking at Pinkerton's Geo-

[1] John Delafield Phelps, of Chevenage House, near Tetbury. (See Memoirs of Sir Samuel Romilly, 1840, vol. III, p. 313.)
[2] See below, p. 220.
[3] Alexandre de Humboldt, Essai politique sur le royaume de la Nouvelle Espagne, 1811.
[4] Sir Alexander Mackenzie, Voyages from Montreal,...through

the Continent of North America, to the Frozen and Pacific Oceans; in the years 1789 and 1793, London, 1801.
[5] Ali Bey el Abbassi [pseudonym], Travels in Morocco, Tripoli, Cyprus, Egypt, Arabia, Syria and Turkey, between the years 1803 and 1807, 2 vols., London, 1816.

12 Sept. 1817 graphy,[1] and at some articles in Bayle's Dictionary. My
object is only amusement. I am fully convinced that you
very far overrate the powers of my mind. It would be mis-
placed modesty in such a case as the present to speak of
myself otherwise than I think I deserve, and therefore I am
to be believed when I conscientiously declare that I think
your opinion of my capabilities far too high. In the first
place I am not very persevering, unless the object for which
I work is steadily before my eyes.—I have all the disadvantages too of a neglected education, which it is now in vain
to seek to repair. It would be wise in me to stop where I am,
and not like a desperate gamester venture my gains to the
fearful odds to which they are exposed. My mind often
misgives me about the Parliamentary scheme, and I think if
you knew me as well as I know myself you would advise
me against it. In my intercourse with you I have always
armed myself with my Political Economy, a subject on
which I have thought a good deal, and in which you are
very much disposed to magnify my success—You have
formed your general opinion from a partial view. Tell
me however what to undertake and I will put my powers
to the test but do not be surprised if I should hereafter
come to you and say that the burden is greater than I can
carry.—

I have bought the ground in Leicester Fields for £3300.—
I hope there will be no difficulty about the Title.[2]

Mrs. Ricardo has been in London about a week, I expect
her home to day.—She has been assisting the young folks
in the selection of furniture for their house, at which, in
spite of your neglect of the rules of etiquette, for which they
freely forgive you, they hope to see you. They are now with

[1] John Pinkerton, *Modern Geo-*   [2] See below, p. 198, n. 1.
graphy, 2 vols., London, 1802.

us, and will stay here till their own house is ready to receive 12 Sept. 1817
them. Pray remember me kindly to Mrs. Mill and Mr.
Bentham
$$Y^{\text{rs}} \text{ truly}$$
$$\text{DAVID RICARDO}$$

230. RICARDO TO MALTHUS[1]

[*Answered by* 231]

Gatcomb Park
10 Oct.[r] 1817

My dear Sir

I said I would write to you when I was going to London, 10 Oct. 1817
and therefore I now do it, but without much hope of seeing
you there. Some law papers which it is necessary I should
sign will take me to London on sunday next[2]—I shall be at
Brook Street in the evening. It is not my intention, if I can
get my business done, to stay in town beyond tuesday morning, unless I had any chance of meeting you there, which
would induce me to defer my return home one day longer.
I fear however that this cannot be, and I write only that I
might not neglect any chance of seeing you however slight
it might be.

Dr. Roget[3] has been on a visit for a few days at Mr.
Smith's,—he stayed one evening with us at Gatcomb.—We
all very much admire his unassuming manner, and are well
disposed to admit his claims on our esteem and affection.
Sir Sam[l] and Lady Romilly have been on a visit at Mr.
Phelps' a near neighbour of mine. They went from here to
Bowood and from thence they were going to Ford Abbey

[1] Addressed: Rev[d] T. R Malthus/
East India College / Hertford'.
MS at Albury.—*Letters to Malthus*, LXII.
[2] 12 October.
[3] Peter Mark Roget (1779–1869),
M.D., F.R.S., famous as a physician in his time, author of the
*Thesaurus of English Words and
Phrases*, 1852. He was a member
of the first Council of the Geological Society.

10 Oct. 1817 Mr. Benthams residence. I have since heard of their arrival there and they are now probably returned to London.

Mr. Smith has not lately heard from Mr. Whishaw the last letter he received was I believe from Genoa with which place he was highly delighted.—

Our harvest in this part of the country is almost entirely got in. The crops are I believe generally good and we are very grateful for the fortunate change in the weather which enabled us to reap and house them in a state of perfection.— We shall now I hope for some years sail before the wind. You and I have always agreed in our opinions of the power and wealth of the country,—we were not in a state of despair at the discouraging circumstances with which we were lately surrounded. We looked forward to the revival which has taken place.

Mrs. Ricardo unites with me in kind regards to Mrs. Malthus.

Ever truly Yours

DAVID RICARDO

If you should write me a line it will reach me sooner by being directed to the Stock Exchange.

231. MALTHUS TO RICARDO[1]

[Reply to 230.—Answered by 233]

My dear Sir   E I Coll Oct 12ᵗʰ 1817

12 Oct. 1817   I am glad to hear of you; and should like much to get a few hours conversation with you in Town; but I am engaged on tuesday and in part indeed on monday; so that altogether the time does not suit, and I can only hope to be more fortunate when you next come to Town.

[1] Addressed: 'Davᵈ Ricardo Esqr / Stock Exchange / London'.
MS in *R.P.*

I have once or twice met Dr. Roget and always thought him an agreeable and amiable man. He was very much liked and respected by poor Horner. I heard the other day from Whishaw. He was at Florence, and thinking of his return round by Venice Milan and the Simplon. He says he cannot sufficiently congratulate himself on having reached Florence, which did not form a part of his original plan. Altogether he seems to have been very much pleased with his tour.

I am glad to hear so good an account of your harvest in Gloucestershire. I believe indeed it has been generally favourable, and this latter fine weather has been a grand thing for the backward counties. I was in the Wolds of Lincolnshire last week, where I found the people much delighted with their *unusual* fine weather. They are very apt to have late and bad harvests.

We have both of us, as you observe, always been confident in the resources of the country, and there is certainly now every appearance that our views will be justified by the result. The present state of things however perhaps tends to contradict one of your opinions respecting profits. Labour has certainly fallen, and though I have no doubt it will rise again gradually and is in fact now rising; yet it must be allowed that now while it is low, profits and interest are also low.

Can you shew me where the fallacy of the following statement lies.

Capital is wholly employed in the purchase of materials and machinery, and the maintenance of labour. If from any cause whatever, materials machinery and the maintenance of the labourer, and his wages, fall considerably in money value, is it *possible* that the same amount of monied capital can be employed in the country?

I quite agree with you in what you said in your previous letter on the effects of a scanty harvest upon the progress of

12 Oct. 1817 national wealth; but I draw from it an inference favourable to my hypothesis that an increase of the value of the general produce determined by the supply and the demand, is the great stimulus to industry and future production and will often more than counteract, in reference to general and future wealth, the evils of a dearth to individuals, if it does not go too far. Abundance without increase of value, (which you contemplate as the result of foreign trade) would, it appears to me, necessarily lead to a stagnation of demand and of industry. If the value of the national produce however abundant will not command more labour this year than the last, the demand for labour must be stationary and the new labourers coming into the market must be unemployed.

By the by you have never told me, in return for my criticisms on your work, how much you think me wrong in my Additions.[1] I am meditating another volume, but hardly know what to call it.[2] Mrs. M desires to be remembered. Suppose you come down to us for a couple of nights.

Ever truly Yours

T R Malthus.

232. MILL TO RICARDO[3]

[Reply to 229.—Answered by 234]

My dear Sir   Ford Abbey 19ᵗʰ Oct. 1817

19 Oct. 1817   I have been more than usually occupied; otherwise you would not have been so long without hearing from me. What I was most anxious to write to you about, was the mode of

---

[1] *Additions to the Essay on Population.*
[2] *Principles of Political Economy*, not published till 1820.

[3] Addressed: 'David Ricardo Esq / Gatcomb Park / Minchinhampton / Gloucestershire.' MS in *R.P.*

directing your studies, that you might lose none of your 19 Oct. 1817 time. But at the moment of receiving your letter I had two burthens laid upon me. One was, the appearance of Col. Wilks's two volumes of the history of Mysore,[1] which laid me under the necessity of a very careful confrontation of his narrative with my M.S., he having enjoyed, from being governor in the country, peculiar opportunities of knowledge; and what he added to my knowledge required a certain portion of my narrative to be written afresh, while I had the printers at my heels. The other burthen was, a promise which the Editor of the Supplement to the Encyclopædia Britannica said I had made him, to write an article for him on *Colonies*. I had a great mind to send to you to write it for me. But at last I concluded that I had no right to lay any such restraint upon you; because I knew your disposition toward me to be such, that you would do it, even if it should put you out of your way. Had I known you to be less obliging, and that you would have said, No, if the thing had displeased, you would have most likely received an application. However, it is now all but finished. I have also not only finished all that Colonel Wilks has created for me to do; but got so far that I have gone to the middle of my last chapter in revising. I therefore reckon that I may now answer your letter.

First of all, as to that task you have laid upon me. "Tell me", you say, "what to undertake, and I will put my powers to the test." I am now very much in the mind to give you nothing to do, till you get my own book to read. No, no; I will not fill your head with other things, when I shall desire to have it presently all applied to one thing. To be serious, however, that book of mine, if it answers my expectation, or rather my wish, will make no bad introduction to the study of civil society in general. The subject afforded an oppor-

[1] See above, p. 183, n. 1.

19 Oct. 1817 tunity of laying open the principles and laws of the social order in almost all its more remarkable states, from the most rude to the most perfect with which we are yet acquainted; and if I have been capable of explaining them, will be of some help to you, in exploring what I wish to see you thoroughly acquainted with, the course which human affairs, upon the great scale, have hitherto taken, the causes of their taking these different courses, the degree in which these courses have severally departed from the best course, and by what means they can best be made to approximate to that course. That is the field of application; and none of the pretexts you set up will avail you. There is nothing in this knowledge mysterious, or hard—there is nothing but what any body, who has common application, a common share of judgement, and is free from prejudice, and sinister interest, may arrive at. He will not do so all at once; time is required; but every step is delightful, and what is gained at every step has an immediate use. I am not at all mistaken, in regard to your capacity, nor in regard to your application. Education defective! If the principal part of what is given to people for education, is only prejudices, you are better without it. Which of our *educated* sparks has written such a book as yours? The best part of every mans education is not that which he gets from others, but that which he gives to himself. Did any man ever write such a book as that which you have written, who had not done more to educate himself than all the world could do for him? I am not sorry you have been reading some things in the Dictionaire de Bayle,[1] if you have hit upon the right ones. He has uncommon skill in the statement of an argument, and in the exposure of prejudices. If you have not read the articles *Manichée*, and *Pauliciens*,

[1] There are in *R.P.* several pages of extracts, copied by Ricardo, from Bayle's *Dictionnaire historique et critique*.

with some others to which these will give you the reference, (Marcion, if I remember right, is one) read them now, and tell me what you think of them—what reflections they suggest to you. If you have not read, or not read lately, Locke's Essay on the Human Understanding, I think you should do so; both because it is perpetually referred to in all books, and in all speculative conversation, and also because it really is an excellent introduction to intellectual matters in general. Lockes mode of proceeding, trains the mind into paths of right inquiry; it gives you the end of the clue, and tells you how you may explore by yourself the labyrinth. This will occupy you till my book comes, which I hope you will have it in your power to see in a month. If not Locke, Humes Essays might occupy you advantageously for some weeks—and you should go through with them *de suite*. Millers historical View of the English Constitution was very instructive to me; but I rather think you told me, you had not a copy of it.[1] I mean to put you (however ungrateful it is in me) to the expence of buying a copy of my book—for I made no stipulation for a certain number of copies (in fact I forgot it) in selling the work, and shall be ashamed to ask many copies from the bookseller. I shall also have a greater number of persons who will think they have claims upon me, and who cannot afford to buy the book, than I can supply; and I have therefore resolved to lay down this rule to myself, to ask a copy for nobody whom I think rich enough to buy the book—so that unless you plead poverty, you must lug out your purse.

I cannot let you pass on the subject of refusing me a large fortune. How envious that is! You think a large fortune

---

[1] John Millar, *An Historical View of the English Government from the Settlement of the Saxons in Britain to the Accession of the House of Stewart*, 4°, London, 1787. Among Ricardo's books at Gatcombe there is a copy of Millar's *The Origin of the Distinction of Ranks in Society*, 3rd ed., London, 1781.

9 Oct. 1817 would not enable any man to effect parliamentary reform. Do you think, prepared for it, as this country is, that the thing would be difficult? It appears to me that the population in this country with regard to some important improvement in their government may be compared to a vessel of water exposed to a temperature at 32°. Leave it perfectly still, and the water will remain uncongealed; shake it a little, and it shoots into ice immediately. All great changes in society, are easily effected, when the time is come. Was it not an individual, without fortune, without name, and in fact without talents, who produced the reformation? Before I have done with you you will reason less timidly on this subject, because you will know more certainly. You would legislate, just now, if sent to legislate, as a man walks who is blind fold, fearing pitfalls and stumbling blocks, at every step. When a man sees his way before him, he walks confidently.

I fear, from what Romilly said when I talked to him here, that Leicester fields will not do. Place writes to me with some hopes, since he went to town. He is for the present proprietor trying the question.[1] I heard from Romilly you had been at Bowood[2]—and Lady Romilly gave me a long history of all the good you and Mrs. Ricardo are doing about Gatcomb. Well, I like to hear you praised. I also must find means to come and see what you are about at Gatcomb, that I may praise you too.—And now I must close—but not till

---

[1] It had been arranged that Ricardo should buy the ground in the centre of Leicester Square for the building of the Chrestomathic School (cp. above, VI, 112). But when he found that the shopkeepers of the Square were 'resolved by every means in their power to prevent the Ground being built on', Ricardo, un-willing to enter into litigation, abandoned this project. (Unpublished letter of Ricardo to Place, 18 Sept. 1817. MS in British Museum Newspaper Library, Place Collection of Newspaper Cuttings, vol. 60, no. 14, fol. 8.)

[2] The seat of Lord Lansdowne in Wiltshire.

I have begged my best compliments to Mrs. Ricardo, and all 19 Oct. 1817
the friends I have that are near you. I am glad to hear that
the young squire and lady are of a forgiving disposition.
I long to kiss their hands—and am always,

My Dear Sir,

very faithfully Yours

J. MILL

P.S. In the character of pupil, you must not be long before
you give your master an account of your progress.

233. RICARDO TO MALTHUS[1]

[*Reply to* 231.—*Answered by* 237]

Gatcomb Park
21 Oct. 1817

My dear Sir

I hope we shall be more fortunate in meeting when I 21 Oct. 1817
again visit London.

You think that the low price of labour which has lately
prevailed, contradicts my theory of profits depending on
wages, because the rate of interest is at the same time very
low. If interest and profits invariably moved in the same
degree, and in the same direction, my theory might be
plausibly opposed, but I consider this as by no means the
case. Although interest is undoubtedly ultimately regulated
by profits, rising when they are high, and falling when they
are low, yet there are considerable intervals during which a
low rate of interest is compatible with a high rate of profit,
and this generally occurs when capital is moving from the
employments of war to those of peace. If goods do not vary
in price, and the cost of manufacturing them falls, it is self

---

[1] Addressed: 'Rev⁴ T. R Malthus / East India College / Hertford'.
MS at Albury.—*Letters to Malthus*, LXIII.

21 Oct. 1817 evident that profits must rise, and if goods do fall in price
generally, then it is not the value of goods or of labour which
falls, but the value of the medium in which they are paid
which rises, and then my theory does not require any rise of
profits—they may even fall.

You ask me if I can shew you the fallacy of the following
statement. "Capital is wholly employed in the purchase of
materials and machinery and the maintenance of labour. If
from any cause whatever materials, machinery and the
maintenance of the labourer, and his wages, fall considerably
in money value is it *possible* that the same amount of monied
capital can be employed in the country?" I answer that it is
possible but by no means probable. Suppose the mines were
to produce a diminished quantity of the precious metals, at
the same time that materials and machinery were greatly increased in quantity; might not the increased aggregate quantity of materials and machinery be of a greater money value
than before, altho each particular portion should be at a less?
Might we not by importation appropriate to ourselves a
larger proportion of the mass of money distributed amongst
all the countries of the world? I cannot doubt the *possibility*
of the case.

In your argument about the stimulus of increased value,
and the effects of demand and supply on future wealth, you
do not really differ from my views on this subject so much
as you suppose, for I make profits and wealth to depend on
the real cheapness of labour, and so do you, for you say that
the evils of a dearth will often be more than counteracted as
it regards wealth by the great stimulus which it may give to
industry. I say the same, for I contend that the evils of a
dearth fall exclusively on the labouring classes, that they
perform frequently more labour not only without receiving
the same allowance of food and necessaries, but often without

receiving the same value for wages or the same recompence 21 Oct. 1817 in money whilst every thing is dearer. When this happens profits which always depend on the value of labour must necessarily rise.

I thought I had written[1] to you about the additional matter in your excellent work, although I had not given it all the examination I intended. I read it as I was travelling, and noticed the pages wherever I saw the shadow of a difference between us that I might look at the passages again when I got home and give them my best consideration.[2] On my passing through London when I returned from France I looked for your book, as I expected you had sent me a copy, which I think you kindly told me you would do,—but Mrs. Ricardo had jumbled that, and many other books in a wardrobe, and it could not be got at till I went to town. I have it now here, and have been reading all the new matter again, and am surprised at the little that I can discover with the utmost ingenuity to differ from.[3]

In every part you are exceedingly clear, and time only is wanted to carry conviction to every mind. The chief difference between us is whether food or population precedes. I could almost agree with the statement of the question in page 47 of 3 vol which I think is in strict conformity with

[1] Replaces 'spoken'. See letter 202.
[2] The MS here and in three other places contains asterisks which mark two sentences quoted by Empson in *Edinburgh Review*, Jan. 1837, p. 495; they do not refer to footnotes by Ricardo, as has been assumed in *Letters to Malthus*, pp. 143–4.
[3] Ricardo when travelling had probably been reading the copy entrusted to him by Malthus for

Say (see above, p. 168, n. 3). His own copy of the *Essay on Population*, 5th ed., 1817, is preserved in the library at Gatcombe and contains, in the second half of vol. II, a series of pencil marks and numbers on the margins, which probably refer to notes written by Ricardo on separate sheets, which are lost. These marks have been used for determining, in the footnotes to this letter, the passages criticised.

21 Oct. 1817 Sir J. Steuart's opinion.¹ —In speaking of the fall of wages you only once mention *corn* wages but must always mean corn wages and not money wages. In the note to page 438 of the 3 vol.² you agree to my doctrine but I think in pages 446, 456, and 457 you forget the admission you had before made.

497. You agree with Smith that the monopoly of the Colony Trade raises profits.³ 502 is in my opinion wrong and inconsistent with 438.⁴ I differ a little from your views in 506.⁵ You do not always appear to me to admit that the tendency of the poor laws is to increase the quantity of food to be divided, but assume in some places that the same quantity is to be divided among a larger number. I can neither agree with Adam Smith nor with you in 326.⁶

¹ Malthus grants that 'nothing is more usual than for the population to increase at certain periods faster than food'. But then, he adds, 'it must be recollected that the great relative increase of population absolutely implies a previous increase of food at some time or other greater than the lowest wants of the people.'
² Should be *second* vol., in which this and all the subsequent references are to be found. The note referred to runs: 'A rise, which is occasioned exclusively by the increased quantity of labour which may be required in the progress of society to raise a given quantity of corn on the last land taken into cultivation, must of course be peculiar to raw produce, and will not be communicated to those commodities, in the production of which there is no increase of labour.'
³ An opinion controverted by Ricardo, above, I, 344.

⁴ On pp. 501–2 Malthus says that, if the ports had been kept open after 1815, in case of a new war the price of wheat would again have risen, and subsequently fallen; and 'the monied incomes of the landholders and industrious classes of society' would have risen and fallen 'nearly in proportion' to the price of wheat; for p. 438 see note 2 above.
⁵ Although Malthus is certain that 'in reference to the interests of Europe in general the most perfect freedom of trade…would be the most advantageous', yet he thinks that 'in reference to the interests of a particular state, a restriction upon the importation of foreign corn may sometimes be advantageous'.
⁶ 'Dr. Smith has clearly shown, that the natural tendency of a year of scarcity is either to throw a number of labourers out of employment, or to oblige them to work for less than they did before,

328 A maximum tends to discourage future production an undue increase of wages, or poor laws, tend to promote it.[1] 360 A fall in the price of commodities and a rise in the value of money are spoken of as the same thing.[2] 361 A diminution of production is another way of expressing an abatement of demand.[3] 371 A combination among the workmen would increase the amount of money to be divided amongst the labouring class.[4] These you will observe are slight objections and I make them that I may preserve my consistency. They would not be understood by the mass of readers but to you who are acquainted with my *peculiar* views, if you please, they need no explanation.—
Kind regards to Mrs. Malthus.

Ever Y^{rs}

DAVID RICARDO

from the inability of masters to employ the same number at the same price.'
[1] Malthus says that the two proposals, to fix a maximum price of provisions, and to proportion the price of labour to the price of provisions, 'are very nearly of the same nature,...both tend directly to famine.'
[2] For Ricardo's distinction, see above, I, 63–4.
[3] Malthus says 'the specific evil of taxation consists in the check which it gives to production, rather than the diminution which it occasions in demand.'

[4] According to Malthus the combinations of 'artificers and manufacturers' are 'not only illegal, but irrational and ineffectual', because if wages in any branch of trade are forcibly kept up this 'must have the effect of throwing so many out of employment, as to make the expense of their support fully equal to the gain acquired by the higher wages, and thus render these higher wages in reference to the whole body perfectly futile.'

234. RICARDO TO MILL[1]

[*Reply to 232.—Answered by 236*]

Gatcomb Park
9 Nov.[r] 1817

My dear Sir

9 Nov. 1817   I may then at length congratulate you on having finished your book, and put it in that state that it may be announced very shortly in the list of "Just Published" in the newspapers. The additional work which Col. Wilks publication has caused you is not to be regretted—nothing is, which has enabled you to make your book more perfect. I am prepared to give to it my whole undivided attention, and shall be well pleased if I can thoroughly understand all the difficult points on which it treats. The subject, as far as it regards the progress of human society, will be highly interesting to me, as I am eager for information on the causes which are constantly obstructing man in the rational pursuit of his own happiness. Legislation would be comparatively an easy science if it were not so much influenced by the characters and dispositions of the people for whom it is to be undertaken. However well we may have examined the end to which all our laws should tend, yet when they are to influence the actions of a different people we have to acquire a thorough knowledge of the peculiar habits, prejudices and objects of desire of such people, which is itself almost an unattainable knowledge, for I am persuaded that from our own peculiar habits and prejudices we should frequently see these things through a false medium, and our judgements would err accordingly. The effect of these habits and prejudices are not inoperative when legislating for the people amongst whom we have been brought up. Are we not

---

[1] Addressed: 'James Mill Esq[r] / Ford Abbey / Chard / Somersetshire'. MS in Mill-Ricardo papers.

witnesses daily of the bias given to our most common 9 Nov. 1817
opinions by party feelings? To an unprejudiced by-stander
it must appear surprising to see truth distorted as it often is
to favour party views. In most of our legislators this is
carried to an extravagant length, but there are perhaps very
few men who are not in some degree biassed either by the
love of their party, or the love of their favourite system.
Legislation then becomes a most difficult science, for first
you have to study the objects which ought to be attained to
promote the general happiness, and then the nature of the
materials on which you have to act for the attainment of that
end. You see that I am not undervaluing the benefits of
legislation, I am only advancing reasons why men of ordinary
minds will necessarily be timid on this important subject,
fearing pitfalls and stumbling blocks at every step. I agree
with you that when a man sees his way before him he walks
confidently, but that does not remove the difficulty which
besets him from the obscurity of his path.—"Great changes
in society may be effected, when the time is come, by comparatively insignificant means",—but the difficulty in such
a question is to decide, first, whether the change be itself
desirable, and secondly, whether the time be come. These
are the points that would puzzle me, and would make me
determine to advance very cautiously. If you will assist me,
as you promise, to get such a knowledge of these matters as
shall enable me to come to satisfactory conclusions, you will
be doing me essential service. I fear however that it augurs
ill for your success in having formed a wrong estimate of the
powers of your pupil. On that subject I shall say no more,
I have acted like an honest man in telling you the truth as it
appears to me,—you are now responsible for any false
judgement you may make.

I have been reading Locke's Essay for the second time,

and although I do not take much pleasure in such subjects as that Essay treats of, I think I understand the author, and have endeavoured to fix in my mind the points which I think he has successfully established. I admire very much his tolerant spirit, and the ardor with which he enforces not only the right but the duty of free enquiry into the grounds of our religious opinions. How very much he undervalues eloquence and Rhetoric. He says they are of no other use but to insinuate wrong ideas, and are perfect cheats. I remember poor Horner observing that his manner of treating an adversary in argument was a model for all writings of that kind, and it appears to me to be a very just remark.

The articles in Bayle that you mention are precisely those which I had been reading. They are very able and I have not a word to offer against them. On these difficult points I keep my mind in a state of doubt from which in this world I never can be relieved. To account for evil in a world governed by a Being of unbounded benevolence and power is or appears to be impossible. It is as puzzling a question now as in the early times of which Bayle writes. Is it much different from the Manichean heresy to say that the Creator's benevolence is unbounded, but that his power is limited—and thus to account for evil?

Excepting in the establishment of schools for the poor, I do not know what good we have done here which should deserve to be well spoken of by Lady Romilly. I shall be grateful to her for her praise, though undeserved, if it should be the means of inducing you to come and examine into the real worth of my claims. I want to see you here and I have no desire to have merit ascribed to me to which I am really not entitled. I hear from my friend Smith that Mr. Whishaw is returned highly pleased with his journey. Warburton too

is at home after a short excursion to Holland and France. 9 Nov. 1817
Mrs. Ricardo and all my young folks join with me in best
wishes.—With kind regards to Mrs. Mill

I am My Dear Sir

Ever truly Y^{rs}

DAVID RICARDO

What a melancholy event is the death of the Princess
Charlotte!

I am glad, and think it quite right, that your rich friends
should pay for your book if they wish to have it. My purse
strings will untie of themselves. I wish you would tell
Baldwin[1] to send me a copy. I shall have it earlier than if I
sent to Murray.

235. TROWER TO RICARDO[2]

[Reply to 226.—Answered by 239]

Unsted Wood—Godalming
Novr 9—1817—

My Dear Ricardo

When a man has been guilty of an *unatoneable* trans- 9 Nov. 1817
gression (if I may coin such an expression) the less he says
about it the better—Now, as I am sensible I have been guilty
of a very aggrivated offence, in suffering your last kind letter
to remain so long unanswered, perhaps my most prudent
course would be to pass it over in silence—But, as I trust it
is not altogether *inexpiable* I feel desirous to urge numerous
excuses as apologies for my neglect. Recollecting, however
that you are not *half* a *country gentleman*, nor a *particle* of
a farmer, I am fearful my extenuations may not be duely

---

[1] C. Baldwin, printer and pub-
lisher of Mill's *History of British
India.*

[2] Addressed: 'To / David Ricardo
Esqr / Gatcomb Park / Minchinhampton'.—MS in *R.P*

9 Nov. 1817 appreciated; and have therefore resolved to throw myself upon your clemency.—And, indeed, as sorrow subdues all our violent passions, I doubt whether, at the present moment, you could find it in your heart to be very angry! The national loss,[1] we have all just sustained, is of such a nature as not merely to awaken our political apprehensions, but even to excite our tenderest sympathies.—This tragical event opens a wide field for speculation, with regard both to the present, and the future—Will advantage be taken of it to try again for a divorce?[2]—and upon surer grounds, and with better success? If obtained, will it be succeeded by a new alliance; and what is still more problematical by another *progeny*? If not, from whose loins is our new race of Kings to spring? No doubt we can boast many broad backs in our royal breed; and they cannot now want inducement to exert their *vigor* in their Country's cause! But their most successful exertions will but provide against a remote contingency; and in the mean time, we cannot view the probable destination of the sceptre with *compleat satisfaction*. The R.[3] does well enough, but we cannot calculate on the continuance of his life. The Commander in chief[4] I should not be afraid of. He has proved himself an active man of business, and has discharged his duties irreproachably, which is no small praise for a man in his exalted station. His strong military attachments, however, do not constitute the best qualifications for the Sovereign of a free people—But I will not pursue the succession; as it forcibly reminds me of the Phantasmagoria with which the Witches tantalized and tormented Macbeth! However, "come what will, what may", I cheer myself with believing, that there is in this happy Country a sufficient

[1] The death on 6 November of Princess Charlotte, the only child of the Prince of Wales (the Regent).

[2] Of the Prince and Princess of Wales.

[3] The Regent.

[4] The Duke of York.

stock of good sense, and right feeling, to secure itself against 9 Nov. 1817
the worst contingency.—

Have you read the Report of the Poor Laws Committee[1]—
I much approve the view it takes of the subject. It contains
many useful suggestions, the adoption of which would
improve the practice of the poor laws; and bring them back
to their original principles, which in the main are just.—
I trust the investigation will be continued, and will lead to
a better system, which in another year will be carried into
execution with less difficulty than at present.—The pressure
in this part of the Country is certainly diminished, but
we have still many poor people out of work upon the
Parishes, and our rates are enormously high—more than
20/- in the pound upon about $\frac{2}{3}$ of the real rent. I hope
you were fortunate in getting in your crops; in our light
soils we succeeded very well, and have above an average
crop.—

We have adopted the provisions of Rose's Bill, and allow
our Depositors a clear 4 pC. upon every 12/6. Deposits are
coming in apace—and I am satisfied, that the well timed
liberality of Government in granting the advantages held out
by the Act, will have the happiest effects. It is true it may
subject them to loss hereafter, but at present it will contribute
much to the stability of the funds.—You ask me if I think
them high? Yes I do—but not despairing of our finances,
thinking that our revenues will recover, that capital will
accumulate rapidly, that these Saving Banks will throw
millions into the Funds, I do not apprehend that they will
decline—I take a sanguine view of our future prospects, if
our ministers have but common sense; and I was delighted
to observe in your book how forcibly you described the

[1] 'Report from the Select Committee on the Poor Laws' [Sturges
Bourne's Committee], *Parliamentary Papers*, 1817, vol. VI.

9 Nov. 1817 inexhaustible energies of this tight little Island. God bless
you my Dear Friend. Mrs. T joins with me in kind regards
to Mrs. Ricardo and your family, and believe me

Yours very sincerely,

H. T.

236. MILL TO RICARDO[1]

[*Reply to* 234.—*Answered by* 242]

Ford Abbey 3ᵈ Decʳ 1817

My Dear Sir

3 Dec. 1817   As I have just got my hand out of two or three jobs, I
will answer your letter before I immerse it in any more. One
reason, I believe, is, that my book[2] being now all printed, and
being likely to be delayed for some little time, by the makers
of maps and index, I have come to the resolution of desiring
Mr. Baldwin to have a copy made up for you, as it is. You
can be supplied with index, and maps, and so forth, hereafter,
with which the books can be bound up; and you will thus
get them a couple of weeks, perhaps, the sooner; a period
which, whatever it may be to your impatience, is no small
one to mine, who am very anxious to hear what you think
of this offspring, and whether it increases or diminishes my
titles to your esteem.

I do not mean to talk to you any more about legislation,
till you have read my book; because after that we shall
probably find some general principles, about which we can
agree, and starting from which we can go on step by step
with some degree of assurance. I have no doubt about
removing all your difficulties; and showing you that instead

[1] Addressed: 'David Ricardo
Esq. / Gatcomb Park / Minchin-
hampton / Gloucestershire'.
MS in *R.P.*

[2] *The History of British India*,
3 vols. in 4to, with two maps,
London, Baldwin, Cradock and
Joy, 1817.

of being a science, the practical results of which must always be uncertain, rendering it always prudent to try to remain in the state we are in, rather than venture the unknown effects of a change, legislation is essentially a science the effects of which may be computed with an extraordinary degree of certainty; and the friends of human nature cannot proceed with too much energy in beating down every obstacle which opposes the progress of human welfare.

I am glad you have been reading Locke. He is admirable not so much for what he establishes, as for leading you into the track of inquiry. He associates your mind with his; and makes it open its own channels of invention. One feels in reading Locke, as if one was the author oneself of the thoughts which he makes to pass through one's mind.

What you observe is exceedingly just as to the pleasure with which one conceives the ardent spirit of free, independent inquiry, which he recommends. How different, the spirit which breathes in his manly, philanthropic pages, and the spirit which oozes out from the gentry of your true church-and-state breed? a breed who would arrest the progress of the human mind, and exert themselves to clamour down every man who shews a desire for its advancement. This too is one of the charms in the writings of Lord Bacon, who urges men to give scope to their minds, and to travel fearlessly in whatsoever road appears to them to lead to the temple of Truth; this being the only course by which the highest improvement and felicity of the race can ever be attained. Dugald Stewart deserves praise for the same virtue.

There are undoubtedly many charms in Lockes method of dealing with an adversary. There is in the first place, and which is the foundation of all, the great perspicacity with which he discerns the flaw in the opposing argument. There is in the next place, the consummate air of good temper

3 Dec. 1817 which attends his refutation. But I know not that you can say there is any other very remarkable virtue. And I should not agree with Mr. Horner in saying that these are all the qualities which constitute a model. There ought undoubtedly to be these qualities, and I think that these are the chief; but there ought to be others. In the first place, I think that Locke, in his controversial writings is excessively verbose, so that you lose the thread of his argument, and are often led to doubt, whether he had any thread. In the next place he heaps terms of respect upon his adversary, till they sometimes amount to affectation, though sometimes also they operate as irony, and very fine irony. And in his points of attack he makes no selection, but takes everything as it comes, and thus overloads the refutation.

I am highly delighted with your observation, that to seek to save the benevolence of a divinity, by supposing his power limited, is to run into Manicheism.[1] It is so most assuredly; and the remark shews that you are no less capable of thinking profoundly on subjects of this class than on those of political Economy. For what is this, but to suppose that there is some power in the universe, which the Deity cannot controul, and which has a tendency to produce evil? And what did the Manicheans do, but give a name to that power: they called it Ahriman, and some of them invented a parcel of fables, which they attached to that name. Poor Mr. Malthus—If I am not mistaken, it is he who solves the difficulty about the existence of evil in this manner.[2] What a misfortune—what a cruel misfortune, it is, for a man to be *obliged* to believe a certain set of opinions, whether they be

[1] On Mill's attitude to Manichæism, which he did not condemn as strongly as he did all other religious beliefs, see J. S. Mill, *Autobiography*, pp. 39–40.

[2] The argument is in *Essay on Population*, 1st ed., 1798, last chapter, which is not reproduced in the later eds.

fit, or not, to be believed! I too was educated to be a priest— 3 Dec. 1817
but I shall never cease feeling gratitude to my own resolution,
for having decreed to be a poor man, rather than be dishonest, either to my own mind, by smothering my convictions, or to my fellow creatures by using language at variance
with my convictions.[1] However, this is too much, indeed, in
the stile of self-applause; and I should be ashamed of having
needlessly run into it, if I knew not to how indulgent a
correspondent I am writing. And I am not sorry you should
know what I think upon those subjects, how far soever you
may settle the point to which my virtues reach below the
point in the scale at which my own vanity would place them.
I believe this last sentence is not very intelligible. But I have
no room to clarify it, if it were worth the pains.

Most truly yours

J. MILL

237. MALTHUS TO RICARDO[2]

[Reply to 233.—Answered by 240]

My dear Sir,   E I Coll Decr 3rd 1817

It was by no means my intention to allow your kind 3 Dec. 1817
letter to remain so long unanswered; but just as I should
naturally have thought of writing, our examinations began,
and I have been immersed in papers almost ever since. Our

---

[1] Mill studied Divinity at the University of Edinburgh, from 1794
to 1798 'at the expense of a fund
established by Lady Jane Stuart
(the wife of Sir John Stuart) and
some other ladies for educating
young men for the Scottish
Church. He there went through
the usual course of study, and was
licensed as a Preacher, but never
followed the profession; having
satisfied himself that he could not
believe the doctrines of that or
any other Church.' (J. S. Mill,
Autobiography, pp. 2–3.)
[2] Addressed: 'D. Ricardo Esqr /
Gatcomb Park / Minchinhampton / Gloucestershire'.
MS in R.P.

term has been shortened a fortnight, and our vacation therefore commences so much earlier. The Directors come down the day after tomorrow, and we shall be then dismissed for six weeks, instead of a month as usual. This change it is hoped will be favourable to peace and quiet. As far as the experiment has yet been tried it has fully answered.

I am much pleased to find that there is so little of my *Additions* in which you differ from me. I have looked carefully at the passages to which you refer, and am inclined to think that the principal causes of our differences on these points, are, as might be expected, your peculiar opinions, in which I cannot yet acquiesce. I must still consider the *necessaries* of life as the *real wages* of labour*; and cannot yet look upon *production* in the same light as *demand*. But it was just after I received your letter when I examined the passages, and I am not now quite *au fait* with regard to all the particulars.

It is impossible I think to doubt that profits have been low, as well as interest during the last two or three years. What destroyed so much agricultural capital, but low profits or rather no profits? and what occasioned so much distress among merchants and manufacturers but a want of demand and fall of prices? Variations in general prices are unquestionably much more common, than variations in value arising from different quantities of labour imployed in producing corn; but such variations of prices, or of the circulating if you please, begin in my opinion perpetually with a rise in the price of corn, and proceed successively, and not immediately, to other commodities. This has certainly been the case with us, during the last 25 years; and I am strongly

[*] I cannot call as I ought to do according to your theories the wages of the American labourer low: He earns both more corn and more money.

disposed to believe, that for nearly the last century or at 3 Dec. 1817 least for 80 or 90 years, no marked increase has taken place in the quantity of labour necessary to produce corn at home. It is your frequent reference to causes which operate only in an inconsiderable degree, or in an unusual state of things, in accounting for great and striking phenomena which are actually occurring, that gives an air of paradox to some of your opinions. The increase in the labour of growing corn has certainly had little or nothing to do with the increase in its price of late years; and surely it would be most unsafe and incorrect to draw any conclusions respecting the rate of profits from the assumption that prices remain the same, in the midst of continual variations in the circulating medium which you yourself acknowledge.

The question I put to you in my last letter was intended to imply the absolute incompatibility of an abundant capital with high profits; and to shew that profits depend entirely upon the competition of capital, or the state of capital compared with labour, and not on the state of the land. The high relative price of labour is an effect, and not an original cause. I am meditating a volume as I believe I have told you,[1] and I want to answer you, without giving my work a controversial air. Can you tell me how to manage this.

We are going into Surrey for about a fortnight or 3 weeks. If you write within that time direct to me Weston House Guildford. Are you likely to be in Town soon. Mrs. M desires to be kindly remembered to Mrs. Ricardo.

Ever truly Yours
T. R. MALTHUS.

[1] Above, p. 194.

238. WAKEFIELD TO RICARDO[1]

Talliaris Park
December 7. 1817.

Dear Sir

7 Dec. 1817   A short time since I was applied to for a sum of money
to be lent on mortgage to the Earl of Portalington[2] in Ireland—the security comprises a Borough—and as Ireland is
a registered country and the legal rate of interest 6 p^r Cent
I felt an inclination to invest a part of my son's money[3]
upon the security—the amount required is from 10 to
£20.000

The application was made to me by Mr. Kirkland of
St James's Street[4]—and I proposed to lend the money—
provided a preferrence was given to me of the nomination
of the member at the market price of the day—leaving to
some distinguished and honourable member of the house
to say how much should be paid—say such a person as
Mr. Grenfell

Mr. Kirkland promised to see Lord Portalington and let
me know—and I have heard nothing since—until the receipt of a letter yesterday—from Lord Portalington's agent
in Dublin asking for the money—he says nothing about the
stipulation to which I have adverted—but I have replied to
his letter telling him that he may have the money but requesting a personal interview with Mr. Kirkland.

[1] Addressed: 'David Ricardo
Esqr / Gatcombe Park / Minching
Hampton / Glostershire'. Franked
by Lord Seymour, from Llandilo.
MS in *R.P.*
[2] Should be 'Portarlington'.
[3] His son was Edward Gibbon
Wakefield (1796–1862), at this
time attached to the British Lega-
tion at Turin. His elopement and
marriage with a wealthy ward in

Chancery, Eliza Pattle, resulted
in the Lord Chancellor's making
'the most liberal settlement on
his ward's husband that had ever
been remembered in the records
of Chancery', giving to him the
equivalent of an income between
£1500 and £2000 per annum
(Irma O'Connor, *Edward Gibbon
Wakefield*, London, 1928, p. 31).
[4] Nugent Kirkland, army agent.

If I cannot lay my son's money out advantageously in a 7 Dec. 1817
landed Estate—I shall wish for the security—and should it
be given with the stipulation to which I have adverted the
seat will be at your service—if I meet directly with a property which will absorb all his money—you may should you
choose it—take the security and advance the 10 or £20.000
which is required—but should you dislike it I shall then offer
it to an employer of mine who I know will be anxious to do
so and take the seat

On tuesday I am going into Herefordshire—and shall
pay a visit to your new purchase of Brinsop Court[1] the contract for which I expect Mr. Crosse[2] has forwarded to you
for execution.

I am in negociation for Lord Oxford's property in that
County for my son

I shall be in London about the 19th In^t against which time
I shall be happy to hear from you about Lord Portalington
—and as the matter of your letter may be as well not to be
made known to my clerks—I will thank you to write
"Private" on the outside of the letter[3]

I am

Your most faithful humble servant

EDWARD WAKEFIELD

David Ricardo Esq.

[1] The Manor of Brinsop Court, in Herefordshire.
[2] Thomas Crosse, Ricardo's solicitor.
[3] For further news from Wakefield on this subject see letters 244 and 288.

239. RICARDO TO TROWER[1]

[*Reply to* 235]

Gatcomb Park
10 Dec.[r] 1817

My dear Trower

10 Dec. 1817   You make your excuses with so good a grace, that
I could not be angry with you if I would, but what perhaps
more certainly determines me to shew charity to you, is the
necessity I am under of frequently throwing myself on the
charitable judgement of others—I shew mercy, that I may
receive it.—

We have here, equally with every other part of the
country, mourned over the untimely fate of our late princess,
and are equally sensible of the great national loss we have
sustained. All the Princes of the Royal Blood probably now
expect to wield the sceptre in their turn, but the probability
is that in this expectation they will be disappointed. It is a
singular circumstance that with so many children our old
King should not have one grand-child. A writer in the
Morning Chronicle whose letter I had not time to read
ascribes this to the Royal Marriage Act, and I think the
remark well founded. Marriage would be a different thing
to all of us, if our partners were selected for us, and were
necessarily strangers to our sympathies. I know that there
are some good state reasons to be advanced in its defence yet
I cannot help thinking that it would be wise not to prevent
the younger branches of the family from marrying subjects,
either with a view to their own happiness and respectability
or to the interests of the country. Our Princes have certainly
not refrained from marriage from a consideration of Malthus'

[1] Addressed: 'Hutches Trower   MS at University College, Lon-
Esq[r]/ Unsted Wood / Godalming /   don.—*Letters to Trower*, XVII.
Surry'.

prudential check, and from a fear of producing a redundant Royal population. If they had they would now be actuated by different motives and we might expect that the great demand for Royal infants would be followed by so ample a supply as to occasion a glut.

I have read the report of the Committee of the House of Commons on the Poor Laws with much satisfaction—I am glad to see sound principles promulgated from that quarter, though I should have been still more pleased if they had insisted more strongly on an *efficient* remedy. On this part of the subject they shew too much hesitation—recommend measures, and then qualify or abandon them. The whole country is feeling the inconvenience of the present system, and will I hope be brought to understand the origin of the evil. All the principal Reviews write well on this subject. In the last number of the British there is a very good review of the Commons' report, which is worth your reading. In the same number there is also a review of my book,[1] in which in every page I am charged with ignorance and absurdity. Yet it is not done in an ungentmanly way, and I have the pleasure to have my friend Malthus associated with me in the censure of having made the subject of rent, which was well explained by Adam Smith, and is perfectly clear, obscure and unintelligible. The writer does not in fact see the important part of the subject—he has read but not studied it. He has kindly left unattacked those points which were most assailable, and has fastened on those which are incontrovertible. My style and arrangement are fortunately for me not mentioned.—A writer in a Scotch paper called the Scotsman has written a short Essay in my vindication, and has I think done it ably, for he has expressed my opinions in

---

[1] *British Review*, Nov. 1817, Art. XV, a review of Ricardo's *Principles* and Say's *Traité*.

10 Dec. 1817 much clearer language than I could do it myself.[1] To compensate me also for the censure of the Reviewer I have been made acquainted with Lord Grenville's opinion of my book, which is favourable beyond my expectations. When I go to London I am, at his Lordship's desire, to be introduced to him. For Lord Grenville's judgement on matters of Political Economy I have always had the highest respect.[2]

We have established a Savings Bank in this neighbourhood in the formation of which I have been very active.[3] I was the only one practically acquainted with such Institutions and therefore my services have been much more highly appreciated than they deserved. We give a half penny per month for every 13/-. In six weeks we have received about £1100 which may be said to be tolerably successful, but we understand that a strong prejudice exists among the manufacturing classes against us. They think that we have some sinister object—that we wish to keep wages down. Time and good temper will overcome this feeling and convince the prejudiced how that the rich have no other personal object in view excepting the interest which every man must feel in good government,—and in the general prosperity. The success of these Banks would be great if the enormous abuses of the Poor Laws were corrected.

Several other banks have been opened since ours within

---

[1] 'Mr. Ricardo and the British Review', in the *Scotsman*, 15 Nov. 1817: the writer justifies Ricardo's assumption of a machine which lasts for a hundred years and works without human assistance as being done merely 'for the sake of *illustrating* his general principles'. Cp. the note added in ed. 2, above, I, 60–1. The *Scotsman* had already reviewed Ricardo's *Principles* in its number of 3 May 1817; McCulloch was no doubt the writer in both cases.

[2] William Wyndham Grenville, Baron Grenville (1759–1834), Prime Minister in 1806–7. 'Lord Grenville pushes the principles of political œconomy of the present school, as far as Ricardo himself' (J. L. Mallet's MS Diary, 22 Nov. 1819).

[3] See above, p. 187, n.

15 miles of us, but every where the same prejudice operates
against them.

Mill's book[1] waits only for the index to be published. He
has from the remarks I have heard him make given me a great
desire to read and study it.

Malthus has a volume ready[2] which I am also anxious to see,
because he expressed in it his views on the subjects on which
I have lately written, and which I know differ materially
from mine.

I shall be in London in Jan.[y], and shall not return again
here. I hope soon to meet you. To secure a meeting I ought
to kill an East India director, a contested election will follow,
and then you will infallibly be brought to town. I am annoyed
by the prospect of being Sheriff of our county this next year.
Of the 3 named Col.[l] Berkeley, son of the late Earl is first and
I second. The Col.[l] it is said is about to try again for the
peerage and therefore it is probable that I may be chosen.

Mrs. Ricardo and my daughter join with me in kind regards
to Mrs. Trower, to whom and to you I wish all manner of
good.

Very truly Yours
DAVID RICARDO.

240. RICARDO TO MALTHUS[3]
[*Reply to* 237]

Gatcomb Park
My dear Sir   16 Dec.[r] 1817

I believe I am within the time stated in your letter for
your visit to Surry, and consequently that this will reach you

[1] *History of British India.*
[2] Malthus had said only that he
was 'meditating a volume' (above,
p. 215); his *Principles of Political
Economy* was not ready for the

press till the end of 1819.
[3] Addressed: 'Rev. T. R Malthus /
Weston House / Guildford'.
MS at Albury.—*Letters to Malthus,* LXIV.

16 Dec. 1817 there. I am sorry that you were not sufficiently loyal to give her majesty some mark of your attention at Bath,[1] during your present vacation, as in that case I might have hoped to have seen you here. As it is we may probably be in London nearly at the same time. We have not yet absolutely fixed on the day for our journey but it will not be deferred beyond the middle of next month. I hope I may see you before your return home.

I am glad to find that we may soon expect another volume from your pen, although, if you attack me, I am prepared for nine tenths of our readers deciding in favour of your view of the question. I want an able pen on my side to put my opinions in a clear light, and to divest them of that appearance of paradox which they now wear. I wish I could assist you to a good title but no one is more able to give a work the best air and arrangement than yourself. Have you seen the Review of M Say and myself in the British?[2] In some of the remarks you would I believe agree, yet it is some consolation to me that after designating every part of my performance absurd, and nonsensical, they attack you on the subject of Rent, and say that both you and I have endeavoured to make the nature of rent, which was before so clear, obscure. Rent is nothing more than the hire paid for land. I feel delighted that they have given me so desirable a companion.—In the Scotsman, a scotch newspaper, I have been ably defended —the writer has evidently understood what I meant to say, which the Reviewer has not done.—

I have been reading Mill's book[3] for this last week, and have got through about half of the first volume. I am not qualified to give an opinion of its merits, but I am very much

[1] On the extreme unpopularity of Queen Charlotte at this particular moment, see Lord Holland's *Memoirs of the Whig Party, 1807–*

1821, London, 1905, pp. 248–9.
[2] See above, p. 219.
[3] *History of British India.*

pleased with it. It is very interesting, and is I think calculated to excite a great deal of attention, for it not only
descants on the religion, manners, laws, arts, and literature,
of the Hindus, but compares them with the religion manners
&c.ᵃ of other nations which the world has generally considered as much inferior to the Hindus, and if these in the
Hindus are to be deemed marks of a high state of civilization,
Africa, Mexico, Peru, Persia, and China, might also lay claim
to the same character. He also gives his own sentiments as
to what constitutes good laws, a good religion, a high state
of civilization, and shews at what a very low degree Hindo-
stan deserves to be estimated for these acquirements. The
Political Economy is I think excellent, and the part that I have
read may be considered as the author's view of the progress
of the human mind.—I hope it will bring him fame and
reputation,—his perseverance, as well as his other qualities
well deserve it.—

I am very glad to hear from Mr. Smith, that Mr. Whishaw
has returned so well pleased with his journey; I should have
been very much pleased to have heard him open his budget
to [you]¹ and Mr. Smyth, when he met the latter at your
house. [He] is very kind in writing to Mr. Smith, from whom
I often hear the little anecdotes which he has communicated
to h[im] of his journey.—

Like the Patriarchs of old I am surrounded by all my
descendants, sons, daughters and grandchildren,—they have
assembled from all quarters to visit us, and if I were not afraid
that they would soon become too numerous for the limits of
our house I should insist on its being an annual custom.—

You have probably seen in the papers that I am gazetted
as one of the three from whom the choice of Sheriff is to be
made, and as Col! Berkeley, the first named, will in all pro-

¹ MS torn here and below.

16 Dec. 1817 bability be excused on account of his intended application to the House of Lords for the Peerage, which must otherwise be given to his brother, who is nearly of age, I shall no doubt be selected. This honour I could well have dispensed with. I hope Mrs. Malthus is well. Mrs. Ricardo joins with me in kind regards to her.

Ever Y^{rs}

DAVID RICARDO

241. SAY TO RICARDO[1]

[Answered by 243]

Monsieur et Respectable Ami

8 Dec. 1817   Je n'ai pas eu d'occasion de vous accuser reception de la bonne lettre que vous m'adressâtes en quittant Paris au mois de juillet dernier.[2] Depuis ce moment je me flatte que votre santé et celle de votre famille, ont été satisfesantes; j'en apprendrai la confirmation avec plaisir.

La derniere recolte des blés n'a point été aussi bonne qu'on s'y etait attendu; le prix des farines, et, par suite des farines de pommes de terre, n'est pas tombé en conséquence aussi bas qu'on s'en etait flatté; ce qui m'a detourné jusqu'à present de spéculer sur cette derniere denrée, comme j'en avais le projet.

Cependant la recolte des pommes de terre a été proportionnellement meilleure que celle des grains, et les fabriques de farine de pommes de terre (de ce que nous nommons *fécule*) se sont fort multipliées.

Il en est resulté que le prix des fécules se maintient au dessous de celui des farines de blé 1re qualité. Les farines

---

[1] Addressed: 'To/David Ricardo Esq^e / 56 Upper brook Street, Grovenor Square/London'. English postmark 11 Dec. Forwarded to Gatcomb on Wednesday, 17 Dec.; see below, p. 230. MS in *R.P.*

[2] Ricardo's letter is wanting.

valent actuellement 27^f le quintal de 100 livres, et la fecule
se vend environ 20^f Tous les boulangers de Paris en mèlent
dans leur pain qui est très beau et très bon à present.

Les renseignemens qui arrivent des diverses parties de la
France sur les subsistances, s'accordent tous en ce point que
la derniere récolte ne suffira pas pour atteindre la récolte
prochaine. Il y a donc grande apparence de hausse dans les
grains et farines, d'ici au mois de septembre prochain.

Cette hausse est encore plus probable sur les fécules de
pommes de terre, car en avril on cesse d'en fabriquer à cause
de la difficulté de garder les pommes de terre plus longtems
sans germination.

Je pense donc que quoique la fécule ne soit pas à très bon
marché, elle subira une hausse d'ici au mois de septembre.
J'aurais desiré faire avec vous une spéculation sur cette
marchandise; mais puisque vous y avez de la répugnance,
j'y consacrerai pour mon compte quinze à vingt mille francs
que je me trouve avoir disponibles, et de plus ce que vous
jugeriez à propos de me confier jusqu'à trente ou quarante
mille francs, pour me mettre à portée de faire une spéculation
d'environ Cinquante mille francs.

Si je peux obtenir de votre amitié ce moyen de profit, la
somme sera exclusivement employée en une marchandise
inaltérable de sa nature, qu'aucun événement possible ne
peut faire baisser beaucoup au dessous de sa valeur actuelle
avant le mois de septembre; et que plusieurs circonstances
peuvent faire monter de 30, de 50 pour cent, et au delà. Il n'y
a pas six mois qu'elle valait 55^f le quintal.

En supposant même que les prix baissassent accidentelle-
ment au dessous du cours actuel, le prix *moyen* de la fécule,
d'après des relevés que j'ai faits avec soins de plusieurs
années antérieures, etant de 20 a 21^f le quintal, je ne risque
en achetant cette marchandise environ à ce prix et en la

8 Dec. 1817 gardant, que mes frais de garde; et toutes les chances de hausse, sont en ma faveur. Si elle etait tombée à 15^f j'aurais speculé sur quelque somme que ce fût.

Je regarderai donc, Monsieur et digne ami, comme une faveur précieuse, la facilité que vous me procurerez de faire une affaire avantageuse dans un moment où j'ai laissé en suspens mon autre affaire. L'incertitude des fermentations m'a empeché de vouloir m'interesser dans les opérations qui se font actuellement dans ma distillerie. Par un arrangement que j'ai fait avec mon associé, il travaille pour son compte particulier, et me paie le loyer du fonds qui m'appartient presqu'en entier.[1]

Vous fixerez vous même le taux de l'interet et la forme que je devrai donner à mon engagement envers vous. Je voudrais s'il etait possible, avoir un credit ouvert chez un de nos banquiers et n'etre chargé des interets que de la somme que je prendrais et pour le tems que je la garderais; car ce sont les prix de la fécule qui me détermineront, soit pour le moment, soit pour la quotité des ventes et des achats. Si pour éviter les frais de commission du banquier de Paris, vous me fesiez des remises sur Paris à un ou deux mois d'échéance, je les escompterais au moment du besoin; et s'il survenait des variations qui m'ôtassent toute idée de spéculation, je vous demanderais la permission d'appliquer vos fonds à l'emploi que vous m'indiqueriez, ou de vous en faire les retours au mieux de votre avantage.

Permettez-moi, Monsieur et respectable ami, de vous transmettre les hommages de ma famille et de vous renouveller les assurances de mon inviolable attachement.

J. B. SAY

Rue du faubourg St Martin N° 92.
Paris 8 Décembre 1817

[1] The working partner was Say's brother Louis.

Je m'occupe toujours à corriger mon Traité d'Economie 8 Dec. 1817
et je fais un grand usage de vos *Principles of Political
Economy.* C'est ce que vous verrez dans ma quatrieme
edition que je vous enverrai peut être avant un an.

242. RICARDO TO MILL[1]
[Reply to 236.—Answered by 245]

Gatcomb Park
My dear Sir   18 Decr 1817

The long desired book has at length arrived, and I have 18 Dec. 1817
been engaged upon it for several days. Before I proceed
further in its perusal, I am desirous of acquainting you with
the impression which it has already made upon me. I have
read as far as the 468th page, and think it admirable.

To express my feelings I should have recourse to the high
sounding words of the people whose history you have been
writing, but unfortunately I am not master even of sufficient
sober English, to enable me to express coldly, and justly,
what I wish to say on this occasion. My gratification has
been great, and I need the talents of a Locke, or a Hume, to
explain from what simple ideas this compound one is made
up. That which gives me most pleasure, is the anticipation
that the public will ratify the opinion which I myself entertain of your performance, and that it may award you a
dignified place amongst the distinguished of our country
men who have contributed to the happiness and well being
of society, and to which your perseverance, and your talents,
so well entitle you. Nothing can be more interesting than
your account of the extraordinary people whose history you
write:—Your comparison of their Government, Laws,
Customs and Religion, with what should be the Govern-

---

[1] Addressed: 'James Mill Esqr / Ford Abbey / Chard / Somersetshire'.
MS in Mill-Ricardo papers.

18 Dec. 1817 ment, Laws, Customs and Religion, of an enlightened, and highly civilized people, is exceedingly curious, and instructive, and is in an uncommon degree clear, and perspicuous. Where it attacks the received opinions too, on which the multitude are so exceedingly susceptible, it is temperate, at the same time that it is powerful in argument. The frequent reference to the state, and exertions of other people, to enable us to form correct conclusions respecting the civilization of the Hindus, brings a grand picture to our view; and tends to improve our knowledge not only of Government, Law, Religion, Arts, and Literature, as things common to all mankind, but also to increase the interest with which we regard the state of each.

The knowledge of each country is not only interesting in itself, but also on account of its becoming a sort of standard by which we may estimate the state of other countries. To this I should add that I think the Political Economy, wherever it is scattered, excellent; had you not brought a blush into my cheek, by mentioning me with such unmeasured approbation as you have done.[1]

I have to thank you for your last excellent letter. I hope you do not suppose me sceptical with respect to the practicability of improvements in legislation. I have the most sanguine expectations on that subject, but then they must be introduced and recommended by those who are able to judge of their effects, and not by the ignorant and inexperienced. If I before had had doubts of what legislation might do, to improve society, I should have none after reading what I have read of your book, but an unskilful, or a designing man, might add to those evils which he pretended to remove, and

---

[1] 'See a Dissertation on the Principles of Taxation, the most profound, by far, which has yet been given to the world, by David Ricardo, Esq. in his work "On the Principles of Political Economy and Taxation."' (*History of British India*, vol. 1, p. 196, note.)

therefore I would know something of his honesty, and more of his qualifications. My plea for caution and timidity was ignorance, a plea of which you would allow the force, although you would endeavour to remove it.—Legislation may not be so difficult as I imagine,—I wish it may not be, for I am anxiously disposed to understand it. One of the great difficulties of the science appears to me to be that which you remark somewhere, (but for which I have been looking over the book in vain) of the Government and laws of one state of society being often very ill adapted for another state of society. You I think apply it to the Tartar hordes.—

I observe you speak with admiration of Berkeley's theory of ideas. I admire exceedingly the ingenuity with which Hume shews from Locke's doctrines that we have no proof of the existence of external objects,—but I wish to know whether you see no weight in the objections, offered by Reid, and I believe by Dugald Stewart, to the mind perceiving only ideas, and not external objects? Why should we as it is said perceive always the image of an object, and never the object itself? This must form the subject of some of our conversations,—I suspect that I do not understand the language that is applied to the operations of the mind.—Your view I observe of the manner in which mankind become acquainted with the idea of a Supreme Being is much the same as that of Hume, if they may be said to have an idea of such a Being, for as you so ably remark the language in which they speak of him, and the adulatory expressions in which they address him afford no proof whatever of any just or sublime conception of him.—We go to London in the middle of Jan.ʸ, when shall I meet you there?—Have you seen the British Review.[1]   Ever Yʳˢ

DAVID RICARDO

[1] Cp. above, p. 219.

243. RICARDO TO SAY[1]

[*Reply to* 241]

Gatcomb Park, Minchinhampton
Gloucestershire
18 Dec.ʳ 1817

My dear Sir

18 Dec. 1817   Your letter, which was directed to my house in London, was not forwarded to me here before wednesday last, which will account to you for the time which will have elapsed between your writing it, and receiving my answer.

Since you were in England I have been gradually withdrawing myself from business, and as our debt is so enormously large, and the price of our funds appeared to me high, I have from time to time withdrawn my money from the funds, and have invested a large portion of it in landed property. When I was in France, and since I left it, I have been tempted by the low relative price of the French Funds to invest another portion of my money in the French 5 pc.ᵗˢ and Bank Actions, so that at present I have really the command of comparatively a small sum of money from which it would be exceedingly inconvenient for me to part.—I regret therefore that I cannot comply with the request contained in your letter.—I hope however that you may speedily meet with some other friend who may be able to supply you with funds which it appears probable from the statement you have given me, you could employ both to his and your advantage. My life has been one of success, but of anxiety, and I am endeavouring so to arrange my affairs, that I shall have no cares for the future, respecting pecuniary matters.

Our friend Mill is just about publishing a work, on which

---

[1] Addressed: 'A Monsieur / Monsieur J. B. Say / Rue du faubourg Sᵗ Martin N⁰ 92 / a / Paris'. MS in the possession of M. Raoul-Duval. — *Mélanges*, pp. 101–2; *Œuvres diverses*, pp. 413–14; (in French translation and incomplete).

he has been employed for some years, on India. With his 18 Dec. 1817
acknowledged talents every thing that comes from his pen
must be interesting, and instructive; but in the present instance, I trust, that he will be found to have surpassed the
expectations of his warmest friends, and sincerest admirers.
The work is printed and will soon be ready for delivery. He
has favoured me with an early copy, and I have read rather
more than half the first volume. I only hope that he may
make the same impression on the minds of those who are
competent judges of literary merit, that he has made on mine.
His views on the subjects of Government, Law, Religion,
Manners are profound; and his application of these views
to the actual, and past state of Hindustan, with a view to
ascertain the validity of the claim which has been set up for
them for high civilization, appears to me to be most masterly,
and cannot I think be refuted.—I hope you will have opportunity and leisure to read and give your opinion of this
highly interesting book.—

The esteem for your excellent book on Political Economy
is daily increasing in this country, and only because it daily
becomes [better][1] known. It has been lately reviewed with
mine in the British Review,[2] and due respect has been paid
to its merits. My work has not been so fortunate, for the
reviewer has found abundant matter for his censure, and
scarcely a passage on which he bestows praise.

I hope Mrs. Say, your son and daughter are well. I think
with pleasure of the happy day which owing to your united
kindness I passed with you in Paris.—Pray make my best
regards acceptable to them.

With great esteem I am My dear Sir

Yours very faithfully

DAVID RICARDO

[1] MS torn.   [2] See above, p. 219.

244. WAKEFIELD TO RICARDO[1]

Dear Sir   Pall Mall December 24. 1817.

24 Dec. 1817   In reply to your letter of yesterday I have already been with Mr. Crosse and furnished him with the necessary instructions about Berrow.[2]

I do not know the price of plants at Bristol—but I apprehend they are no where so cheap as the Scotch ones. My friend Mr. Dickinson the member for Somersetshire has the last two or three years been planting largely—and he finds—that the best way—is the having his plants from Beck and Allen—and he has I know tried most of the nurserymen in his neighbourhood—he is a successful planter and I believe that no better method can be pursued—than that which he has adopted.

Mr. Kirkland[3] has just left me—and I am glad to hear that Lord Portalington is in a hurry for his money—I told Mr. Kirkland—that if Lord Portalington's Brother, Sir Henry Parnell[4] member for the Queens County, would give me his word—that you should be returned at the next election for the Borough, that he should have the money which he wants for the security—and that I would subsequently pay him any sum which Mr. Grenfell or any equally respectable member of the House of Commons, should say was right.

Lord Portalington is in Ireland. Mr. Kirkland writes to him to night and expects his acquiescence to these terms— in the course of a fortnight the matter will be determined one way or other. I have not any confident expectation of buying Lord Oxford's property for my son—but a few days will

[1] MS in *R.P.*
[2] An estate which Ricardo had just arranged to buy, adjoining

his property of Bromesberrow.
[3] See letter 238.
[4] See below, p. 346, n. 2.

determine it—should I not—I shall then wish for Lord 24 Dec. 1817
Portalington's security for him.

I am

Most faithfully yours

EDWARD WAKEFIELD

David Ricardo Esqre

245. MILL TO RICARDO[1]

[*Reply to* 242.—*Answered by* 246]

My Dear Sir

    I must confess that your letter gave me uncommon 27 Dec. 1817
pleasure, notwithstanding the extravagance of the praise,
and notwithstanding the allowance which I know ought to
be made for the partiality with which you regard me, and all
that I do. I am quite sure that you never speak, except as you
think. And I shall need to be supported by the good opinion
of such men as you. For you will see by and bye how I shall
be treated by the men and the creatures of party, and by all
those who aim at being the great ones of this world, upon
whose craft I have endeavoured to let in some light more than
ordinary. You will see how I shall be treated by some of my
own friends and yours; and it will amuse you to contemplate
the awkward shifts they will be put to, between the necessity
they may think themselves under to speak somewhat in
praise, and the real hearty inclination to backbite, and undervalue. You will see more of this than I shall, because there
will be less reason to disguise before you. And I hope you
will note it carefully, as an instructive specimen of the moral
temperament engendered by the present vicious state of our
social institutions; and the motion to be dishonest and wicked

---

[1] Addressed: 'David Ricardo Esq. / Gatcomb Park / Minchinhampton / Gloucestershire'.—MS in *R.P.*

27 Dec. 1817 which they create. And I shall beg you to note it carefully not only for your own sake, but for mine, to let me know all the particulars of it which present themselves before you. From what I have said, you may judge of the sort of impression which it will make upon me.

But why do I trouble you with this stuff, in such a hurry after receiving your flattery? Why, truly, in the first place, to give vent to a little of the satisfaction which I feel, that those points of knowledge which I chiefly wished my book to communicate, are exactly those points which you describe it as likely to be successful in communicating. This is the first of the reasons for so much haste. The next is, to urge you to lose no time to repeat your dose of flattery. The second volume is a very different kind of a subject;[1] and I am hardly less impatient to know what you think of the manner in which that has been treated. I calculate, that at the pace at which you seem to have been reading, you will, by the time this reaches you, be nearly done with the reading of the second volume. This, therefore, is to intreat that as soon as you are, you will sit down and tell me what you think of it. You must not however, because I have told how much I like your praise, be the less faithful in telling me wherein you think there is any thing to blame.

On the subject of legislation I have no doubt that we shall now understand one another. Doubtless, the laws which are adapted to an improved state of society, would not be adapted to a state of society much behind. But it will not be difficult when we have a standard of excellence, to determine what is to be done, in all cases. The ends are there, in the first place, known—they are clear and definite. What you have

[1] Vol. 1 of *History of British India* contains a general survey of the state of civilisation among the Hindus, and the early history; vol. II, the history from 1708 to 1784.

after that to determine is the choice of the means, and under glorious helps for directing the judgement. But we shall have plenty of time to talk of all those matters, when we meet in London. You will not be there much before us; for we shall be before the end of January; and I shall have a little more time for conversation, I hope, than I had last year.

Yes, we must talk about Berkeleys theory; and Reid's and Stewart's conclusions upon it. You will observe that where I praise the ingenuity and refinement of the reasonings of Berkeley, I do not express concurrence in his opinions.[1]

I have not seen the British Review. But Place writes to me—"I have read a review of Ricardo and Say in the last No. &.c. It is a wretched performance. The author is utterly incapable of reasoning, and, being ignorant himself, he throws the words *ignorance*, and *nonsense*, and *folly*, at Ricardo". &.c.

Did I ever tell you that Place is not only a convert to your book, but an enthusiast for it? I have told him my doubts, whether he understands the whole—but I have not had an opportunity by conversation of ascertaining. You are with him one of the heroes in mind.[2]

I dare say you have a nice parcel of those that belong to you, all about you, at this social time, and doing all that depends upon you to make them all happy. I should like to thrust my nose in among you, and enjoy a little of it along with you. Present my best compliments

[1] *History of British India*, vol. 1, p. 378 ff. Mill attacks Hindu metaphysics and criticises its English admirers for confusing 'the vague and unmeaning jargon' of the Hindu philosophers with the speculations of Berkeley. After describing their doctrines he ex-

claims: 'How different is all this from the curious result of the refined and ingenious reasonings of Berkeley! And how shallow the heads that confound them!' (p. 388, n.).
[2] See above, p. 183.

27 Dec. 1817 to all, and my kind regards and remembrance to all that know me.

I shall say no more, till I get your next letter, than that I am, my Dear Sir

Ever most truly yours

J. MILL

Ford Abbey
27ᵗʰ Decʳ 1817

246. RICARDO TO MILL[1]

[*Reply to* 245]

Gatcomb Park.
30ᵗʰ Decʳ 1817.

My dear Sir

30 Dec. 1817   You are a most accurate calculator, for your kind letter reached me just as I had closed the second volume of your book, and was commencing the third. If my approbation can give you the least satisfaction I am happy I am able to give it in as unqualified a degree to the volume I have just finished, as to that which preceded it. I wish however that I was a more competent judge, as I should then be more fully assured that the decision which I pronounced would be ratified by those who must ultimately decide on the real merits of your performance. I have little fear however of your success, and cannot anticipate from any quarter, or from any party, the sort of criticism which you appear to expect. It is probable indeed that many may not agree with your notions of government—they may think that you give too much weight to some of the motives to human action, and too little to others; but they cannot fail to acknowledge the great proof of talents which your work displays, as well as the evidence it affords of the purity of your views, and of the

[1] Addressed: 'James Mill Esqʳ / Ford Abbey / Chard / Somersetshire'.
MS in Mill-Ricardo papers.

absence of all sinister interest. Who can deny that it leads
the mind into the right track of consideration respecting the
philosophy of laws and government, and the means of promoting and securing the happiness of the human race? What
subject can be more important or interesting? You may be
criticized, but you will not be condemned, and you will I
think certainly obtain the prize which in these days is given
to successful literary merit.—The narrative of the progress
of the English in India has been highly instructive to me, as
I was very imperfectly acquainted even with the great transactions of our countrymen in that quarter of the world. The
style is very clear, and the only difficulty I find in fixing the
facts on my mind, besides that which arises from a very bad
memory, proceeds from the difficult names of the heroes of
Indian story. Much as I am pleased with the narrative I am
still more so with the reflections with which it is interspersed,
to all which I have paid peculiar attention, and have marked
them for further consideration.—The three last chapters are
more particularly interesting. The account of Mr. Hastings
government appears to me to be very ably done, and the
sentence you finally pronounce upon him more lenient than
he deserves. Nothing can be more atrocious than the conduct
he pursued towards Nuncomar, Cheyt Sing, and the Begums,
to say nothing of that towards the Nabob of Oude, Mahomed
Reza Khan, and the Rajah Shitabroy.

Your account of the Supreme Court of Justice has given
you an opportunity of which you have ably availed yourself
to reflect on the constitution of Courts generally and the bias
of judges. I never considered the establishment of the trial
by Jury as a corrective to this bias, but as a security against
corruption—it appears however to be so, though perhaps
this is not the only advantage which results from that institution.—Do you not give too much weight to the influence

o Dec. 1817 of fees on the administration of justice, particularly when the fees do not increase the emoluments of the judge but of those who are appointed by the judge?—Is not the love of ease, which is natural to the judge as well as to others, a corrective against the multiplication of causes in which he (the judge) has no direct interest? The love of patronage so trifling in degree must be more than balanced by a fear of censure and the love of ease.

The friends of Mr. Fox will not be satisfied with the correction which your note gives to the text,[1]—nor perhaps with your remarks on his India Bill. To me they mostly appear very satisfactory. The opposition made by King and people to the nomination by the House of Commons, of the Rulers of India, on the ground that such Rulers would in fact be chosen by the Minister, is an acknowledgment of the imperfect constitution of that body, and is the most conclusive argument for Reform. This is very ingeniously argued, and I do not see how it can be answered. You admit the advantage of the Directors recording, as Mr. Fox proposed, their reasons for doing or forbearing to do certain acts, provided such reasons be made public. Under Mr. Fox's bill would not those reasons have been made public as often as Parliament chose to call for them? If Parliament neglected its duty that was no fault of the Bill. You are I think a little too severe when you speak of the rare occurrence of parliamentary influence with knowledge and talent, in all places where much either of money or power is to be enjoyed. If money and power were the only things desirable to man your conclusion could not be denied, but while public opinion and public sympathy are so much valued by all ranks of men, sufficient motives exist for the acquirement of knowledge and talent independent of the power and money which

[1] *History of British India*, vol. II, p. 698.

they may chance to bring along with them. Would not theory
lead us to expect that the sanction of public opinion would
have most weight with those who had no other object of
ambition?

In the Government of so distant a country as India, connected with us as it is by very peculiar ties, there must be the
greatest difficulty in securing it against misrule. The people
of England, who are governors, have an interest opposed to
that of the people of India, who are the governed, in the
same manner as the interest of a despotic sovereign is opposed
to that of his people. In both cases there are no other limits
to the abuse of power but those which the Governors themselves chuse to impose. That apathy of the public which you
deplore as one of the causes of bad government in the country
in which almost all their interests are centered, acts with
tenfold effect when the question is respecting a foreign
government which is chiefly regarded as it will afford revenues
and power. On the mal administration of such a government
public opinion will not be very active and will therefore not
much tend to the correction of abuses. I hope I shall see in
your last volume your opinion of the sort of Government
which it would be wise to establish for India. This would
afford a practical application of your principles.—

I have only left myself room to communicate some
afflicting events which have lately pressed hard on my family
in London, and I am sure that you will sympathise with the
sufferers. Mrs. Samuda[1] had to witness the gradual decay by
consumption of her eldest son whom she finally lost about
6 weeks since. This was not her only affliction for during his
illness her youngest child was seized with fever and in a few
days was consigned to the grave. The admirable manner in
which she felt and endeavoured to conquer her feelings

[1] Ricardo's sister Hannah.

30 Dec. 1817 on these melancholy events endeared her more than ever to every one that knew her, but she had yet in common with the rest of her brothers and sisters another most painful trial to endure. Mr. Keyser's[1] affairs it appears have not lately been prosperous which had such an effect on his mind as to produce every symptom of permanent insanity. Happily however for his family this will not be his fate for after a few days of violence he was attacked with violent and frequent epileptic fits which in less than a week closed his mortal existence,—he died on saturday last. You may judge of the severe trial which his poor wife has endured. All that the kindest sympathy could bestow she has received from my excellent brothers and sisters.   Ever Y^{rs}

D Ricardo

247. RICARDO TO MILL[2]

Gatcomb Park
6th Jan^y [1818][3]

My dear Sir

6 Jan. 1818   Having finished your third volume[4] I must again write to you, to say that you have in my opinion sustained your reputation to the last, or rather in this volume exceeded it. From the manner in which you have, in the 6th Chap^r, treated of Courts of Justice, and Police, I begin to think that you are correct in an opinion I have heard you give, that the most intricate parts of Political Economy might be made familiar to the people's understanding, for you have expressed yourself with a clearness and precision that can not fail to be understood by the least attentive reader; and a

---

[1] Ricardo's brother-in-law.
[2] Addressed: 'James Mill Esqr / Ford Abbey / Chard / Somerset-shire'.

MS in Mill-Ricardo papers.
[3] In MS '1817'; docketed by Mill '1818'.
[4] Of *History of British India.*

subject which appears at first view so difficult is within the grasp of a moderate share of talents.

Nothing can be more satisfactory than your review of Lord Wellesley's administration, and the insufficiency of his reasons for the treaty of Bassein. The steps by which we have made our progress in India appear to have been first to get our troops into the dominions of our allies for a stipulated monthly payment, and then under various pretences to obtain all the powers of Government. Your arguments are convincing that the first step was the most injurious to the people of India, as it took away from the native governments the salutary dread of insurrection, and therefore opened the door to all manner of misrule and oppression. If Lord Wellesley had continued in the Government of India he would have soon discovered that the Peshwa's administration was radically bad, and he would not have been at a loss for excuses to take it into his own hands, and thus this system might have been extended till all India was under British rule. The difficulty of the question seems to be this. In the first step, stipulating that your ally shall have the service of your troops in consideration of his paying for it, there may be a want of policy and wisdom, but there appears to be no injustice,—but in the second step there is the greatest injustice although it is demonstrable that it may greatly promote the happiness of the people. That which is free from the taint of injustice is the cause of misery to the people,— that which is manifestly unjust is the cause of their happiness. Are we to fix our eyes steadily on the end, the happiness of the governed, and pursue it at the expence of those principles which all men are agreed in calling virtuous? If so might not Lord Wellesley, or any other ruler, disregard all the engagements of his predecessors, and by force of arms compel the submission of all the native powers of India if he

6 Jan. 1818 could shew that there was a great probability of adding to the happiness of the people by the introduction of better instruments of government. If he accomplished this end at the expence of much treasure to England I do not think the plea would be admitted by a British House of Commons however freely chosen. The difficulty of the doctrine of expediency or utility is to know how to balance one object of utility against another—there being no standard in nature, it must vary with the tastes, the passions and the habits of mankind. This is one of the subjects on which I require to be enlightened.—

Your remarks on the effects of indigence are excellent, it is the cause of selfishness, cruelty and crime.

One great cause of the misrule in India appears to be the little interest taken by the English in Indian affairs. This has been the constant complaint in Parliament. I hope your book will tend to remove this apathy. The difficulty of punishing offenders made the subject distasteful in the House of Commons.—

I shall want you when we meet to give me some additional reasons for the following opinions expressed in the pages stated. 106. How can the enormities committed by an agent prove the corruption of the person appointing that agent? 295. Did not most of the difficulties of the Zemindars arise from their inability to enforce the payment of rent? If that abuse had been removed would not the object have been obtained? 296 Did the Ryots pay a fixed rent to the Zemindars or did they not. If they did what is meant by the Zemindars farming out the lands by Auction at the end of the lease? 302 If the expence of justice falls on the dishonest litigator will it in any great degree prevent the honest man from seeking redress by law, if law is purely administered. 303. Is it a fair conclusion from your premises that the

chances of success to the honest and dishonest litigant are 6 Jan. 1818
equal? 304 I agree that the evil complained of exists, but in
the absence of absolute corruption in the judge, it appears
to me inconceivable, that granting every obstruction to
justice complained of, the expectation of success in the dishonest litigant can ever equal the like expectation of the
honest[1] litigant. 328 What a frightful obstruction to improvement does the immoral character of the people of India
present! 338 In your argument respecting the Zemindars
you contend that rich landholders are not eager after small
additions to their fortunes, and therefore will not improve
the cultivation of the land. On the same principle may it not
be contended that rich police officers would not be anxious
about the small gains from corruption? 502 If it be injustice
and robbery to take from any people more than the lowest
sum for which they can be defended, what business have the
English in India, unless it be to confer favours from a pure
principle of benevolence? 600–1 Do you not leave out of
your calculation the effects which would have resulted to
British Interests if the treaty of Bassein had not been made
and the country of the Peshwa had been forcibly wrested
from him by the Rajah of Berar and Scindia? 602 Is it right
to enumerate among the advantages of Scindia of which we
had no right to deprive him the expectations which he had
formed of obtaining justly or unjustly an influence in the
Government of the Peshwa which he did not then possess.
721 In the estimate of the revenue is any deduction made for
the provision established for the payment of the Nabob of
Arcot's debts? 723 Does not the expenditure of 15,551,000
include the interest of the debt contracted by Lord Wellesly?
Is not the Company's Capital included in the amount of
debts? Should any thing be allowed for a redemption fund?

[1] In MS 'dishonest'.

6 Jan. 1818 These are the passages which I have marked for enquiry.—
I have been particularly pleased with your observations on
the numerous or rather powerful sanctions necessary to an
efficient army—they shew the deepest reflection.—The same
army in France or in the service of Scindia would be stimulated to action by a very different set of motives. Another
observation which is very striking is that made in page 602
of the astonishing self delusion which prevents men from
seeing in their own acts those very qualities which they are
so loud in condemning in the acts of others. In Lord
Wellesley's conduct this self delusion almost surpasses belief.
Your arguments in favour of colonization are very satisfactory, and to me are particularly so, because they happen
to agree with the opinion which I had formed on that
subject.—On the whole then I am more than ever satisfied
that your labours have been eminently successful and that
you will be entitled to, and will receive an ample portion of
public approbation and esteem; at which no one will rejoice
more than

Y^{rs} ever

DAVID RICARDO

248. MᶜCULLOCH TO RICARDO[1]

Dear Sir   Edinburgh 13th Jany 1818

13 Jan. 1818   The bearer of this note, a man of good education and
of respectable character, having been reduced by the pressure
of the times to a situation of great difficulty and distress, had
been advised by some of his friends to publish a little work,

[1] Addressed: 'David Ricardo   marked: 'Hand by J. Laing
Esquire / Upper Brook Street /   Surgeon'.—MS in *R.P.*—*Letters*
Grosvenor Square / London' and   *of MᶜCulloch to Ricardo*, I.

giving an account of a voyage to Spitzbergen[1]—He has 13 Jan. 1818
already sold one edition, chiefly in this city and Glasgow,
which has enabled him to put his family into a somewhat
better state, and to pay of a few small debts; and has now
published another edition with the view of realizing a little
capital—He has taken this edition with him to London, and
I hope you will excuse the liberty I now take of recommending him to your patronage—The subscription of a
gentleman of such high respectability, and so well known in
the city of London and in the literary world, would be of the
greatest service to this poor man, and for these reasons I have
presumed to introduce Mr Laing to you—

I am with the greatest respect

Dear Sir

Your Mt Ob St

J. R. MᶜCULLOCH

David Ricardo Esqre

249. RICARDO TO TROWER[2]

[*Answered by* 254]

My Dear Trower
London 26 Jan? 1818

Your last kind letter[3] reached London before I arrived 26 Jan. 1818
there, and after performing a journey to Gatcomb, was again

[1] John Laing, *An Account of a Voyage to Spitzbergen; containing a Full Description of that Country, of the Zoology of the North, and of the Shetland Isles; with an Account of the Whale Fishery*, London, Mawman, 1815; 2nd ed., with slightly altered title, Edinburgh, Black, 1818; 3rd ed., Edinburgh, Tait, 1821. See *Edinburgh Review*, June 1818, Art. I. The book is dedicated to MᶜCulloch, who was probably related to the author, his mother being a Laing. On the tribulations of John Laing, see Historical MSS Commission, *Report on the MSS of J. B. Fortescue*, vol. x, p. 438.

[2] Addressed: 'Hutches Trower Esqr/Unsted Wood/Godalming' —not passed through the Post. MS at University College, London.—*Letters to Trower*, XVIII.

[3] Trower's letter is wanting.

26 Jan. 1818 brought to town in my pocket on the 15th inst. I should have answered it before but I have been incessantly employed in business that required my immediate attention. I heartily wish with you that we had chanced to fix our residences near to each other, that we might in the calm of the country, have pursued those discussions which on many occasions engaged our attention even in the tumultuous scenes where we were accustomed to meet, but where we had neither leisure, nor favourable opportunities, to make them so serviceable to us as we should have done amidst groves, and fields, undisturbed by the stimulating interests which formerly engrossed us. I remember well the pleasure I felt, when I first discovered that you, as well as myself, was a great admirer of the work of Adam Smith, and of the early articles on Political Economy which had appeared in the Edinburgh Review. Meeting as we did every day, these afforded us often an agreeable subject for half an hour's chat, when business did not engage us. Every thing that has since occurred has stimulated me to give a great deal of attention to such subjects: first, the Bullion controversy, and then my intimacy with Mill and Malthus, which was the consequence of the part I took in that question. My discussions with Malthus have been innumerable, and in my eagerness to convince him that he was wrong, on some points on which we differed, I was led into a deeper consideration of many parts of the subject than I had before given them, and though I have failed to convince him, and may not have satisfied others, I have convinced myself; and think that I have a very consistent theory in my own mind. This theory I have attempted to commit to paper that I might communicate it to others, but owing to my little knowledge of the art of composition I have not succeeded to my wish, and I now quite despair of ever knowing how to wield that admirable instrument for conveying information.

The new publication of Malthus, which I mentioned to you,[1] is not yet in the press. It has no connection with any former work of his. Among other things it is to contain some examination of my opinions, to which I wish them to be submitted. He has a great aversion to controversy,— I hope this aversion may not induce him to withhold it. The Review of his Essay in the Quarterly[2] is I think well done, and I am glad to see that so popular a Review is at length employed in advocating the cause of truth. The reveries of Southey on questions of Political Economy[3] will I hope no longer be admitted in any respectable journal. He quite mistakes his talent when he writes on such subjects, and is really no more deserving of attention than Mr. Owen or any other visionary. The writer of the article in the Quarterly I suppose you know is Mr. Sumner, a clergyman, the author of a clever book on the Records of the Creation, in which Malthus' system is not only defended for its truth, but for its affording proofs of the benevolence and goodness of the Creator.[4] Mr. Sumner's work was reviewed in the Quarterly,[5] and report says that Mr. Weyland was the reviewer.—He has of course carried his own erroneous principles into the Review, and does not do the author justice.—I am sorry to hear that Mr. Sumner does not intend writing any more on

[1] Above, p. 221, n. 2.
[2] *Quarterly Review*, July 1817, Art. IV.
[3] The latest article by Robert Southey, the poet, on political economy had been one on 'The Poor' in the *Quarterly Review* for April 1816; it concluded with the maxim, 'as certain as the laws of nature and of God', that 'the more they [the people] multiply, the greater will be the wealth, and strength, and security of the state'.

[4] John Bird Sumner, *A Treatise on the Records of the Creation, and on the Moral Attributes of the Creator; with particular reference to the Jewish History, and to the Consistency of the Principle of Population with the Wisdom and Goodness of the Deity*, 2 vols., London, Hatchard, 1816. The author was afterwards Archbishop of Canterbury.
[5] Oct. 1816, Art. III.

26 Jan. 1818 Political Economy—his whole attention in future is to be devoted to the study of Theology. Whether in this latter pursuit he will have an equal chance of benefiting mankind, as in the former, I have great doubts, or rather I have no doubt at all; and I very much regret that the science will no longer be assisted by his distinguished talents.

I would gladly compound for such a change in the Poor Laws as should restore them to what appears to have been the original intention in framing them; namely, the relieving only the aged and infirm and under some circumstances, children. Any change would be an improvement which had not a tendency to increase the evil which it proposes to remedy. The present plan creates objects of distress, and these must necessarily go on increasing in a geometrical ratio.

No man in his sober senses would wish for any sudden alteration of the present plan. The great object should be to teach the labouring classes that they must themselves provide for those casualties to which they are exposed from occasional variations in the demand for particular manufactured goods, and which should not be the subject of legislation. A man's wages should, and would on a really good system, be sufficient not only to maintain himself and family when he is in full work, but also to enable him to lay up a provision in a Savings Bank for those extraordinary calls which you mention.

To relieve the poor by any *extended* exercise of private charity would hardly be less objectionable than the evil of which we now complain. Your objection to this tax, or any of the taxes being paid by voluntary contribution, is most sound,—the selfish would pay nothing, and the whole burden would fall on the generous and humane. Great evils however result from the idea which the Poor Laws inculcate that the poor have a *right* to relief. In the British Review which I send you I think you will find a good article on this subject.[1]

I have gone through my friend Mill's book "The History of India." It is not a mere dry detail of facts, but contains ample discussions on the most important points, which refer not only to the Government of India, but to the Government of every other country. His observations on Legislation, on Law, and on the rules of Evidence, are very interesting, and he shews most triumphantly, I think, that the administration of Justice on which so much of the happiness of every people depends, is still very deficient in these countries which are considered the most civilized in Europe. I do not see what plausible objections can be made to him. Hastings' Trial, Mr. Fox's and Mr. Pitt's India bills give him very good opportunities for entering into these discussions. He endeavours to refute the prevailing opinion that the Hindus are now, or ever have been a highly civilized people, and enters very fully into an examination of the state of their religious opinions, their customs, their laws, their literature, and their knowledge of the arts and sciences, with a view to prove that they have never made more than the first steps in refinement and civilization. I am exceedingly pleased with the work,— it is replete with entertainment and instruction, and cannot fail to be acknowledged as a proof of great talents in the author. By special favour I had it before the maps and indexes were completed, and therefore several weeks before it was published. Mrs. Ricardo joins with me in kind regards to you and Mrs. Trower.

Very sincerely Yours
DAVID RICARDO

[1] See above, p. 219.

250. RICARDO TO MALTHUS[1]

My dear Sir   London 30 Jan.ʸ [1818][2]

30 Jan. 1818   During your visit in London next week I hope you will
stay with us in Brook Street, and I am commissioned by Mrs.
Ricardo to add her solicitations to mine to induce Mrs.
Malthus to accompany you.—

Lord King,[3] Mr. Whishaw and you have done me a great
deal of honour in making my work the subject of your discussions, but I confess it fills me with astonishment to find
that you think, and from what you say[4] they appear to agree
with you, that the measure of value is not what I have represented it to be; but that *natural price*, as well as *market price*,
is determined by the demand and supply,—the only difference being that the former is governed by the average and
permanent demand and supply, the latter by the accidental
and temporary.—In saying this do you mean to deny that
facility of production will lower natural price and difficulty
of production raise it? Will not these effects be produced;
after a very short interval, although the absolute demand and
supply, or the proportion of one to the other, should remain
permanently the same? At any rate then demand and supply
are not the sole regulators of price. I should be glad to
understand what Lord King and you mean by supply and
demand. However abundant the demand it can never permanently raise the price of a commodity above the expence
of its production, including in that expence the profits of the

---

[1] Addressed: 'To / The Revᵈ
T. R. Malthus / East India College /
Hertford'.
    MS at Albury.—*Letters to Mal-
thus*, LXV.
[2] In MS '1817'; postmark, 1818.
[3] The author of *Thoughts on the*

Restriction of Payments in Specie,
1803, a pamphlet to the merit of
which, according to Romilly,
Whishaw had 'contributed something' (*Memoirs of Sir Samuel
Romilly*, 1840, vol. II, p. 105).
[4] Malthus's letter is wanting.

producers. It seems natural therefore to seek for the cause of the variation of permanent price in the expences of production. Diminish these and the commodity must finally fall, increase them and it must as certainly rise. What has this to do with demand?

I may be so foolishly partial to my own doctrine, that I may be blind to its absurdity. I know the strong disposition of every man to deceive himself in his eagerness to prove a favourite theory, yet I cannot help viewing this question as a truth which admits of demonstration and I am full of wonder that it should admit of a doubt. If indeed this fundamental doctrine of mine were proved false I admit that my whole theory falls with it, but I should not on that account be satisfied with the measure of value which you would substitute in its place.

I am sorry that you have determined not to publish this spring.

I have not seen Torrens, and do not know what his intentions are respecting the work which he promised to give to the public.—[1]

Sir James Mackintosh is indeed a great acquisition in more respects than one to your College.[2] It must be particularly agreeable to you.

I thank you for your congratulations on the honor [which][3] has been conferred on me by the appointment [to] the office of Sheriff—an honour which I could well have

---

[1] Cp. above, p. 35, n. 2.
[2] He had been appointed Professor of General Polity and the Laws of England. 'Poor Mackintosh, I am heartily sorry for him, but his situation at Hertford will suit very well (pelting and contusions always excepted.) He should stipulate for *pebble money*, as it is there technically called, or an annual pension in case he is disabled by the pelting of the students!' (Sydney Smith to Whishaw, 7 Jan. 1818, in *The 'Pope' of Holland House*, p. 313.)
[3] MS torn here and below.

30 Jan. 1818 dispensed with. Under all circumstances I think it best not to offer an objection to it.—

I wish you were of our party to day. Mr. Whishaw Mr. Smyth, Mr. Mallet, Mr. Sharp and Mr. Warburton dine with me.

I am glad that you have heard Mill's book favourably spoken of. I hope it may be as well thought of by others as it is by me.

Very truly Yours
DAVID RICARDO

251. GRENFELL TO RICARDO[1]

My dear Sir   Cassiobury[2] 15 Febry 1818

15 Feb. 1818   I forgot to tell you before I came away yesterday that my *friend* will *agree* to nothing short of the *Five*—*without* a Guarantee[3]—This appears enormous.

You have seen that Vansittart did away what he had before said as to the payment to the Bank of the 6 Mill. *before July*.[4]

Will you dine with me on Wednesday at Seven—and meet Tierney—Calcraft[5] &c

Yours very truly
P G.

I shall be in Town tomorrow by two.

[1] Addressed: 'David Ricardo Esq / Upper Brook Street / Grosvenor Square'. Franked by Grenfell, from Watford. MS in *R.P.*

[2] Cassiobury House, in Hertfordshire, seat of the Earl of Essex.

[3] £5000 for a seat in Parliament without guarantee of re-election in the event of an early dissolution; cp. below, pp. 276 and 355.

[4] On 13 February, in the House of Commons, Tierney and Grenfell having reminded the Chancellor of the Exchequer that he had formerly declared that the loan would be repaid to the Bank before 5 April, he replied that it would be repaid 'in the course of the year' (*Hansard*, XXXVII, 419–23).

[5] John Calcraft (1765–1831), M.P. for Rochester.

252. MALTHUS TO RICARDO[1]

E I Coll. Feb[y] 24th [1818]

My dear Sir,

Your letter[2] did not reach me till this morning, from which I conclude, that notwithstanding its date of the 21st, it did not leave Town till the 23rd. 24 Feb. 1818

We are engaged to dinner tomorrow with Sir James M.[3] at Mr. Le Bas's; and Mr. George Eckersall and Miss Bray[4] being with us shall have our beds full in the evening, so that probably you will prefer coming on saturday, when we shall have ample room, and be most happy to see you.

I am surprised, with you that Major Torrens should puzzle himself so long with his peculiar objections to your measure of value. For myself, I own, I am quite satisfied with your own concessions; and if as you yourself acknowledge, taxation, foreign materials, and the different quantities of fixed and circulating capitals employed, all prevent the exchangeable value of commodities from being determined by the labour which they have cost in production, I should say, it followed that your theory was only true *caeteris paribus*, which might be equally said of the cost of the materials.

Given the wages of labour, the profits of stock, and the taxes, the exchangeable value of commodities will vary with the cost of the materials.

I am glad however that Mill remains staunch to the *true* faith; and I assure you I have a high opinion of his knowledge and talents since I have read the first volume of his work on India, though I fear it is not very popular.

---

[1] Addressed: 'D. Ricardo Esqr / Upper Brook Street. / Grosvenor Square.' Postmark, 1818. MS in *R.P.*

[2] Ricardo's letter is wanting.
[3] Mackintosh.
[4] Malthus's niece.

24 Feb. 1818   We shall fully expect you to dinner on saturday. You must take another opportunity of coming down when Mackintosh is with us. He would be very happy to take a chaise with you some wednesday morning. But it is now too late for tomorrow. He is obliged to be here before twelve on wednesday morning.

Mrs. M joins me in kind regards to Mrs. Ricardo.

Ever truly Yours
T R MALTHUS.

253. WAKEFIELD TO RICARDO[1]

Pall Mall   Monday morning
feb: 28   1818

Dear Sir

28 Feb. 1818   Mr. Daniel Moore of Lincolns Inn—whom I believe you know—yesterday evening sent a gentleman Mr. Marnell to offer a seat in the ensuing parliament. Mr. Marnell states the Borough to be 260 miles from London to have 76 voters —who are discontented with their present patron and have deputed a confidential person to London to find one[2]— the terms asked are £3000 for each seat not to be paid until the day after the party is beyond the power of petition—except £100 from each candidate to defray the expences of a dinner and some charges which have already been incurred. Mr. Marnell has engaged one seat and is to be with me at 11 OClock to day—

---

[1] MS in *R.P.*

[2] Mallet describes a change which was gradually taking place in the constitution of Parliament. In corrupt boroughs, the 'independent interest', that is the voters, coalesced against the Patron, and sold their votes to the best bidder. 'The *independent interest* is the interest opposed in these places to the interest of the Patron; but the word independent is not by any means descriptive of it, for generally speaking it is the *interest of Money* opposed to the interest of Landed property and aristocratical influence.' (MS Diary, entry 27 Oct. 1819.)

Mr. Mill tells me that you are going to Hertford to day, 28 Feb. 1818
but I hope there will be time for us to meet first as Mr.
Marnell states the agent to be in town and seeking to close
with the first person who is willing.

I am the moment after writing this going to Mr. Moore
to learn the degree of confidence which may be placed in
Mr. Marnell—should that be such as I expect from Mr.·
Moore having sent him to me—I then think it will be
worth the risk of the £100 and minute enquiry.

I am

Most faithfully yours

EDWARD WAKEFIELD

David Ricardo Esq.

254. TROWER TO RICARDO[1]

[*Reply to* 249.—*Answered by* 255]

Unsted Wood—Godalming
Febry 28—1818.

My Dear Ricardo—

Having first thanked you for your last kind letter, and 28 Feb. 1818
for the Papers you sent me, I must, without loss of time,
congratulate you upon the *high Honors* with which you are
at present surrounded, and which, I doubt not, you *yourself
will Honor*: I shall be curious to obtain from you, by and by,
some account of the duties of this *High Office*, as I have the
misfortune to be in this black list for 1820.[2]—I was in hope,
I should have escaped, but the fates have ordained it otherwise.—If you should happen to have a contested election for
Glocestershire, your powers and your duties will then be
displayed in full array!—I think myself lucky in having

---

[1] Addressed: 'To / David Ricardo
Esqr / Upper Brook Street / Grosvenor Square'.

MS in *R.P.*
[2] Ricardo was Sheriff of Gloucestershire for 1818.

28 Feb. 1818 escaped such an evil at least. Is it an expencive office in your County? ours, I believe, costs the high Sheriff about 6. or 7. hundred pounds.—

I have read with attention the Article in the British Review[1]. You need not be afraid of any harm your antagonist there has done you. He is much too violent in his language, and much too hasty in his conclusions, to entitle his view of the subject to attention. And I should rather say, it was fortunate to have been so weakly attacked, as it has produced so admirable a defence from your northern ally. The writer in the British has taken a very imperfect view of your theory; he has reasoned merely upon its immediate effects, and has not pushed, as he should have done, his enquiries to its more remote and general effects. He cannot deny the *truth* of your *principles*, yet he argues against their necessary effects; and not seeing so far as you do, he entangles himself in his own inconsistencies. Believe me, you do not do yourself justice, in attributing any want of success in convincing your opponents to the manner in which you have communicated your ideas, or to want of knowledge in the art of composition—I perfectly agree in what your Scotch friend has said upon that subject. Be assured, the difficulty is in the *nature of the enquiry*, which requires a more close and constant attention than most readers are disposed, or perhaps capable, of devoting to any subject.—If there be anything, which I should wish different in the manner of treating it, it would be the making a greater point of *defining accurately* and *rigidly*, the *terms employed*—The Equivocality of language is the pregnant source of the endless contests that arise upon all scientific and abstruse subjects; and has been especially so in all the discussions upon political economy.— In spite of the formality, or *apparent affectation*, of such a

---

[1] 'and Scotch Paper' is del. here. Cp. above, p. 219–20.

mode of treating the question, I would begin with a *copious*
chapter of clear and concise definitions (that is as clear and
concise as the nature of the subject will admit,) just as if I was
about to demonstrate a mathematical problem. For I firmly
believe, that the subject is capable of being demonstrated.
I hope Malthus will discuss the points in which he differs
from you, in his new publication; as I always find the most
effectual mode of thoroughly understanding a question, is to
grapple with the objections that are urged against it.—

Have you read Burkbecks short account of his expedition
to the back settlements of America in the Illinois Country?[1]
It is interesting and amusing, and shews what I was not
prepared to see, that the emigration from what is now termed
old America to the new settlements, are even more numerous
than those from Europe.

You excite my curiosity to read your friend Mill's account
of India; but it is so costly a publication in its present bulky
state,[2] that I must wait patiently till it is cut down to an
octavo edition.—

Does not your pulse beat quicker now you learn, that
18000 squares miles of Ice have disappeared? This curious
subject opens a new field for speculation; and emboldens one
to look forward to those good old times when a man *literally*
earned his bread by *the sweat of his brow*.—

I begin to think of covering the sides of some of my
sloping hills with the clambering vine; and who knows but
the time may come when we shall sacrifice to Bacchus in
British Burgundy, instead of poisoning ourselves with
Portuguese Port!—I hope to be in Town, for a short time,
in the course of the Spring, when of course I shall have the

---

[1] Morris Birkbeck, *Notes on a
Journey in America from the Coast
of Virginia to the Territory of*   *Illinois*, London, Ridgway, 1818.
[2] 3 vols. in 4to, priced 6 guineas.

28 Feb. 1818   pleasure of seeing you—I will then carry to Town with me
the publications you have lent me, unless you should wish
to have them sooner.—Mrs. Trower desires to join with me
in kind remembrances to Mrs. Ricardo and family, and
believe me my Dear Friend

yours very truly,

HUTCHES TROWER.

Have you read the Bishop of Landaffs Memoirs?[1] They
are very interesting. He is a man very much after my own
heart. I admire and love his sturdy independence; but, at the
same time, think he frequently carried it too far. He did not
think it worth while to attend to the "suaviter in modo
fortiter in re". Adieu. H. T.

255. RICARDO TO TROWER[2]

[Reply to 254]

London 22 March 1818

My dear Trower

22 March 1818   I thank you for your congratulations on the occasion
of the high honours which I have attained. The hour is fast
approaching when I shall have to appear before the Judges,
arrayed in the masquerade suit which I have been obliged to
provide. The Assizes for our County commence on the
1ˢᵗ April. I hope I shall sustain my high office with becoming
dignity—the difficulty is much increased by my being so
much a stranger in the county, never having been present on
any public occasion whatever. From this moment however

[1] *Anecdotes of the Life of Richard
Watson, D.D., Bishop of Llandaff,
written by himself at different
intervals, and revised in 1814*, ed.
by his son, 4to, London, Cadell,
1817.

[2] Addressed: 'Hutches Trower
Esqʳ/Unsted Wood/Godalming'.
MS at University College, Lon-
don.—*Letters to Trower*, XIX.

I may date my public life; as the ice once broken, I shall not 22 March 1818
fail to meet my neighbours 2 or 3 times a year at Gloucester.
The expence of the office in our county does not exceed
£450, so that on that score I shall be better off than you. You
may depend on having all the advantage which my experience
can give you in the way of instruction previous to your
election.

The perusal of the article in the British Review, has called
forth much too favourable a criticism from you on my book.
I am well aware of its great deficiencies which I much fear
I shall not be able to remedy in a new edition, if it should be
called for. Your suggestion of a copious chapter of clear and
concise definitions would be of great use, but it requires
a degree of precision and accuracy beyond what I could
furnish. My scotch friend continues every now and then to
allude to my work with the greatest respect,[1] and in an interview which I lately had with Lord Grenville I received from
him the most flattering testimony of his favourable opinion
of my endeavours to throw additional light on the science
of Political Economy. Praise from Lord Grenville on this
subject is particularly gratifying to me, because he has given
many proofs of his persevering attention to it, and on all
great discussions, of the correctness of his opinions.—

Birkbeck's account of his expedition to the back settlements of America is highly interesting—I hope he will from
time to time furnish us with an account of the progress of the
little colony which he will soon have about him.[2] His success
will not fail to induce many from Europe to follow his
example, and there is some reason to fear that the artificial
state of things in England in consequence of our enormous

[1] McCulloch, in the *Scotsman.*
[2] Later in the year appeared
Morris Birkbeck's *Letters from*

Illinois, London, Taylor and
Hessey.

22 March 1818 debt will co-operate with the natural advantages of a new and fertile country to attract capital to a place where profits are so high that with moderate industry a certain provision may be made for a family. I am told that many individuals with an aggregate capital of £100,000 are preparing to follow Mr. Birkbeck to the Illinois Country.—

It is not expected that the dissolution of Parliament will take place before Octr. It is said that no attempt will be made to increase taxation, so that our nominal sinking fund of 15 millions, will be really reduced to 3 millions. Mr. Vansittart had a ridiculous project I hear of creating a new circulating medium and legal tender, called stock notes, which were to be advanced, without any limit, on stock, at the rate of £50 for every £100 stock. If such a plan had been carried into execution it was possible that our money might have been increased to 400 millions. I am told that he has now abandoned it, and indeed it is difficult to believe that he ever entertained so ridiculous a project, tho' my authority for the fact is no less than that of Mr. Tierney.[1]

If I could, without much trouble, get into the New Parliament I would. I should neither be Whig nor Tory but should be anxiously desirous of promoting every measure which should give us a chance of good government. This I think [will][2] never be obtained without a reform in Parliament. I do not go so far as Mr. Bentham, I regret that his

[1] Vansittart had not yet abandoned his project, and, on 9 April 1818, he introduced in the House of Commons a measure authorizing bankers to issue notes 'secured upon a deposit of public Funds, or other Government securities'; this idea, he said, had been suggested to him by a pamphlet by Ambrose Weston *(Two Letters, Describing a Method of Increasing* the Quantity of Circulating-Money: Upon a new and solid Principle, London, 1799, reprinted in *Pamphleteer*, 1817 and as a separate pamphlet, 1818). Owing to the strong opposition encountered the bill was withdrawn on 30 April. (See *Hansard*, XXXVII, 1253–4 and XXXVIII, 410.)

[2] MS torn.

book[1] is so full of invective against those from whom he differs, yet I am convinced by his arguments. There is no class in the community whose interests are so clearly on the side of good government as the people,—all other classes may have private interests opposed to those of the people. The great problem then is to obtain security that the representatives shall be chosen by the unbiassed good sense of the people. The suffrage must be extensive to secure the voters against corrupt influence and the voting must be by ballot for the same reason. There must be an intimate union between representatives and their constituents in order to destroy the dependence of the former on the executive government. The elections should not be less than triennial. Mr. Burke has said that the people may err but it can never be from design.[2] The ability of representatives when their interests are opposed to those of their constituents is a great evil because it can only be employed in promoting objects which are mischievous to the latter. If the suffrage is not universal there can be no danger of anarchy. A man with a very small property can have no wish for confusion if he be actuated by those motives which have always been found to influence mankind. I have only partially read the memoirs of the Bishop of Landaff and like much what I have read. He was a reformer and saw pretty clearly the evils of our present representation but I doubt whether he as clearly saw the remedy.

I am glad to hear that we shall soon see you in London. Mrs. Ricardo joins with me in kind remembrances to Mrs. Trower. Believe me

Ever most truly Y^{rs}

DAVID RICARDO

[1] Bentham's *Plan of Parliamentary Reform, in the Form of a Catechism, with Reasons for each Article, with an Introduction, shewing the Necessity of Radical, and* the *Inadequacy of Moderate, Reform,* London, Hunter, 1817.
[2] *Thoughts on the Cause of the Present Discontents,* 1770; in Burke's *Works,* 1792, vol. I, p. 416.

256. RICARDO TO MALTHUS[1]

[Answered by 258]

London 25 May 1818

My dear Sir

25 May 1818   I have again to regret that I shall not have you as an inmate of my house on your next visit to London. Sylla has left us; but Osman, his wife, child, and nurse, are coming immediately—these, with the Clutterbucks, will exhaust all our resources in the way of house room. I am therefore deprived of a pleasure which I had promised myself in your and Mrs. Malthus' company during your stay in London. I hope however that you will be our daily visitors, or as often as engagements will permit. I trust that those on our part will be exhausted before you come, for at no period have I led so dissipated a life as during this season. The King of Clubs will meet on the 6th. Let me know whether Mrs. Malthus and you will favor us with your company on the 8th, as we should be glad to ask a few friends to meet you on that day.—

The general opinion here is that Parliament will be dissolved immediately after the prorogation, but as the election in that case will interfere with the Circuit I cannot believe that ministers will chuse so inconvenient a time.—

To morrow evening there is to be a long debate in the House of Lords on the Bank Restriction Bill, on which occasion Lord Grenville means to speak. Lord King mentioned to me his idea of proposing that the Bank should be forbid making any dividend on their stock while the price of gold was above the mint price. I have no doubt that practically such a measure would operate a reduction of the cur-

---

[1] Addressed: 'To/The Revd T.R.   MS at Albury.—*Letters to Mal-*
Malthus/East India College/Hert-   *thus*, LXVI.
ford'.

rency and its rise to par, but if the Bank Directors were 25 May 1818 obstinate it might be attended with the most serious consequences to widows, orphans, and others who might depend on the Bank Dividends only for their support.

My walks with Mill continue almost daily—I hope you will sometimes honour us with your company when in London. We could make a very tolerable reformer of you in six walks if your prejudices be not too strongly fixed. Indeed I should expect to find that our differences were not very great, as if you are favourable to reform at all, and that I believe you are, we should agree on all the important principles.—Sir James Mackintosh has been reading Bentham [1] and was just beginning to give me his opinion of the book when we were interrupted. I hope I shall find another opportunity of hearing his sentiments, which I am very eager to do. In a conversation which I yesterday had with Sharp he told me what he conceived Sir James' sentiments on reform to be. If he is correct I do not think that Sir James and I should be so much opposed to each other as he now thinks [2].—

Mrs. Ricardo joins with me in kind regards to Mrs. Malthus.

Very truly Yours
DAVID RICARDO

[1] The copy of *Plan of Parliamentary Reform*, presented by Bentham to Mackintosh, which is in the British Museum (8007. ee. 10), bears at the end this MS note: 'Read in the Hall at Haileybury Saturday 16 May 1818 from 10 A.M. to 3 P.M. J. Mackintosh'.

[2] For Mackintosh's opinions see his article in the *Edinburgh Review*, Dec. 1818, Art. VIII, where he attacked all of Bentham's proposals for Parliamentary Reform, and upheld the existing system of representation. Cp. below, VIII, 328, n. 1.

257. WHISHAW TO RICARDO[1]

My dear Sir

27 May 1818   I am sorry to hear from Mr Abercromby[2] that you have any concern with Stafford, and am afraid from what he says that you have no certain prospect of a Seat in the next Parliament at the General Election which is now fast approaching. I have been out of town lately, which has prevented me from calling or enquiring after you. But I had understood from Mr Vizard[3] that you had some prospect of Wooton Basset. I am afraid that my advice or suggestions, at present, can be of little use—but, if you think my opinion worth having on any of these occasions, I hope you will apply to me without scruple. I am so circumstanced to-day that it will be impossible for me to call on you; but I shall be at Mrs Weddle's[4] tomorrow, and will look in upon you in the evening

I remain

Y[rs] most truly,

J. Whishaw

Lincolns Inn
Wednesday May 27th [1818][5]

I was at the E I College last week. All was very quiet, and the Vacation commences immediately—but the Malthus's remain there till the 5th or 6th of next month, and then go into Surry.

---

[1] MS in *R.P.*
[2] James Abercromby(1776–1858), M.P. for Calne, afterwards Speaker of the House of Commons; created Baron Dunfermline in 1839.
[3] William Vizard, the Queen's Solicitor during her trial in 1820.

[4] A 'most agreeable old lady, sister to Lady Rockingham' (*Life and Letters of Maria Edgeworth*, vol. 1, p. 211).
[5] Omitted in MS. The General Election took place in June and July 1818.

258. MALTHUS TO RICARDO[1]

[Reply to 256]

My dear Sir,   E I Coll May 31ˢᵗ 1818.

The bustle of the Directors on thursday, and an un-   31 May 1818
expected engagement on friday, in the afternoon when I
generally write my letters, prevented me, (quite contrary to
my intention) from answering your former letter before I
received the latter.[2]

I am much afraid that Mrs. Ricardo has been kindly putting
herself to some inconvenience to receive us, when there was
no sort of occasion for it. Mrs. Malthus on account of having
the children with her, whom she meant to leave with Mrs.
Bray, could not have staid in Town more than two days, in
her way into Surrey, and these she has now engaged to spend
with her sister Mrs. Wynne at Mrs. Baillie's; and with regard
to myself, you know a *single* man may be any where. I hope
therefore Mrs. Ricardo has not made any changes or new
arrangements in her bed rooms on our account. Mr. and
Mrs. Wynne leave us on wednesday. Mrs. Malthus will
either go with Mrs. Wynne or join her the next day, and
set off for Surrey on saturday. I shall be in Town I believe
on thursday, and stay perhaps a week. If you have a Batchelors
room quite vacant, without any removals, I will take it with
great pleasure, but not otherwise. At all events I will dine
with you on monday, and Mrs. Malthus will be most happy
to join me, if by any accident, (which I think not probable)
she should stay in Town till that time.

What do you think of Lord Lauderdale's Protest?[3] He
certainly does not understand the nature of a Seignorage.

[1] Addressed: 'D. Ricardo Esqr /
56. Upper Brook Street / Grosvenor Square'.
MS in *R.P.*
[2] The second letter is wanting.

[3] The Protests of Lord Lauderdale, on 22 and 27 May, against
the Bank Restriction Bill (*Journals
of the House of Lords*, 1817–1818,
pp. 678, 698); cp. above, I, 371.

31 May 1818   I am afraid I shall hardly be able to give six walks of three
hours each to Mr. Mill; but if I could, I doubt if I should be
quite converted. You know from experience that I am a
little obstinate, when I think I am right; but I hope I should
not shew any such disposition if I believed myself wrong.
Mrs. M joins me in kind regards to Mrs. Ricardo.

Ever most truly Yours

T Robᵀ Malthus.

259. TROWER TO RICARDO[1]

[Answered by 261]

Unsted Wood—Godalming
June 7—1818.

My Dear Ricardo

7 June 1818   As I know your inclination will not lead you to be
among the first to quit "the flaunting town," I think I may
safely venture to direct this letter to Brook Street; unless,
indeed, you should have posted away to assure the Electors
of —— that you are most anxious to devote your life to their
interests; and that you are the most incorruptible of Patriots!
If you should be engaged in any such good cause, my best
wishes attend your success; *taking it for granted*, that you are
not such a *radical reformer* as your friend Mill; and that you
would not support the notable resolutions of Sᴿ Francis
Burdett![2] Indeed I trust, that even Mill himself would have
shrunk from a participation of the Baronets extravagant
propositions.—I hear the scene they occasioned in the House
was very curious, and that Broughams retort was admirable.
The Game *he* is playing is evidently that of becoming leader

---

[1] Addressed: 'To / David Ricardo
Esqr / Upper Brook Street / Gros-
venor Square'.
MS in *R.P.*

[2] The Resolutions for a Reform
of Parliament, introduced on 2
June 1818.

of the opposition; and his talents will obtain for him that
honor, which he would never procure from the consent of
the party. I grieve to see the Restriction Bill was suffered to
pass with so little opposition.[1]—In the Commons there was
little or no struggle but in the Lords the Speeches of Lords
Grenville and Lauderdale appeared very good; and, upon
the whole, I liked Lord Lauderdales protests.[2]—When you
write pray let me know how your day went off at the former
Lord's.—We are to have a fierce contest for Surrey, and
canvassing has been going on actively in this neighbourhood.
Dennison[3] is the new Candidate. I shall vote for the old
Members, because, although I differ from Ministers in many
points, and disapprove much of their policy, yet, I am no
friend to triennial parliaments, and find it difficult to coalesce
with those, who deprecate the war, and would have secured
to Bonaparte his seat on the Throne of France.—

I have been strongly urged by some of my neighbours to
stand for Guildford; and, if it had entered into my plans,
I think it probable I might have succeeded, at no great
expence.—A seat in Parliament is an object well worthy a
man's ambition, and as such is not a matter of indifference to
me; but to enjoy it properly would require greater sacrifices
than are consistent with my circumstances and situation.—
I am surprised Ministers did not suffer the Parliament to run
out its time—They could not have lost by the delay, and
I think would have gained—As it is I hear the opposition
expect to gain 10 or 12 votes.—I should like to see a union
between the enlightened and moderate of both parties; and
sure I am, that in the present dearth of talent, you could not

[1] The bill for continuing the
restriction of cash payments had
been finally passed by the House
of Lords on 27 May.

[2] See above, p. 265, n. 3.
[3] W. J. Denison, a banker.

7 June 1818 find among our politicians more wisdom and virtue than are requisite for an efficient administration.—

Pray remember me kindly to Mill—I often think with pleasure of our walks in Kensington Gardens; and when I take my solitary stroll, feel the want of those active and intelligent minds, which amused and instructed me, and excited me to intellectual exertion. How true it is, we are the creatures of circumstances. In the society of men of letters we become enamoured with science, and ambition to be Philosophers. Living with Country Gentlemen, we become accustomed to rural pursuits, and I fear *must be contented* to become—Farmers!

Adieu My Dear Ricardo let me hear from you soon—and pray remember Mrs. Trower and myself very kindly to Mrs. Ricardo and your family and believe me

Yrs very affectionately

HUTCHES TROWER

260. RICARDO TO MALTHUS[1]

[Answered by 264]

London 24ᵗʰ June 1818

My dear Sir

24 June 1818   Your letter[2] arrived here whilst I was in Gloucestershire. I came to town last night, having on monday presided at the County Meeting, and made a return of our two members.

I thank you for your enquiries after the infant[3] that you left so ill. Its miseries lasted but a short time, for it died at

---

[1] Addressed: 'To / The Revᵈ T R Malthus/Albury/Guildford/ Surrey'.
MS at Albury.—*Letters to Malthus*, LXVII.

[2] Malthus's letter is wanting.

[3] The only child of Osman Ricardo.

2 oClock on the day you left London. Dr. Holland[1] was 24 June 1818
surprised at the rapidity with which the disease advanced,
but has since ascertained that it was entirely confined to the
bowels, and is indeed the complaint to which children are
most subject. Mrs. Osman Ricardo's distress was very great,
but I am happy to say that she soon became calm and resigned. In my journey to Gloucester I conveyed her home
on saturday last, and left her yesterday morning tolerably
well and comfortable.—

I believe it is now finally settled that I am not to be in
Parliament, and truly glad I am that the question is at any
rate settled, for the certainty of a seat could hardly compensate me for the disagreeables attending the negociation
for it. Mr. Clutterbuck's answer announced to me that the
seat he had in view for me was disposed of, and thus end my
dreams of ambition.

Having once consented to yield to the opinion of my
friends I let no opportunity slip of getting into the Honourable House, but I am fully persuaded that if I consult my
own happiness only I shall do wisely in stopping where I am.
It is easier to animadvert on the actions of others, than to act
with wisdom ourselves, and I strongly fear that I want both
the judgment and discretion which are requisite to make a
tolerable senator. I am surprised at the kindness and consideration with which my friends now treat me, and it would
be a great want of prudence to afford them more easy means
of sifting my claims.

I am equally pleased with you that Sir Samuel Romilly's
election is going on so well in Westminster, and more
pleased than you will be at Sir Francis Burdett's recent suc-

---

[1] Henry Holland (1788–1873),
M.D., F.R.S., a member of the
Council of the Geological Society.
On his acquaintance with Malthus
and Ricardo see his *Recollections
of Past Life*, London, 1872, p. 241.

24 June 1818 cess on the Poll.[1] Sir Francis is I think a consistent man.
I believe Bentham's book[2] has satisfied him that there would
be no danger in Universal Suffrage but his main object I am
sure is to get a real representative Government, and he would
think that object might be [obtain]ed[3] by stopping very
far short of Universal suffrage. [With] such opinions it is a
mere question of pru[dence] (as to the obtaining of his
object) whether he shall ask for the more, or the less extended suffrage. I agree with you that it would be more
prudent to ask for the less, and I agree also with you in
thinking that with our present experience we should not
venture on Universal Suffrage if it could be had.—I am glad
however to find that you think the election in Westminster
will afford us a fair sample of the sense of the nation.—
   I will take care that all demands against you shall be
faithfully discharged.—
   I have not left myself room to enter at any length into the
question of the comparative advantage of employing capital
in agriculture or on manufactures[4]. If by wealth you mean,

[1] The poll for returning two
members for Westminster was
open from 18 June to 4 July. The
candidates were Romilly for the
Whigs, Burdett for the Reformers, Maxwell for the Tories,
and Hunt for the Radicals. Burdett, whose vote in the first few
days of the poll had been far
below that of the Tory, had over-
taken him on 23 June, and steadily
increased his majority in the
following days. Romilly headed
the poll throughout the election
and was returned together with
Burdett.
   By nominating Romilly, himself a moderate Reformer, the
Whigs had caused a split in the
ranks of the Reformers: 'Ben-

tham who has been intimately
connected with Romilly near
forty years, refused to support
him and gave no vote. Mill voted
singly for Burdett; and Ricardo
at first hesitated, but at length
voted for Romilly, and gave him
a cordial support.' (Whishaw's
letter to Thomas Smith, 10 July
1818, in The 'Pope' of Holland
House, p. 200.) The Poll Book
for the Westminster election of
1818, published by Stockdale,
shows that Ricardo gave his two
votes to Burdett and Romilly
while Mill plumped for Burdett.
[2] Plan of Parliamentary Reform.
[3] MS torn here and below.
[4] 'but it appears to me that our
difference is occasioned by what

as I do, all those things which[1] are desirable to man, wealth, 24 June 1818
I think, would be most effectually increased by allowing corn
to be grown, or imported, as best suits those concerned in
the trade. You say that in the one case the corn obtained
would only be sufficient to support the workmen employed
and *pay fully the profits of stock*; and in the other case it
would pay in addition the increased amount of rent, and support an additional population proportioned to it. Now *if
the profits of stock to be paid fully* in one case would be much
greater both in value as defined by you, and in value, as
defined by me than in the other, it is evident that the
difference might not only equal the additional amount of rent,
but exceed it. I contend that the profits of stock would be
higher than this whole amount, if we consented to import
corn;[2] and therefore, although I will admit, that in the case
supposed, our wealth has increased by the increase of rent,
from 1793 to 1813, yet I would contend that if the trade had
been free, and corn had been imported in preference to growing it, under the new and improved circumstances of agriculture, our wealth would have increased in a still greater
ratio than it now has done.

Mrs. Ricardo begs to be kindly remembered to you.

Truly Y^{rs}

DAVID RICARDO

[1] I think the improper sense in which you use the word wealth' is del. here.

[1] 'contribute' is del. here.

[2] See the paragraph added in ed. 2 of *Principles*, above, I, 428–9.

261. RICARDO TO TROWER[1]

[*Reply to* 259.—*Answered by* 268]

London 27 June 1818

My dear Trower

27 June 1818   Your kind letter dated the 7th June ought not to have
remained so long unanswered, but various things have en-
croached on my time, and I have also been a journey to
Gatcomb, and Gloucester, for the purpose of returning the
members for our County to Parliament. As there was no
contest my task was easy, and we have, with our usual consistency, sent one member to vote with ministers, and another
to vote with the opposition, both I believe disposed im-
plicitly to follow their leaders.[2]

My own endeavors to get a seat in the House have not
been attended with success, but I believe that amongst all
those who are disappointed, in a similar manner, there is not
one more resigned than I am. I could meet with nothing
where I should not have had a contest, which I was exceedingly
unwilling to encounter, particularly as I should have been
thrown, alone, amongst persons with whom I was wholly
unacquainted, and therefore ignorant how far I might depend
on their statements. From all that I have seen I am more and
more convinced that the system requires great amendment—
that Parliament should really represent the good sense of the
nation—that the expences of election should be reduced to
the minimum—and that the choice should be made by ballot.
Under such a mode of choosing representatives we should
get rid of the disgusting spectacle of the lowest blackguards
in every town assembling about the Hustings, and insulting

---

[1] Addressed: 'Hutches Trower
Esq[re]/Unsted Wood/Godalming/
Surrey'.

MS at University College, London.—*Letters to Trower*, XX.
[2] Lord R. E. H. Somerset, Tory,
and Sir B. W. Guise, Whig.

in the grossest, and most cruel manner, those respectable candidates against whom their antipathies are excited. Why is such a man as Sir Murray Maxwell to be exposed to the disgraceful treatment which he has received?[1]—I am for Sir Sam! Romilly's system of Reform, as avowed to a gentleman whom he authorised to communicate it to Mr. Bentham, and to any other person.—His system is to extend the suffrage to Householders—to limit the duration of parliament to 3 years, and to vote by ballot. This is all the reform that I desire,[2] and I cannot help thinking that if you had continued your walks with Mr. Mill and me, we should have got you to join in so moderate a scheme. Mill says you distinctly admitted that there should be an effectual check on the Government in the people, and as you are a fair and candid reasoner, he is persuaded that you could not fail to admit the conclusions also which would follow from that principle. Those conclusions are that the House of Commons as at present constituted does not afford that check—that it really represents the Aristocracy, or rather a narrow Oligarchy, and not the people.—You are I fear surrounded by Anti-reformers,— wealthy alarmists who have in consequence of the French Revolution and the unhappy circumstances which attended it, associated the idea of insecurity of property with the exercise of popular priveleges. They must necessarily have some influence on your opinions, but I pray you to counteract

[1] Captain Maxwell, whose ship had been wrecked in the East Indies the previous year, had recently been knighted for his conduct on that occasion; as Tory candidate for Westminster he was insulted and pelted with mud by the mob.

[2] On 14 March 1818 Bentham had written to Ricardo: 'I told Burdett you had got down to *trienniality*, and were wavering between that and annuality, where I could not help flattering myself you would fix; also, in respect of extent, down to *householders*, for which, though I should prefer universality on account of its simplicity and unexclusiveness, I myself should be glad to compound.' (Quoted by Bowring, in *Works of Bentham*, vol. x, p. 498.)

27 June 1818　the effect by reading what the rational reformers have to urge in favour of their view of the question—read Madame de Stael's posthumous work on the French Revolution which contains an admirable defence of liberal institutions.[1]

I cannot agree with you in thinking that Brougham's was a good speech in answer to Burdett,—it was not in the least degree argumentative, nor did it shew what his own principles now are respecting reform. Brougham is a very clever man, but will never rank very high as a politician, for there is no steadiness in his opinions, and he appears to me sacrifice too much to his immediate objects. Sometimes he wishes to conciliate the Whigs, and then the violent reformers receive no mercy at his hands,—at other times one would conclude that he went as far in the cause of reform as even Burdett himself. A man who wishes to obtain a lasting name should not be a vacillating statesman too eager for immediate applause.

I am sorry that you could not consistently with your ideas of prudence seek to be returned for Guildford. You would be quite in your element in the House of Commons, and provided you started with the opinions which I deem right, there are few among my acquaintance whom I think would be more useful members, or whose talents would be more likely to be made manifest by the discipline which the business of the House of Commons would afford.

We shall leave London in little more than a fortnight for Gatcomb. If Mrs. Trower and you should at any time during the next six months find it convenient to absent yourselves for a short time from home you will give both Mrs. Ricardo and me great pleasure if you will come into Gloucestershire,

[1] *Considérations sur les principaux événements de la Révolution française, ouvrage posthume de Madame la baronne de Staël, publié par* M. le duc de Broglie et M. le baron de Staël, 3 vols., Paris, Delaunay, 1818.

and let me shew you the beauties of our country. We might take our walks and rides on the banks of the Severn instead of in Kensington Gardens, and might too have Mill for our companion, for he has positively agreed to make me a visit this summer. Pray think of it and if practicable come to us.— Mrs. Ricardo joins with me in kind regards to Mrs. Trower.

Believe me ever

My dear Trower

very sincerely Y^{rs}

DAVID RICARDO

27 June 1818

262. WARBURTON TO RICARDO[1]

My Dear Sir,   18. Cadogan Place. July 8. 1818

I return you many thanks for the loan of the enclosed[2] which Whishaw has transmitted to me. Not knowing whether you have left town, I have sent my servant with it to Brook S^t, with orders to take it to the post if you are at Gatcombe.—

I hope that one of the wishes expressed by Smith, will be gratified; and that you will succeed in finding a seat in the ensuing Parliament; the Elections upon the whole seem to have prospered, and you would find yourself in rather better company than was assembled there during the last session. The feeling which seems to prevail through the

8 July 1818

[1] Addressed: 'David Ricardo Esqre/Gatcombe Park/Minching Hampton / Stroud / Gloucestershire'. Not passed through the post. Presumably Ricardo had not yet left London (see above, p. 274), and it was delivered to him in Brook Street by Warburton's servant. MS in *R.P.*

Henry Warburton (1784–1858), F.R.S., a timber merchant, was an original member of the Political Economy Club and Vice-President of the Geological Society. Mallet describes him as 'a man of considerable talents and acquirements' and 'a great scholar and mathematician' (MS Diary, entry of March 1819).

[2] Probably a letter from Thomas Smith who was travelling on the Continent.

8 July 1818 country is the natural consequence of the cessation of war, with the prosecution of which, while it lasted, the whole attention of the people was occupied, all other matters appearing dull and uninteresting. The great exertions that have been made to improve the education of the people will soon begin to tell, and I really believe that the popular cause will receive great accession of strength in the next few years.

I understand that in spite of the insecure tenure by which a seat would be held owing to the King's advanced age, that the usual price, £5000, has been given for being returned during the continuance of the Parliament. I would advise you, if you have not secured a seat, and give up the thoughts of finding one at present, to be already upon the look out for one in the next Parliament; the present is not likely to endure more than 2 or three years.—

M. Binda is gone to join Count Palmella[1] at Paris, and expects to sail to the Brazils in the course of the summer; he will however first return to this country. Pray make my Comp^{ts} to Mrs. Ricardo, and

Believe me,

Yours truly

HENRY WARBURTON

263. RICARDO TO MILL[2]

My dear Sir   Gloucester 12 Augt 1818

12 Aug. 1818   I arrived here this morning, and have been busily engaged, ever since, in visiting the Prison, and in the other duties which my office imposes on me.[3] I am happy to say

---

[1] The leader of the Constitutional Party in Portugal.
[2] Addressed: 'James Mill Esqr /

Queen Square / Westminster / London'.
MS in Mill-Ricardo papers.
[3] As Sheriff of Gloucestershire.

that our Calendar is not very heavy, so that there is no doubt of my being able to return home on sunday, if not on saturday evening. I look forward with great pleasure to your visit at Gatcomb; I hope you will be ready to leave London on sunday or monday next. If you send me a line to Gatcomb to inform me by what coach you intend to travel I will take care either to meet you myself, or send some one to meet you. At the 96, or 97 miles stone, there is a public house, just before the roads part, where one goes to Chalford and Stroud, the other to Minchinhampton and Stroud. You will do well to stop at this public house, as the coach goes the Chalford road, and we cannot miss each other if we have a fixed place of meeting.

The judges will not come into Gloucester till the evening, they have sent word that they shall not have got through their business at Monmouth in time to allow them to arrive here early. I only regret this as it will make our sitting longer at the very formal dinner, at which I am called upon to preside.

The long continuance of dry weather has given a very bad complexion to our fields—we shall not appear to you in our favourable dress, and therefore to estimate the beauty of our country, you must make due allowance for the effects of this uncommonly hot season. When I left London Hyde Park appeared to look as brown as possible—it could hardly be made worse. Do you continue to cross it in your way to Kensington gardens? and does Mr. Bentham make his usual circuit?—The poor deer with their fawns must be nearly starved.

I have not yet tried what I can do in the way of composition. I have been reading part of Berkeley's works, part of Warburtons, and Dr. Beattie's answer to Hume and the other sceptical Philosophers.—Warburton and Beattie are both very scurrilous, and do not remove the difficulties

12 Aug. 1818 which make the subject of metaphysics so perplexing. Indeed
these cannot be removed for from the nature of the enquiry
if they satisfied you on some points you would only transfer
your difficulties to some other. I shall in due time make the
effort to write which you recommend, but it will be after the
fine weather has passed away, and I am less taken up with
the subjects which now engage my attention.—

The attention of my neighbours, and of the gentlemen
who are assembling in this town, has subjected me to several
interruptions since I commenced this letter, for they deem it
respectful to the Sheriff to call at his room.

This must be my excuse if my letter is more than usually
unintelligible, and must also account for its briefness.

Very truly Y^{rs}

DAVID RICARDO

264. MALTHUS TO RICARDO[1]
[Reply to 260.—Answered by 266]

My dear Sir,   E I Coll Augst 16th 1818

16 Aug. 1818   I congratulate you most sincerely on your success in
the Edinburgh Review, I think I hardly ever met with an
article in that journal, which so entirely approved of the
views of the work under consideration.[2] Perhaps the review
might have had more effect, if the writer had had the *appearance* of thinking more for himself; but if he really did
agree with you on every point, as he seems to have done, this
might not have been easy; and at all events the review cannot
fail of greatly contributing to the publicity and general
circulation of your book, and the extension of your fame.

[1] Addressed: 'D. Ricardo Esqr /   MS in *R.P.*
Gatcomb Park / Minchinhamp-   [2] See below, p. 280, n. 2.
ton'.

I am curious to know who is the writer. My conjectures fall
on Mill and Buchanan, and rather more on the former than the
latter; but I have only just finished the Review and have no
grounds to go upon, but the great coincidence of opinion.

You answered the question in my last letter just as I should
have expected; and quite consistently with your general principles. But does it not follow as an unavoidable conclusion,
that if as a matter of incontrovertible fact, general profits have
risen, and labour has not fallen, after the outlay of a great
quantity of capital upon the land, and a great increase of the
national income from the increase of rents, then rents are a
creation not a transfer; and if they have risen chiefly from
improvements in agriculture occasioned by the direction of
so much capital to the land in consequence of a high price of
corn, is it not an increase of wealth which would not otherwise have been obtained?

We returned to the College the end of July and spent the
last week of our absence in a very pleasant excursion to the
isle of Wight, which Mrs. Malthus had not seen before. We
were present at a grand sailing match at Cowes, which
afforded a most gay and animated scene; and frequent
bathings while we remained in the neighbourhood of the
sea enabled us to get through the hot weather without being
oppressed by it.

I was quite grieved to hear of poor Mrs. Osmans Ricardo's
loss, and hope she has now fully recovered her health and
spirits.

I did little or nothing, as I expected, in the vacation, but
am trying to get on a little now, though I have had all my
books to move which has been a great interruption, and the
job is not yet completed. They were moved into another
room before the vacation in order to allow the study to be
painted, and I have now been moving them back again.

16 Aug. 1818 The confidence of your reviewer ought to alarm me, but I am a very obstinate heretic, and I think my convictions remain undisturbed. I dined at Mackintosh's with Whishaw the other day. They were both well and inquired after you. Mack^{sh} says that he cannot yet understand you as he ought, which he cannot account for.

Mrs. M joins with me in kind regards to Mrs. Ricardo. All well at the College.

Ever truly Yours
T R Malthus

265. McCULLOCH TO RICARDO[1]

[*Answered by 267*]

College Street Edinburgh
15 July 1818

Dear Sir

15 July 1818 I take the liberty to send you herewith a copy of a critique on your work on the "Principles of Political Economy and Taxation", which I have written for the next number of the Edinburgh Review.[2] It will, I hope, meet with your approbation—And I shall consider myself as having done no small service to the science if I have succeeded in giving a correct view of the leading doctrines contained in your great work, and if I shall have been anywise instrumental in attracting to it that share of the public attention to which it is so justly entitled—

There is no part of your work which I admire more than that in which you treat of the theory of taxation—But although I am fully convinced that the more your general principles on this subject are inquired into, the more correct

---

[1] MS in *R.P.*—Received by Ricardo on 20 August (see below, p. 287). [2] June 1818 [published in August], Art. II.

they will be found; still it appears to me that you give as it were a reluctant assent to those arguments, and they are of the most decisive nature, which shew the impolicy and ruinous effects of a heavy taxation—Such at least is the impression which a repeated perusal of this part of your work has made upon me—I regret this exceedingly—All governments are but too much inclined to tax and overburden their subjects; and when a philosopher has pointed out the bad effects of excessive taxation in general, it is quite uncalled for and can serve no good purpose for him to attempt by afterwards modifying his expressions to apologise for the mischief by which it must in every case be attended—I have not alluded to this in the Review because I consider [it][1] as a matter of only secondary importance—But when you come to print a second edition, I am not without hopes you will revise this part[2]; and that you will see the impropriety of contaminating a work destined to be immortal, with any thing that can be construed into an excuse or palliation of that system of profligate extravagance according to which the economical affairs of the different European nations have long been managed—

I know you will forgive the freedom with which I have made these remarks—It is because I entertain the most profound admiration for the "Principles of Political Economy" and for its author, that I have thus candidly stated my opinion respecting what I consider as almost the only blemish in the former

I am

Dear Sir

Yours respectfully and sincerely

J. R. M^CCULLOCH

David Ricardo Esqre

[1] Omitted in MS.   [2] Cp. below, p. 353.

266. RICARDO TO MALTHUS[1]

[*Reply to* 264]

My dear Sir   [Gatcomb Park, 20 Aug. 1818]

20 Aug. 1818   I am very much obliged to you for the kind manner in
which you express yourself respecting the praise that has
been so lavishly bestowed on me by the reviewer of my book,
in the Edinburgh Review. Immediately on reading it, I
guessed that the writer of the article was Mr. M'Cullock, for
from the publication of my book he appears sincerely to have
embraced the views which I wished to impress on all my
readers. I cannot but feel highly gratified at his praise, which
I should not have been, in any thing like an equal degree, if
it had come from Mr. Mill, because, though I should not have
doubted his sincerity, I should have imputed much to his
friendship and good opinion.

The praise indeed is far beyond my merits, and would
perhaps have really told more if the writer had mixed with it
an objection[2] here and there.—

I do not remember what the question was which I answered consistently with my general principles in my last
letter, and not having your letter here I cannot refer to it.—
I admit that by improvements in agriculture an enormous
quantity of wealth may be created, and that in the natural
progress of society much of that wealth may ultimately[3] go
to landlords in the shape of rent,[4] but that does not alter the
fact of rent being always a transfer, and never a creation of

---

[1] Addressed: 'The Rev⁴ T. R.
Malthus / East India College /
Hertford'; franked by H. J.
Shepherd, M.P. 'Minching
Hampton August twenty 1818'.
MS at Albury.—*Letters to Mal-
thus*, LXVIII.

[2] 'to my theory' is del. here.
[3] 'ultimately' is ins.
[4] Cp. the alteration to this effect
in ed. 2 of *Principles*, above, I, 412,
n. 5.

wealth—for before it is paid to the landlords as rent it must 20 Aug. 1818 have constituted the profits of stock, and a portion is made over to the landlord only because lands of a poorer quality are taken into cultivation.

Mrs. Malthus and you must have found your excursion to the Isle of Wight very pleasant. I remember being there many years ago, and finding it a very agreeable place.

You will have seen by the newspapers that I have been through all the parade and expence, which my office of sheriff imposes on me, when the judges attend the Assizes, without any advantage. The judge came in to the town after midnight, by which his commission became void, and after sending to London, Jury, Witnesses, Counsel, and Sheriff, were all dismissed to their respective homes. It is expected that we shall have a new commission in 2 or 3 weeks.—[1]

[1] The incident was reported in the *Courier* of Saturday, 15 Aug. 1818: 'SINGULAR LEGAL DIFFICULTY.—A most extraordinary, and indeed an unprecedented circumstance has just occurred in the city of Gloucester. On the evening of Wednesday last, Mr. Ricardo, the High Sheriff, and his retinue, proceeded about ten o'clock, in order to meet the Judges... Sir William Garrow [one of the judges] had come forward from Monmouth with the utmost expedition, but all his efforts did not enable him to reach Gloucester before twelve o'clock. When Sir William was in the Sheriff's carriage, Mr. Ricardo suggested the probability of the illegality of opening the Commission on Thursday, instead of Wednesday, which was the specific day.... The Court was therefore adjourned.... Gloucester then became a scene of considerable confusion. Lawyers and their clients were seen running in all directions. The witnesses, all of whom were obliged to remain at Gloucester, were lamenting the loss of time they should sustain. Barristers were renewing their terms of lodgings and indeed nothing could equal the confusion of the city of Gloucester when the tidings of the adjournment were made known. The consequences of proceeding to trial were not at first conjectured. They might have been of the most lamentable and mischievous kind. Prisoners might have been deemed illegally punished; decisions, if lawsuits, would have been null and void, and even the Sheriff himself, had he proceeded to the execution of a sentence of death, might have been indicted for wilful murder.'

Mrs. Osman Ricardo has recovered her health and spirits, and is daily more endeared to us by the sweetness of her temper, and her obliging disposition.—

I am sorry that you have not made any great progress in the work that you are about. After the reflection you have given to the subject I am not surprised that my reviewer has not shaken your confidence in your opinions. It would have been little flattering to me if he had, for I have had many opportunities, and have taken a great deal of pains to bring you round to my way of thinking without success. Why should he be so fortunate on the first trial? The truth I begin to suspect is, that we do not differ so much as we have hitherto thought. I differed very little from the opinions expressed in that part of your MS which you read to me, but I wish to have an opportunity of judging of your system as a whole, and therefore shall be glad when it comes in its printed form.

I am glad to hear that Sir J. Mackintosh and Mr. Whishaw are well, pray remember me kindly to them. If either, or both of them, should go to Bowood this season, I shall take it very kind of them if they will come for a few days to me. The Marquis of Lansdown[1] has promised me a visit, and it would be particularly agreeable if they would all come at the same time. Should Mr. Whishaw be as near to me as Bowood he is already under an engagement to come. I met the Marquis and March.ᵉ of Lansdown at Gloucester—they entered the town on their way home, from a tour, just as I was about leaving it, and owing to the breaking up of the courts were detained some time for want of horses.

I suppose that you will be confined at Hertford till the

---

[1] Henry Petty-Fitzmaurice, third Marquis of Lansdowne (1780–1863), Chancellor of the Ex- chequer in 1806–7, at this time one of the leaders of the Whig opposition.

Xmas vacation. I very much wish that Mrs. Malthus and you 20 Aug. 1818
would pass a part of that vacation with us. Perhaps you may
direct your steps westerly. If so you will not mind deviating
a little from your course.

Mr. Mill arrived here yesterday evening to pay me his long
promised visit. He brings me no news, excepting that he
dined at Mr. Bentham's with Mr. Brougham, Mr. Rush the
American Ambassador, and Sir Sam! Romilly. The old gentleman is becoming gay. A party of four must to him be a
formidably large one.

Mrs. Ricardo joins with me in kind regards to Mrs.
Malthus.

Ever truly Y^{rs}

D. RICARDO

267. RICARDO TO M^{C}CULLOCH[1]

[Reply to 265.—Answered by 271]

Gatcomb Park, Minchinhampton
Gloucestershire 22^d Augt 1818

Dear Sir

After I had sufficiently enjoyed the pleasure which I 22 Aug. 1818
derived from reading the flattering critique on my work in
the last number of the Edinburgh Review, I naturally began
to speculate on the probable writer of it, and immediately
my suspicions fell upon you, because I had no reason to
believe that any other person who was likely to be a writer
in the Review so fully agreed with the doctrines which I have
endeavoured to establish as yourself, excepting only my
friend Mr. Mill, and he I knew had not written it.

Having at various times had reason to believe that you
took a favourable view of my opinions, I settled the point

[1] Addressed: 'J. R. McCulloch Esqr / College Street / Edinburgh'.
MS in British Museum.—*Letters to McCulloch*, III.

22 Aug. 1818 at once, and felt assured that you were the person who had distinguished me so very far beyond my deserts. I know not whether I ought to thank you, but I have been exceedingly gratified. My own doctrines appear doubly convincing as explained by your able pen, and I have already heard in this retreat that those who could not understand *me*, most clearly comprehend *you*. For this service I may thank you, and I may also be permitted to express my satisfaction that I have succeeded in impressing you with the same view of the general principles of Political Economy which I myself entertain. I have not many converts of which to boast, but when I can number amongst them yourself and Mr. Mill I think mine is no mean triumph. The latter gentleman is now on a visit to me here, and I am sure you will be pleased to know that he thinks your review a masterly essay on the science, and will very much assist to disseminate correct views on a very intricate part of it.

I rather regret that you did not notice those passages, in the Review, which you think give encouragement to ministers to be profuse in the public expenditure, contrary to the general principles which are in other parts of the work maintained. They should have been noticed to have been condemned. I have only the poor apology to offer in my defence that I had no such intention, and shall be glad if the book goes to a second edition to leave such passages out, or so to modify them that they shall not bear such a construction. I am as great a friend to economy in Governments as you can wish me to be; every guinea that is spent unnecessarily I think is a public wrong, and I should therefore be sorry to give the slightest encouragement to waste and extravagance. I will not fail carefully to revise that part of my book, and shall be happy to have my attention drawn by you to the particular pages from which you think it may be inferred that my

opinions are not so strong as I have now[1] expressed 22 Aug. 1818
them.

Before I conclude I must account for not writing to you
sooner, for your letter being dated the 15ᵗʰ July you might
otherwise be surprised that I did not answer it before the
22ᵈ of August. Your letter, and the sheets that accompanied
it, only reached me here on the 20ᵗʰ inst., and consequently
I had seen the published number of the Review before I
received your letter. Some delay must have occurred in the
conveyance of your parcel to London, for as I have a dispatch, at least once every week from Brook Street, it could
not I think have been there before the 13ᵗʰ Augᵗ. I hope that
business or pleasure may during the next winter call you to
London, that I may have an opportunity personally to assure
you of my esteem.

> I am Dear Sir
> Very sincerely Yours
> DAVID RICARDO

J. R. MᶜCulloch Esqʳ

268. TROWER TO RICARDO[2]

[Reply to 261.—Answered by 272]

Unsted Wood—Aug: 23. 1818

My Dear Ricardo

I have been absent from home, or your last kind letter 23 Aug. 1818
should not have remained so terribly long unanswered.
Many thanks for your friendly invitation to Gatcomb, which
I should rejoice to think were practicable. But there is a vast
gulph between us, and Mrs. Trower is very much devoted to
her nursery. I hope, however, at some time or other, to be

---

[1] 'now' is ins.
[2] Addressed: 'To / David Ricardo Esqr / Gatcomb Park / Minchin-hampton Glocestershire'.
MS in *R.P.*

23 Aug. 1818 able to steal away from my family, for a short time, that I may
have the pleasure of taking a glance of you.—

I have just been reading, with great attention, and still
greater interest, the criticism on your Book, in the Ending-
burgh Review; which, from what I have heard you say,
I conclude is from the pen of Major Torrens.[1] He does not
say one word in your praise more than you deserve. I am
desirous of hearing your opinion of it. To me it appears, upon
the whole, very well done. He is master of the subject, and
the general view he has given of your system, and opinions,
is clear and satisfactory. He is however much too sparing of
quotations from your Book, and, upon some occasions, I
think, where the *text* would have been more convincing than
the *comment*.—He appears to me, in one part of his Review,
rather to puzzle himself in endeavoring to explain the difficult
question of exchangeable value, and price. In page 68. he
says, if the labor of production should be encreased, equally
on all articles, "their exchangeable value would remain unaltered, while *their real price would however be augmented*,"
and lower down, in the same page, he says—"In such circumstances although the *prices of commodities would remain
stationary*, the wealth and comfort of the whole society
would be diminished." This surely is a contradiction. In the
next page, in endeavoring to shew, that a rise in wages
would not affect the *prices* of commodities, I think he *shows
only*, that it would not affect *their relative values*. The quotation, which follows, from your Book,[2] is conclusive on that
point; but *his* reasoning appears to me defective.—He is
most forcible in that part of the Article, that relates to the
origin of rent; which I think he has managed well; and his

[1] See above, p. 179. The review
was by McCulloch.

[2] Above, I, 105 ('To say that commodities' to the end of the paragraph).

answer to the objection of the quarterly Review, on that point, is to me very satisfactory.[1] No doubt, the same effect would be produced (as far as the argument goes) by *fresh capital* employed upon land, which *merely affords the ordinary profit on Stock*, as by *land not affording any rent.*—By the by, how is the fact with respect to America? Does *no land pay any rent*; because his argument proceeds upon that idea; as he speaks of the boundless extent of fertile and unoccupied land, and of the workmen operating with the best machinery &. &. &. Pray who is "the Fellow of the University of Oxford," what is the title of his Book.[2] I have never heard of it—must I read it? Upon the whole, then, I think this Review will do your book a great deal of good. It will dispose many to read it, who otherwise might not have looked at it; and it will facilitate their comprehension of it, by the clear and concise general view which it gives of its objects.—What says Mill of the Review? Pray remember me kindly to him, and say I have derived much useful information from Naysmith.[3]

I observe by your letter, that both Mill and you are disposed to strain my admissions beyond their legitimate extent; making good the old adage; "if you grant an inch they'll take an ell." But, since you are both much too clear sighted seriously to contend, "that because I admit there should be an effectual check on the Government, in the people"; that *therefore* "I cannot fail to admit that the House of Commons,

---

[1] p. 77. McCulloch answers the objection based on Adam Smith's statement that even 'the most desert moors in Norway and Scotland...afford some small rent to the landlord'; he does not mention the *Quarterly Review*, and is no doubt controverting the *British Review*, which raises that objection against Ricardo (Nov. 1817, p. 315; cp. above, p. 219, n. 1).

[2] See below, p. 297, n. 1.

[3] Perhaps *The Duties of Overseers of the Poor, and the Sufficiency of the Present System of Poor Laws considered*, by James Nasmith, D.D., Wisbech, 1799.

23 Aug. 1818 as at present constituted, does not afford that check; that it really represents the Aristocracy or rather a narrow Oligarchy and not the people." So far from admitting this, I contend, that the House of Commons practically, and in effect, affords that check, which the people ought to have on the Government; that the force of public opinion *is*, and *must be* felt in Parliament; and that the rapid and inevitable growth of that opinion makes it a much more important consideration how the influence of that opinion should be properly regulated, than how it should be encreased. The natural tendency of the course of events in a Country circumstanced as this is, where wealth, and knowledge, and independent spirit, are spreading rapidly among the people, is to give too much force to the popular part of our Constitution, to render it *too republican*. Those who prefer that form of Government, will naturally be disposed to encourage these tendencies, but for myself I give the preference to the mixed government we at present enjoy.—That it is capable of improvement in *practice* I do not mean to deny, and should gladly acquiesce in any mode of election which, whilst it checked the disgraceful scenes witnessed at our Polls, did not expose us to greater mischiefs. And I think it probable, that some mode of ballot might be proposed, which would diminish if not entirely remove the existing evils. Adieu. Remember us very kindly to Mrs. Ricardo and your family, and believe me my Dear Ricardo

Yours very sincerely
HUTCHES TROWER

Judge Garrow seems to have put you to great inconvenience at the Assizes. Why did he not send on one of the Council to open the Court. There are always some named in the Commission.[1]

[1] See above, p. 283, n.

269. RICARDO TO SHARP[1]

Gatcomb Park
Minchinhampton
27th Augt 1818

Dear Sharp

When I yesterday saw your name on the outside of your letter,[2] I hoped that its contents would inform me that you designed soon to pay me a visit, instead of which I was sorry to see that there was little probability of your being in Wiltshire, or Gloucestershire, this year. I am concerned to find that Mr. Boddington[3] is still suffering from the effects of his accident. From what I had heard I hoped that he had entirely recovered. Should any favourable circumstance occur to render your presence in, or near, London unnecessary, pray let me see you here:— if you would come I am not without hopes that Lord Lansdown would meet you.

I am obliged to you for the interest you take in my fame, and for the pleasure you express on the occasion of the favourable review which my book has received in the Edinburgh Review.[4]—I have certainly been much gratified by it, both on account of the clear manner in which the Reviewer has explained my doctrines, and the approbation which he expresses of them. It is satisfactory to know that an able man has so completely understood me. You probably know that the writer of the article on which we are now commenting is Mr. McCulloch, the reputed editor of the Scotsman newspaper.

From what you say, I fear that you have some reason to think, that the Bank will not place themselves in a situation

27 Aug. 1818

---

[1] Addressed: 'Richard Sharp Esqre M.P./Mansion House Place/ London'.
  MS in the possession of the Hon. Mrs Eustace Hills.
[2] Sharp's letter is missing.

[3] Samuel Boddington, Sharp's partner in business and a member of the King of Clubs. (See *The 'Pope' of Holland House*, p. 335.)
[4] See above, p. 280, n. 2.

27 Aug. 1818 to resume cash payments next year. What possible excuse can now be offered, either by the Bank, or by ministers, for not fulfilling the engagement which they have so solemnly contracted?[1]

Mr. Mill has been passing a few days with me at Gatcomb, and is very much pleased with our country, although we are not able to shew her in her best dress. Even in the valleys we cannot meet with a field that is green, and in many places the springs are dry, and the cattle are driven miles in search of water.

I hope that you will encounter no other difficulties in your studies but such as will give an agreeable stimulus to exertion, —and make your success more gratifying.

Mrs. Ricardo begs to be kindly remembered. My young ladies are all absent from home.

To-morrow I leave Gatcomb for Gloucester, and shall not return till after our *third* Assizes, which will commence on monday next.

Ever truly Y[rs]

DAVID RICARDO

270. RICARDO TO MILL[2]

[Answered by 273]

Bow 8 Sep[r] 1818

My dear Sir

8 Sept. 1818   I should have written to you some days ago, but I was desirous of informing you of the progress I had made in the procuring of a seat in Par.~[t] I have however waited for no

[1] The 'excuse' of the Chancellor of the Exchequer for continuing the suspension of cash payments for another year had been the magnitude of the loans to France which were being negotiated by Baring. (Vansittart's speech, 9 April 1818, *Hansard*, XXXVII, 1229 ff.)

[2] Addressed: 'James Mill Esq[r] / Professor Wallace's / Royal Military College / Bagshot'.

MS in Mill-Ricardo papers.

Mill was 'on a visit to his old friend Mr. Wallace, then one of the Mathematical Professors at Sandhurst' (J. S. Mill, *Autobiography*, p. 18).

purpose for I know no more about it than I did when you communicated to me the contents of the letter which you
received at Gloucester.[1]—I called twice last week at Mr.
Brougham's residence in St James' Square, the last time on
friday but he was not then come to London. On saturday
I sent him a few lines by the Post telling him where I was,
and expressing my readiness to attend him whenever he
should require it. As I have not received an answer and as
my solicitor has not heard from Lord P.'s solicitor, it is
probable that Mr. Brougham is still enjoying his rustic
amusements. I do not know that my presence or absence can
be of the least importance—you have acquainted Mr.
Brougham with my consent to the terms proposed, and it
now lies with my solicitor to see that all is right and secure.
A general dislike I find prevails against Irish securities from
the extreme difficulty of getting the legal remedies put in
force, when from necessity or choice a borrower refuses to
pay the interest for which he is engaged.[2]—

I very quickly followed you to London from Gloucester.
On monday morning I went in due form to meet Mr. Justice
Holroyd, attended him and the other judge to the Cathedral
and then into court. Osman had mentioned to Mr. Hicks
and others my fears concerning my brother, and of my
intention to go to London immediately after the Assizes.
This passed from one magistrate to another and as soon as
they had an opportunity of speaking to me they strongly
recommended me to mention the case to Sir W Garrow.
I did, and he instantly insisted on my leaving Gloucester,
and assured me that my presence was not necessary,—

[1] Ricardo and Mill had gone to Gloucester on Friday, 28 August. See above, p. 292, and below, next paragraph.
[2] On 2 Sept. 1818 Ricardo's solicitor T. Crosse had written to him: 'I was duly favored with your Letter as to a proposed advance to Lord Portarlington but have not yet seen his Solicitor on the subject. There is a general prejudice here against Irish securities'. (MS in *R.P.*)

8 Sept. 1818 accordingly I immediately set off for Gatcomb, and the next morning accompanied Mrs. Ricardo in her journey to this place, where we arrived at night.—I found my brother Moses much less ill than I had expected—he was not considered here to be in danger, and although he continues very weak I should pronounce him decidedly better now than when I came. He gets little sleep at nights, and can bear very little food without feeling intolerable oppression, which appeared to be his chief complaint. He has now left off all medicine, and contents himself, notwithstanding he has appetite, with the smallest allowance of light food, and the effect is very marked and promising. His spirits are very much mended, and I think he is decidedly advancing in recovery.—His mind is at case about his business—We have got an able man to conduct it for him for the present and have a scheme to enable him to quit it altogether,—in which case he will retire to Bath, and live on the moderate income which he will possess.

I intend staying here till monday next when I shall again direct my steps towards Gatcomb, and shall expect to see its appearance much improved by the rain which has lately fallen. I hope that you are pleased with the country about your present residence and that you found Mrs. Mill and all your young family well. Ever Y^{rs}

DAVID RICARDO

271. M^{c}CULLOCH TO RICARDO[1]

[*Reply to* 267.—*Answered by* 285]

Dear Sir   Edinburgh 3rd Septr 1818.

3 Sept. 1818   I was duly favoured with your very kind letter of the 22nd ulto for which I ought ere now to have returned you my best thanks—Although I am perfectly aware that the

[1] Addressed: 'David Ricardo Esquire / Gatcomb Park / Minchinhampton/Gloucestershire'.— (Received after writing letter 270; cp. postscript to letter 274.) MS in *R.P.*

manner in which you have spoken of my review of your great work is much too flattering, it has, I will confess, afforded me the greatest possible gratification—Laudem a viris laudatis is a species of praise which I do not affect to despise; and on which, in the present instance, I set the highest value, because I am sure it would not have been given had you not judged it deserved—

I do not know that you have as yet got many converts in Edinburgh—Smith was here worshipped as a demigod; and when your work appeared it was reckoned little better than petty treason to presume to doubt one of his dogmas—This thorough paced belief in the accuracy of *all* that is stated in the Wealth of Nations, has now, however, been a good deal modified—and although there are a considerable number who continue as warm and as indiscriminating in their praise as ever, I am quite confident that at no distant period it will be generally admitted that it is to *your* work, and to Smith's, that those who wish to cultivate an acquaintance with the real doctrines of the science must have recourse—

I have written a paper on the Corn Laws, and another on the Cottage System for the Supplement to the Encyclopaedia Brittannica, which I have entirely founded on your principles —I gave one of them to your brother, Mr Ralph, whom I was fortunate enough to meet with here, to deliver to you—

I have never been in London, and there is nothing that I should like more than to pay a visit to that city—Unfortunately however I see no near prospect of my being able to gratify my wishes in that respect; but you may be assured that if I ever am in London, a short period only will elapse before I do myself the honour of waiting upon you—I remain

With the sincerest respect and esteem

Yours faithfully

J. R. M^cCULLOCH

David Ricardo Esqre

272. RICARDO TO TROWER[1]

[Reply to 268.—Answered by 276]

                                              Gatcomb Park 18th Sept.r 1818
My dear Trower

18 Sept. 1818   Our third Assizes this year, as they may without much
inaccuracy be called, commenced on the 31 Aug., and on that
day I had again to go through all the ceremonies of meeting
the Judges, attending them to the Court, and then to the
Cathedral, all which had been so needlessly gone through
on the former occasion; but here my active services ended,
for I had received the night before such an account of the
alarming illness of one of my brothers, whom I believe you
do not know, and of his wish to see me, that I was anxious to
hurry to London as soon as my presence could be dispensed
with. Nothing could be more humane and considerate than
the Judges behaviour to me;—they no sooner knew how I
was circumstanced than they insisted on my leaving Glocester
immediately. I accepted their indulgence, and on my arrival
in London found my brother in a less alarming state than
I expected to find him. I passed a fortnight from home, and
am but just returned. I am happy to say that my brother's
health improved daily while I was in London, and I left him
with a fair prospect of complete recovery. It is to this interruption that you are to attribute my long silence after the
receipt of your kind letter.

I am glad to hear that you are pleased with the review of
my book in the Edinburgh Review. It gives me great satisfaction, and principally because the writer (Mr MCullock)
appears to have well understood me, and to have explained
my doctrines with great clearness and perspicuity. I am glad
too to have had your observations on the review, for you

[1] Addressed: 'Hutches Trower Esq.r / Unsted Wood / Godalming'.
MS at University College, London.—*Letters to Trower*, XXI.

have called my attention to the inaccuracy of the reviewer in a passage which had not before been noticed by me. In page 68 he has in the first quotation you make, used the word *price* instead of the word *value*; substitute the latter word and the whole is consistent, though perhaps not quite satisfactory, for it supposes my definition of value to be correct, which may by many be disputed. In the next page he again speaks of real price as synonymous with real value, but his meaning is obvious. The word *price* I think should be confined wholly to the value of commodities estimated in *money*, and money only. If so confined, a commodity may rise in *real value* without rising in *price*. If more labour should be required than before to work the mines, and to manufacture shoes, it is possible that shoes may continue unaltered in *price*, but both the shoes, and gold (or money) will have *risen in value*. He is very able on the subject of rent, but if he answers the objections of any Review, it cannot be the Quarterly, for the work has not been noticed by it. In America I should think that there was no land for which a rent was not paid, but that is to be attributed to their particular institutions. The Government is proprietor of all uncultivated lands in the interior of the country, which it is ready to sell, and daily sells, at the moderate price at 2 dollars per acre. Rent then must amount in every part of America to the interest which 2 dollars would make, p^r acre, at the least; but this fact makes no difference in the principle, as you seem to be fully aware.

"The Fellow of The University of Oxford"[1] is Mr. West, a barrister. His pamphlet was ingenious, and he had a glimpse

---

[1] First written "'The fellow of University College'", which is the correct description of the author of *An Essay on the Application of Capital to Land*, 1815; then altered to accord with the description in the *Edinburgh Review*, June 1818, p. 73, which had been copied by Trower, above, p. 289.

18 Sept. 1818 of the true doctrine of rent and profits. I am acquainted
with him. He has I believe given up the study of Polit.
Economy.[1]

Mr. Mill has been staying a fortnight with me—he returned
to London a day before I went there. He is very much
pleased with the review—he thinks it very well done.

Both he, and I, I observe, have mistaken the extent of your
admission respecting the House of Commons. You admit
that there should be an effectual check on the Government
in the people, but you think that as that House is at present
constituted it practically and in effect affords such a check,
because it feels the force of public opinion. We are of opinion
with you that the force of public opinion is felt, and strongly
felt in Parliament, but not in consequence of its good constitution, but in spite of the badness of it. The Parliament
itself is controuled by public opinion as manifested through
the means of the Press, and therefore it is the Press which is
the real check on our Government. The Public opinion and
p[opular][2] force is irresistible, and it is of this both the
monarchy and the oligarchy stand in awe, and to it we are
indebted for all the liberty we enjoy. *Instead* of having this
check for the people *out* of parliament,—would it not be
better to have it *constitutionally* exerted *within it*—would
it not be more efficacious *there* as an instrument of good
Government? It would in that case be powerful in correcting abuses on which the fear of insurrection does not now
operate. As Parliament is at present constituted can we

---

[1] Cp. above, VI, 179. Edward West
was now practising as a barrister.
In 1822 he became Recorder of
Bombay, but he continued his economic studies and before sailing
to India began his *Price of Corn
and Wages of Labour, with Observations upon Dr. Smith's, Mr.*

*Ricardo's, and Mr. Malthus's
Doctrines upon those Subjects...,*
not published till 1826. (See A.
Plummer, 'Sir Edward West,
1782–1828', in *Journal of Political
Economy*, Oct. 1929, pp. 573–82.)
[2] MS torn; 'popular' is Trower's
reading (below, p. 310).

reasonably expect any important improvements in the *law*, 18 Sept. 1818
while there is such a phalanx of interested men who have the
power to oppose them? Why is not a general inclosure bill
passed? because the lawyers interest is opposed to the general
interest. Why are there so many obstacles to the transfer of
landed property? Why is justice so tardy, and its expences
so great? and a thousand more whys,—all for the same reason.
No, my friend, Parliament is no check *for* the people, but
happily is yet checked *by* the people, whose voice and power
cannot be wholly stifled while the press is tolerably free. You
talk of your preference to a *mixed* Government, over that of
a republican. I have *no objection* to the former provided it be
administered for the happiness of the *many*, and not for the
benefit of the *few*. I know of no security under any form of
Government for the happiness of the people, but that the
people themselves, through the means of their representatives, should have a preponderating voice. I rejoice that you
are not one of those who have an *antipathy* to election by
ballot, for of all those, who object to that mode of election
I have never heard any solid reasons for their objection:—
they are all to be resolved to an antipathy, for which they can
give no account.

Mill was exceedingly pleased with the view of some parts
of our County. We performed a little tour to some estates
which I have at 27 miles distance from home,[1] and then we
went to Hereford, and surveyed the beautiful country about
the cities of Hereford and Ross. I think you have been in
those places.

---

[1] Wakefield had arranged for
Ricardo, his son Osman and Mill
to stay for a few days from 28
August with the farmer at Paunt-
ley Court, while visiting that estate
and the neighbouring ones of
Bromesberrow Place and Berrow
Court. (Wakefield's letter of
13 Aug. 1818, MS in *R.P.*)

18 Sept. 1818   Pray remember us all most kindly to Mrs. Trower and
believe me very sincerely   Yrs

DAVID RICARDO

I believe a Serjeant only can open the Court, and no
serjeant accompanies the Judges in this Circuit.

273. MILL TO RICARDO[1]

[*Reply to* 270.—*Answered by* 274]

My Dear Sir   College Bagshot 23ᵈ Septʳ 1818

23 Sept. 1818   I have a letter from Brougham this morning, which
contains the following words—

"I have arranged all about Ricardo—Pray let him know
how much I regretted not seeing him—But Sir H. Parnell
came to town on purpose, and we settled every thing as he (R)
could wish—The titles will take some little time—but all
is sure. I should write to him, but have lost his address."

This letter to me is sent from Oxford, where he had got
on his way to Westmoreland, and will be back in 3 weeks.

I now reckon that I may congratulate myself on seeing you
in Hon. House, where I am sure you will do as much honour
to my prognostications, as you have done by your book:
where, if you live and keep your strength, the cause of good
government, the first of all causes for poor human nature,
will owe enough to your exertions to hand down your name
with honour to the latest posterity. You need not laugh. That
is a subject on which I reckon myself one of the best of judges.
Nor are you to imagine that I am paying you a very high
compliment. There are two things which contribute mightily
to reduce it: The first is, the very moderate qualifications of

[1] Addressed: 'David Ricardo Esq. / Gatcomb Park / Minchinhampton / Glostershire'.—MS in *R.P.*

those among whom you are to work, few of whom it will be difficult to excell; and the second is, that the cause itself is now, by the progress of the human mind, brought into such a situation, that very moderate exertions will produce great results, that every operation will *tell*, because it falls in with the current in which things are running of their own accord. This, therefore, is the course which all high ambition, even *selfish* ambition, would take into, in the present state of the human mind. No high and permanent reputation, will ever again be acquired by merely fighting up the pretensions of one aristocratical party, against another. There will be no great character, hereafter, for any thing else than great service to the cause of causes, the cause of *good government*. What then are the things which must go to the composition of good government, and how the proper combination of these things is best to be attained in this country; these are the grand points which you are to familiarize to your mind; and then there will be no fear about the language in which your thoughts will spontaneously clothe themselves. Let those discourses, therefore, which we have so often talked about, be written without delay. And do not stay, in the first instance, to be very nice and punctilious about any thing; run the matter off while the vein is open. I would, if I were you, set down in the first place, on a separate piece of paper, in a distinct proposition or propositions, the subject which I meant to handle, and then under it I would state the different points which I meant to take up, as well my own propositions as the answers to them. I would pass and repass these in my mind; to see as far as I could recollect, if they contained every thing, and if I had them in the best possible order; that is, the order in which that is taken first which needs nothing of what follows to explain it, and which serves to explain what follows; that is taken second which is explained by what

23 Sept. 1818 precedes, and is serviceable for explaining what follows, without needing what follows for explaining itself. This is the plain rule of utility, which will always guide you right, and in which there is no mystery. After this, I would sit down to write, and expand. When the writing is done, you should *talk* over the subject to yourself. I mean not *harangue*, but as you would talk about it in conversation at your own table; talk audibly, however, walking about in your room. This will practice your memory, and will also practice you in finding words at the moment to express your thoughts. After this you shall talk the various subjects over to me, when we have again an opportunity of being together: and after this you may have perfect confidence in yourself. One thing more, however; you must write your discourses, with the purpose of sending them to me. Depend upon it, this will be a stimulus, not without its use. I will be the representative of an audience, of a public; and even if you had in your eye a person whom you respect much less than you do me, it would be a motive both to bestow the labour more regularly, as it should be; and to increase the force of your attention. Therefore no apologies, and no excuses will be listened to.[1]

I have left myself no room either to speak, or to enquire about family matters. It was a great relief to have such favourable accounts as you gave me of Mr. Moses. I found my incumbrances here enjoying themselves highly. It is an admirable place for walking, all dry sand, and well made roads in every direction. The weather too has all along been and continues delightful. I often think of Gatcomb, and all its inmates and neighbours. It is a great pleasure to me to be now properly acquainted with it, and its doings. I hope

[1] Two of these 'discourses' (*Observations on Parliamentary Reform* and *Defence of the Plan* of *Voting by Ballot*) have been preserved and are printed above, V, 487 ff.

Mrs. Ricardo has still some friendship for me, though I fear 23 Sept. 1818 she reckons me amongst the *immoderate*, as she calls them, by which she means all those who think on the other side from her. But she has so much both of good meaning and good acting about her, that I am resolved to be a friend of hers whether she will or not. I beg to present my best respects to Mr. Osman and lady, for whom I hope you carried from Brook Street, the Nouvelle Heloise, and which I hope she does not think so immoral a book as either Tom Jones, or Gil Blas.

Ever truly yours

J. MILL

I shall be here probably a fortnight or three weeks more, after which I must pay a visit of 8 or 10 days to Hume, either at Bognor or Worthing, and then I am in London for good. Did you read in the Morning Chron. the Aberdeen Memorial, against the decision about their magistracy.[1] Hume had sent it to me, and has been corresponding with me about it. I may now congratulate him upon having *you* for a co-adjutor in bringing it forward. I have been endeavouring to fill him with matter. And Brougham promises me that he will be a captain in the field. This is a point that must be agitated, and will bring on the questions of reform very early. I fear the influence of the ladies with some people. *They* are not for parl.ᵞ reform, because it is not fashionable: It, and its advocates, are not spoken well of in high circles. But ladies like only that which is spoken well of in high circles. And we know well why it is spoken ill of in high circles: Excise officers are not popular in circles of smugglers.

N.B. Brougham wishes an account from as many places as possible (and mentions Gatcomb) of the proportion of

[1] The Memorial of the Burgesses of Aberdeen to the Privy Council praying that the right of electing the Magistrates by poll should be restored to their Burgh. (*Morning Chronicle*, 18 Sept. 1818.)

23 Sept. 1818 persons, receiving Parish relief, who can read and write. Ascertain this in as many parishes as you can. You are at liberty to use his name. I shall do what I can, both here and in Devonshire. You may get from Mr. Austins parish, and Mr. Hickeses, and Mr. Escots,[1] and Mr. Clutterbuck might get from some parishes. Brougham reckons it a capital point.[2]

274. RICARDO TO MILL[3]

[Reply to 273]

Gatcomb Park
29th Sept[r] 1818

My dear Sir

29 Sept. 1818 I thank you much for the communication of the passage, from Mr. Brougham's letter, respecting me. It appears indeed more probable than it has ever yet done, that I shall have a seat in the House of Commons, and in proportion to the increased probability do my fears also increase, that I shall never be fit for any other duty in it, but to say aye, or no, accordingly as my judgement may direct me, on the different questions offered for discussion. Because you have been successful in one of your prognostics, and my book has excited more attention than I had dared to hope, you, like other prophets, begin to think that you may foretell the most improbable of events, and like them too you trust to chance or good fortune for their proving true,—for to suppose that the discipline you recommend will enable me to take a part in the debates, and offer any thing which shall do me, and

[1] H. Hicks and T. Estcourt, two neighbours of Ricardo in Gloucestershire.

[2] Brougham was Chairman of the Select Committee to enquire into the state of the Education of the Lower Orders, appointed in 1816 and renewed in 1818.

[3] Addressed: 'James Mill Esq[r] / at Professor Wallace's / College / Bagshot'.
MS in Mill-Ricardo papers.

my instructor, credit, is building on good fortune alone. The ground work is wanting. Years of neglect at the most essential period of life cannot be balanced by weeks or months of application. Not only do I labour under a defect of memory which prevents me from retaining to any useful purpose what has been the object of my study, but I have difficulties in composition—in clothing my thoughts in words, in a degree that I seldom witness in others. This defect I fear is unconquerable, and you will agree with me that no man can write or speak well, if he cannot express his ideas with facility and ease. Look at the evidence before the Usury Committee, and you will observe that, in point of expression, mine is the worst evidence given before them. As I told you on a former occasion I tell you now: I have no disinclination to work, and it is sufficient for me that you recommend the course which you have pointed out, that I will follow it, but I prepare you before hand for disappointment, for most assuredly I shall never be able to speak in an Assembly which can boast of the talents of a Romilly, a Tierney, a Canning, and a Brougham.

My brother Moses continues to improve in health. He now takes a little exercise on horseback, and I have great hopes that he will be restored to that standard of health at which he was for some years fixed, before his late attack.

Gatcomb is now quite a different place from the Gatcomb you saw—the change that took place during my absence in London was surprising. When I left the country every thing was burnt up, so that not a green blade of grass could be seen; on my return to it the verdure was every where beautiful, and every field was sending forth in abundance its supply of food for the cattle which were before half-starved. I regretted that you had seen us under such disadvantageous circumstances but I comfort myself in the hope that you will

29 Sept. 1818 often repeat your visit and perhaps again make the little tour from which we had so much pleasure.

I am glad that you are so pleasantly situated at Bagshot, and that your family are enjoying themselves highly. I have no doubt but that the pure air they are breathing will be very serviceable to them.

Mrs. Osman Ricardo is in the 4th vol of Heloise and is very much pleased with it. She as well as Mrs. Ricardo and all our circle request to be kindly remembered to you.

I am told that it will be difficult to obtain the information respecting the proportion of Paupers in the surrounding parishes who can read and write, as the information in many cases cannot without much trouble be got from the paupers themselves, as perhaps the persons receiving the money are few, although they receive it on behalf of many,—and the few are often unacquainted with facts of that description which regard the many. I will however use my best efforts to comply with Mr. Brougham's wishes.

I am now doing very little either in reading or writing, having Mr. Basevis family here. I cannot settle to any regular employment till I am alone or till I can separate myself entirely of a morning from the rest of the inmates of this house.—

Since I commenced this letter I have rec^d a letter from Messrs Bleasdale & Co my solicitors in which to my great surprise they tell me that they have not yet received any communication from Lord Portalington or his solicitor on the subject of the proposed advance. They add "Should this business go off I am told a seat may be procured elsewhere upon eligible terms but I am not at present in possession of particulars." To this last intimation I cannot of course attend as I consider the business which Mr. Brougham has managed for me as really settled if the title to the property is good,— yet I may after all be disappointed and I cannot be quite

certain of the seat till I know that my solicitor or one equally 29 Sept. 1818
capable of judging is satisfied with the security.—

Ever truly Y^{rs}

DAVID RICARDO

I have had another friendly letter from Mr. McCulloch.[1]

275. RICARDO TO MILL[2]

[*Answered by* 278]

Gatcomb Park
15 Octr 1818

My dear Sir

Since receiving your letter[3] I have been at Bath with 15 Oct. 1818
Mrs. Ricardo to see Mrs. Clutterbuck who was very unexpectedly delivered, long before the completion of her time,
of a dead child. We found her pretty well—she had a good
night while we stayed with her, and we left her with every
prospect of being soon reinstated in health and strength.

You tell me that in sending me Mr. Place's application on
behalf of Mr. Evans[4] you send me no advice—that you do
not know the young man, and that I must judge for myself.
I must deal with it then as wholly Mr. Place's application, in
which you are quite neuter, doing only as you are asked to
do. So regarding it, I must frankly confess that I am not
disposed to give even the lowest sum of £5– to the case in
question. Mr. Evans' name is connected with political transactions, of his merits in which I am wholly ignorant. I wish
to avoid connecting myself with any party, or to be mentioned as the supporter of any man whose political conduct
may have been violent and intemperate. I do not say that

[1] Letter 271.
[2] MS in Mill-Ricardo papers.
[3] Mill's letter is missing.
[4] 'Thomas Evans the Spencean'
notes Place on a letter from Sir

Francis Burdett, who sent a contribution, 17 Oct. 1818 (MS in
British Museum, Add. 37949,
f. 72).

15 Oct. 1818 Evans' has been such, and I have no particular inducement to examine into it. Had you felt any particular interest for the young man I should at any rate have given the money, although I might have asked you not to let my name appear, but as it is I have no particular motive to prefer this application to others. You will be kind enough to make my refusal appear as little ungracious to Mr. Place as possible, as I entertain great respect for him.

The additional postage which a note will occasion if inclosed in this letter will not compensate you for the loss of interest on £2, and therefore I request you to pay that sum for me, in discharge of my engagement. I will repay you the first time we meet.—

I wish you a pleasant journey to Worthing.

Truly Y.rs

DAVID RICARDO

Mr. Basevi is still here—his presence, and many domestic concerns, which have particularly engaged my attention, have hitherto prevented me from making much progress in my writing. Next week I hope to be more diligent.

My solicitors have not yet received the abstract of the title of Lord P.'s estate, but they have heard from his solicitor, who has promised very soon to send it to them.—

276. TROWER TO RICARDO[1]
[*Reply to* 272.—*Answered by* 279]

My Dear Ricardo   October 18. 1818. Unsted Wood

18 Oct. 1818   This is the Country Gentlemens Season of dissipation, when shooting parties, and other schemes of idleness, occupy

[1] Addressed: 'To / David Ricardo Esqr. / Gatcomb Park / Minchinhampton'.—MS in *R.P.*

too large a portion of our time. Although a very indifferent
sportsman I occasionally engage in these active exercises, and
have lately been waging war (though not very destructive,)
against peaceful Partridges and Pheasants! You, I believe,
will not have this sin to answer for; but do not plume yourself
too much on this account, for, as the *receiver* of stolen goods
is considered as bad as the thief, I flatter myself you will not
fare much better, than I shall—No doubt *you* have been
partaking largely of other mens plunder!

I was sorry to hear by your last kind letter of the ill health
of one of your brothers, and hope, that his recovery has been
long since completed. Your absence during the Assizes was
unfortunate, as you would naturally wish to have fully discharged all the duties of your office; which are now I believe,
practically though not really concluded; excepting, indeed,
your attendance at the approaching Quarter Sessions.—I was
surprised to find Mr. McCullock the Author of the Review,
not being aware, that he added the study of Political Economy
to his other numerous acquirements—He is generally considered a very able man.[1] How happen'd it, that Major
Torrens declined the undertaking?—I was pleased in conversation, the other day, with some men, *addicted* to Political
Economy, to hear your book spoken of as now becoming a
Text Book on the subject.—"Magna est veritas et prævalebit"
and no doubt, ere long, the important truths you have
exhibited to the public will be properly appretiated.—

I wish your *political* opinions were equally in unison with
my own; but they appear to be much more at variance than
I was aware of.—You say, you have "*no objection*" to a mixed
Government! What! have you any *doubt* that *that* is the form
of Government, (when properly administered,) best calcu-

---

[1] Trower mistakes Dr. John Macculloch (1773–1835), the geologist,
for the economist.

18 Oct. 1818 lated to promote the happiness and prosperity of the people? Can there be any question on this point? Are you tremblingly alive to the evils of Monarchy, and do you shut your eyes against the dangers of democracy? If you are in favor of a Republic there is an end of the question. But, if you agree, that the principles of our mixed Government are to be preserved; then, the dangers to which it is exposed from the too great preponderance of *either* of the three powers of which it is composed must be equally kept in view.—My firm persuasion is that that *balance* of the Constitution, which is essential to its wholesome operation, and even its existence, is most in danger from the *popular* part of the Constitution; from that force, which you truly say is *irresistible*, and which, if not regulated and restrained, must eventually destroy our Constitution. In fact my fear is, that the House of Commons should really become *too popular*—for, should such be the case, there is no sufficient power in the other branches of the Constitution to control it. I prefer therefore, that the public opinion should occasionally, and upon sufficient emergencies operate from *without*, than constantly predominate *within*. You ask, whether *Instead* of having this check for the people *out* of Parliament, would it not be better to have it constitutionally exerted *within it*. I answer, that it would not be *instead*; and that the two powers acting constantly *within and without*, would set at nought the other branches of the Constitution, and presently precipitate us into a Democracy.— No doubt, many reforms are necessary, many obvious improvements require to be put in practice, and those you have mentioned in the *law* are some of the most glaring, and the most necessary. But, I should prefer gradually obtaining these great ends by means which I could calculate and control, rather than by a force, which when let loose would be incalculable in its objects, and irresistible in its effects. My

paper forces me to cut short my remarks upon this most 18 Oct. 1818 interesting and important subject. This Country is greatly blessed in its capabilities and resources, both mental and physical. Let there be but peace abroad, and *wisdom at home*, and I feel satisfied, that a glorious career awaits us. Pray make our united kind regards to Mrs. Ricardo and family, and believe me My Dear Ricardo

Your very affectionate friend
HUTCHES TROWER

277. MALTHUS TO RICARDO[1]

My dear Sir,   E I Coll Oct 21ˢᵗ 1818

Whishaw in a letter to me the other day told me that he 21 Oct. 1818 understood you were coming in for Portarlington. I hope this is true, and wish to hear it confirmed by you, as I should be sorry that you should not come into Parliament, having once determined to take any steps towards it. Portarlington I think was the place for which Sharpe formerly came in, and I should suppose it was an agreeable and very quiet sort of borough.

We have some thoughts of going to Bath this winter for the whole or part of the vacation, in which case I shall certainly make a point of paying you a visit at Gatcomb; but it will probably be from Bath, and not in our way down, as on our journey, we shall be too large a party. I believe we shall have one of the Miss Eckersall's as well as our children. Shall you be at Bath any part of the winter?

Whishaw is returned from his autumnal tour, and we hope to see him and Smyth here, early in the next month. But he talks a little of going previously to Bowood if he can

---

[1] Addressed: 'D. Ricardo Esqr / Gatcomb Park/Minchinhampton./ Gloucestershire.'—MS in *R.P.*

21 Oct. 1818 find the time, to meet Dugald Stewart and Miss Edgeworth who are there. He can hardly be expected to resist such temptations.

I am going on with my volume, though slowly, and with more interruptions than I intended or expected. I boggle ever at the title; and it [is]¹ not till after some delay and difficulty, that I have at length determined upon "The Principles of Political Economy considered, with a view to their practical application". I could not find any term like tracts or essays which I liked. Will the title do? what do you say?—But though I have at length determined on what I am going to write about, I doubt whether I shall finish this spring.

I hear the sale of your work goes on swimmingly, and that you are preparing another edition; but pray don't render all my fine arguments useless. I am inclined to think that where we shall most essentially differ in our practical conclusions is on the point where Say and Mill are distinctly with you. Your conclusions however naturally follow from your original definition of value in exchange and your too decided seperation of wealth and value, which I have always thought fundamentally wrong. You have quite overlooked the consideration of *value* as the prime power of industry and the grand stimulus to production.

I hope Mrs. Ricardo and your family are quite well Mrs. Malthus joins with me in kind regards:

Ever truly Yours
T R MALTHUS

¹ Omitted in MS.

278. MILL TO RICARDO[1]

[*Reply to 275.—Answered by 280*]

My Dear Sir

4 College Terrace, Bagshot, 26th Octr 1818

I am inclined to bring up the rear of my part of our 26 Oct. 1818
correspondence just now, fearing I may have less leisure in
future. We are still here, as you see; to which several things
have contributed. Besides the continuance of good weather,
a still stronger cause has been accidentally added. To the
course of education destined for the gentlemen cadets at this
college, has been recently added a course of chemical
lectures, which began to be delivered for the first time about
three weeks ago, by a gentleman from London. Although
these lectures have been held very sacred, and even the sons
of the Professors and officers of the institution excluded
from them, the great authorities of the place united in an
invitation to John to attend them, and the opportunity I
thought of some importance, as now the time was come when
I wished him to see a course of chemical experiments.[2] The
distinction of this invitation he owed to a little reputation he
has acquired, very accidentally. Among the Professors here
are two or three gentlemen of Oxford and Cambridge, really
clever men, and another very accomplished Oxford scholar,
tutor to the Governor's sons.[3] These gentlemen and I having
got intimate, and taking our walks together, one of them

---

[1] Addressed: 'David Ricardo Esq / Gatcomb Park / Minchinhampton. / Glo'ster Shire'. MS in *R.P.*
[2] J. S. Mill, giving an account of his studies in a letter to Sir Samuel Bentham, dated 30 July 1819, says: 'having had an opportunity of attending a course of lectures on chemistry, delivered by Mr.

Phillips, at the Royal Military College, Bagshot, I have applied myself particularly to that science'. (Quoted by Bain, *J. S. Mill. A Criticism*, 1882, p. 8.)
[3] Probably William Mills, of Magdalen College, Oxford, afterwards Whyte Professor of Moral Philosophy. The Governor was Maj.-Gen. Sir Alexander Hope.

26 Oct. 1818 called upon me one evening when I was out, and missing me fell into conversation with John, and asked him about his studies. The account the boy gave him of what he had done he mentioned to the rest; and the whole appeared either folly or cheat; that I was either fool enough to let the boy pass over a multitude of things without knowing them, or wished to impose upon others by making the semblance of knowledge in him pass for the reality; as no child they concluded could possibly know all that he told his interrogator he had done. An occasion was soon taken to put him to the test, by inviting me to the house of one of them, when I was requested to bring the boy along with me. All were present, and as their purpose was to me unknown, I was a little surprised when they began a rigid examination. The consequence was that they expressed extravagant admiration, as absurd, I told them, as their scepticism which they mentioned to me, had been before. Nevertheless they trumpeted their admiration, and he began to be taken too much notice of; the governor begged he might be allowed to go to his house as much as possible, and make friendship with his boys, and so the thing has gone on. I was anxious he should hear the lectures, and I was unwilling to appear to slight the compliment which had been paid him, by taking him away: and I was still more unwilling to leave him to the spoiling of the notice he is receiving. I have arranged matters accordingly, thus. This week and the next will finish the said lectures, all but a few on geology which he can learn from books. I shall remain here till the end of this week, when I must pay my promised visit to Hume: Mrs. Mill will remain here with the children till the end of the week following, when we shall all assemble in London. And this is the principal part of my history since my last—except that I have not at all been well. A bowel complaint, consisting of costiveness attended with severe

gripings, has been prevalent here for the last three weeks, 26 Oct. 1818
and I have had too great a share of it; the pain, and the medicines necessary for relief, have kept me in a very uncomfort-
able state of body, and have unfitted my mind for study—
I have done little but read. My wife is also now ill in the same
way. Your family I hope are all well, and Mr. Moses fast
recovering. I am truly sorry for the misfortune of Mrs.
Clutterbuck, but comfort myself from what you say that
her own constitution has suffered as little as could well be in
such a case. Pray what are the news of Mr. Ralph? If he is
with you, or if you see him before I do, tell him I shall make
up for the delinquency of not answering his letter, by talk
in abundance when we meet in London, or its neighbourhood.

I had a short scrawl from Torrens the other day, about his
son who is at the college here, and who, he is afraid, will be
dismissed—the boy is too idle to get knowledge enough to
pass; and he wishes me to see what I can do among the
professors and office-bearers for him. He adds: "I have
just returned from Edin. which I liked extremely. I introduced myself to McCulloch and was highly pleased with him.
We had much discussion on Ricardo's doctrine of value. I
threw my arguments upon paper, and they will be printed in
the next N^o of the Edin. Magazine.[1] McCulloch answers me

[1] Robert Torrens's article, entitled 'Strictures on Mr. Ricardo's Doctrine Respecting Exchangeable Value', appeared in the *Edinburgh Magazine* for Oct. 1818, pp. 335-8; it was written in the form of a letter to the editor and signed 'R'. Torrens criticised Ricardo's theory of value and contended that 'when capitalists and labourers become distinct, it is always the amount of capital, and never the quantity of labour, expended on production, which determines the exchangeable value of commodities.' McCulloch replied in the number for November, pp. 429-31, under the title 'Mr. Ricardo's Theory of Exchangeable Value Vindicated from the Objections of R.'; his article is signed 'M.' and dated 2 Nov. 1818. He says: 'Mr. Ricardo has not, as far as I can discern, anywhere affirmed, that when equal capitals are of different degrees of durability, the products of equal quantities of labour will not be of equal value. He has, I am quite

26 Oct. 1818 in the ensuing N°, and each is quite confident of gaining the victory over the other. The battle, however, is a most perfectly amicable one."¹ I am very glad of this—it will promote the reputation both of the doctrine and its author. I should not wonder if it is Blackwoods Mag. he means; as I see in the advertisement of the present N° an article entitled Ricardo and the Edin. Rev.²

certain, made no such statement. He contends, and justly too, that the products of equal quantities of Labour are always equal.' He asks 'What is capital but *accumulated labour?*' and concludes: 'to tell us that the value of commodities depends on the amount of capital consumed in their production is only another, but an extremely cumbrous, roundabout and incorrect way of telling us, that their value depends on the *total quantity of labour* required to bring them to market.' Ricardo, no doubt sharing Mill's dissatisfaction with this vindication (cp. below, p. 364), wrote a reply of his own (see below, p. 360). This reply has not been found; see however the series of parallel passages quoted by Ricardo in refutation of Torrens, above, IV, 315. Cp. below, p. 338.
¹ Some additional details are given by Torrens in a letter from Edinburgh, 30 Sept. 1818, to Place, in London: 'On Sunday I dined with Constable the Bookseller we had a pleasant literary party American and English and I had the good fortune to be placed beside MᶜCulloch who reviewed Ricardo. He is about thirty; very good humoured, and unaffected. We had much con-

versation. He says he is the only Edinburgh economist who has embraced the doctrines of Ricardo; and seemed glad to meet one of the converts though not agreeing in all points. I have given him my intended review [cp. above, p. 179, n. 2] to read and it is my present purpose to publish it in the form of a letter to Mr. Philips. I make progress in my Work upon political Economy and shall be soon ready to go to press. If Mill has returned to Town remember me kindly to him'. In a postscript he adds: 'I leave this on Friday and shall be in London in about a fortnight. I have been this instant introduced to Buchanan who edited Adam Smith. We entered upon Economy instantly. He admits as far as I can learn in a short conversation none of Ricardos doctrines. He admires Malthus highly. MᶜCulloch does not'. (MS in British Museum, Add. 37949, fols. 70–1.) Cp. below, p. 354.
² The article in *Blackwood's Magazine*, Oct. 1818, on 'Ricardo and the Edinburgh Review', signed J. G. deals with MᶜCulloch's review of Ricardo and has no connection with Torrens's criticism. Cp. below, p. 332.

I am quite pleased with your declaration that you would 26 Oct. 1818
betake yourself to the writing of the discourses[1] we have so
often talked about, as soon as Mr. Basevi left you; and I doubt
not you are now deeply engaged, and already feeling delight
in your progress. The exercise will be of prodigious advantage to you—and as I know well how much it would have
accelerated my own progress, had a man of more experience
than myself looked at the productions of my pen when my
experience in expressing my thoughts to others was not yet
great, I shall not at all mind delicacy in urging you to let me
see yours. A few lines shewing where you may have de-
veloped too sparingly, or where on another occasion you may
have dwelt too long, where you have divided less advantageously than you might, or made a less perfect arrangement
than the subject admitted of, given your thoughts in one
order when another would have been either more clear, or
more impressive; where you may have omitted any thing
necessary, or used any thing not necessary; where a flaw may
occur in your reasoning; or where you may have used a
fallacy instead of a proof—these things pointed out a few
times in a composition of your own, when your mind has
been attentive to the subject, will give you such an insight
into the whole mystery of these errors and their opposite
perfections, that you will carry the command of it to every
subject you undertake. Nor do I speak all this at random;
but from a very exact register of the experience I have had
first of my own mind, and then of all the minds with which
I have dealt. Your mind in fact is in that state of maturity,
in which a small portion of new instruction of the right kind
goes a great way with it. And do not take this as a compliment: the same is the case with every mind which has taken
as much pains with itself. Now your habits of attentive

[1] See above, p. 301.

26 Oct. 1818 observation, and attentive reflection, in your course through life, on all you have seen, and heard, and read, is that sort of pains I speak of; and that is the best part of education. You over-rate what is got in the schools; when you think that it places you irrecoverably behind. The best things the schools could give would be those habits of attention observation and reflection which you have got without the schools; and which our imperfect schools are so very ill calculated to give. Therefore no mistrust. You will soon find how little occasion you have for it. Who of them has a mind to compare with yours? Some of the very best among them profess they are unable with all their efforts to understand what you have demonstrated. In fact I have set my heart upon your making a figure: that is the short and the long of it—and you must not disappoint me. Compliments to the whole of your fire side, whose kind remembrance I am so anxious to retain: with best regards to Mrs. Osman and her lord—glad to hear of the profound studies in La Nouvelle Heloise—by the bye she ought to write to me all she thinks about it, all the remarks and discoveries, and criticisms she has made.

Ever yours

J. MILL

279. RICARDO TO TROWER[1]

[*Reply to* 276.—*Answered by* 287]

Gatcomb Park 2ᵈ Novʳ 1818

My dear Trower

2 Nov. 1818   I am not so guilty as you, in the affair of the Partridges, and pheasants.—I eat them it is true, but their death, or that of some other animal, is necessary for my subsistence, and

[1] Addressed: 'Hutches Trower   MS at University College, London. Esqʳ/Unsted Wood/Godalming/   don.—*Letters to Trower*, XXII. Surry'.

I may legitimately pursue them for that purpose. I employ a skilful man who brings them down with the least sum of pain, that can be inflicted in such a warfare. Are you no more guilty than this? If our judges were the birds themselves, I should be condemned to the guilotine simply—you would have to sustain the death of Damiens.[1]

I think it is possible by what you say that you may be mistaking the[2] gentleman who reviewed my book: it was not Dr. MCulloch of London, but Mr. MCulloch, of Edinburgh, the editor of the Scotsman. I am very much pleased at the approbation you express yourself, and which has been expressed by others, in your presence, of my humble efforts to improve the science of Polit. Economy. The reward which I have received for my labours has far exceeded my expectations.

I wish, with you, that we could more nearly agree in our political opinions, this agreement we shall not probably be able to effect, but we may continue to esteem each other, and give each other credit for sincerity, whether we do or not. You speak with energy of the superior advantages of a mixed government, over that of a republic, as of a question not admitting of a doubt, and seem shocked that any hesitation should be expressed in agreeing to so clear a proposition, and you place it so far on the proper footing, that you prefer a mixed government, only, because, in your opinion, it is best calculated to promote the happiness, and prosperity, of the people. This you appear to agree is the only legitimate end of all government. Democracy, Aristocracy, Monarchy— or the three mixed, wherever they prevail *ought* only to be considered as means to that end. Yours is either a solid well founded opinion, or it is not. If it is not, then, as you observe,

---

[1] The soldier who stabbed Louis XV in 1757; he was tortured and torn in pieces by horses.   [2] 'name and' is del. here.

2 Nov. 1818 there is an end of that argument against a reform of parliament, that it will make the popular branch of our constitution too strong, and so destroy the other branches; for if a republic be the best form of government, and will best promote the happiness of the people, we must not quarrel with reform for its tendency to give us a republican government. But let us suppose, or take for granted, which I do, that the contrary opinion is well founded, and that a mixed government such as ours, consisting of King, Lords, and Commons, is the best form of government, and let us examine the question of a reform in parliament on that supposition. You and I, and all *reasonable persons*, impressed with this opinion, having representatives to chuse, would select those only who acknowledged this demonstrable principle, and who would engage to maintain the monarchical and aristocratical branches. Having no *private interest* to serve, it would be folly or madness in us, if thinking that one form of government would be productive of advantage and happiness, another of disadvantage and misery, we should obstinately and deliberately reject the former, and prefer the latter. This is evidently improbable, if not impossible. If then the representatives of the people were fairly, and unbiassedly chosen, by the *reasonable part of the country*, you cannot shew that any motive could exist for chusing any but such as would uphold those branches of the constitution which are demonstrably essential to good government. If you say that the superiority of a mixed government, over a republic, cannot be demonstrated, but can only be inferred as a probable truth, I ask to whom would you refer the question for decision? not to the King, nor to the House of Peers, but to the *reasonable* part of mankind in the country, and who have no *sinister interest* to influence their decision. This then brings us again to the conclusion which I wish to establish, that there is no such

security for good government as that of leaving the choice
of representatives to the *reasonable part* of the community for
they have every motive to wish to be well governed, none
to be ill-governed. This being *demonstrated*, we must extend
the elective franchise to all *reasonable men* who have no
particular interest in opposition to the general interest, and
the most you can require of the friends of reform is the right
to challenge such electors as are *without the necessary
qualifications*. Now this right I freely yield to you; shew the
sinister interest, or the probability of a bad choice, and I will
consent to deprive the individual to whom they attach of the
right of electing members. But I will not allow you to
challenge peremptorily, and without shewing cause. Does
not your argument run thus? The advantages of a mixed
government are so evident that I am surprised any reasonable
man can have a doubt on the subject—let me but fairly state
the case, and all who are not biassed by prejudice, or interest,
will admit my conclusion. Yet, though they admit it, I dare
not trust them with the choice between a mixed government,
and a republic—these *reasonable people* are so besotted that
they will give up a *greater good, for a smaller*, and if once
I allow the democratic part of our constitution to prepon-
derate, there will be immediately an end of the Monarchical
and Aristocratical branches, although it is proved that they
are essential to good government. It is not sufficient for your
argument to prove, as you appear to think, that the popular
part of the constitution would become irresistible if we had
a reform, you are bound also to show that this irresistible
power would be mischievously employed, and to do that
you must shew an *adequate motive* for such an abuse.
Men have the power, which is almost uncontroulable, of
destroying themselves, but we confine them in straight
waistcoats only when we discover that they think they have

2 Nov. 1818 adequate motives for employing this power to their own destruction.

In answer to my question whether it would not be better that the operation of public opinion should be within the House of Commons, instead of without, you say that it would not be *instead*, but that the *two* powers acting constantly within, and without, would set at nought the other branches of the constitution, and presently precipitate us into a democracy. To the last of these propositions I have already replied, and you must shew me where my argument is defective. To the first, I say that it is a fallacy to speak of two powers, one acting within the house, the other without. I know only of one power that we were speaking of, the power of public opinion. If it operated within the house, it would be inert without, as indeed it always is there, until the people actually resist. It is only by its operation on the fears of those *within* the house that public opinion produces any effect in our government. If the opinions of the representatives of the people within the House of Commons after a reform coincided with those [of][1] their constituents without, one power, namely, public opinion, would controul the government, as it ought to do in all governments whose end, and object, is the happiness of the people. If they did not coincide, those within would have the power of opposing public opinion no longer than till the following election, when if the constituents were not convinced that they had been in error, representatives would be chosen more obedient to their views. It surely cannot be correct to say that because you take measures to ascertain the real opinion of the people in their own house of Parliament, that you double the effect of public opinion, and give it a strength which would be mischievously employed. According to your view of this

[1] MS torn.

question the right of electing the House of Commons might be safely left with the house of Lords, or we might get rid of the House of Commons, and preserve the house of Lords only. The check from without, whilst we have a free press, would continue to exist, and would operate on the fears of the Lords, as it now operates on the house of Commons, and all the objects of good government would be obtained, for it would still be a mixed government of Monarchy, Aristocracy, and Democracy. The democratic part of it indeed would shew itself somewhat irregularly, as it now does, without, but that is the way in which you think its operation is salutary. If this is not your opinion shew me what the advantages are of the present House of Commons for it seems to be agreed upon between us that it does not fairly represent the people, and that you seem to consider one of its great merits. All the advantage that I can find out in it is that it is a more enlarged representation of the aristocracy than the House of Peers would be—that it admits the great landholders and wealthy merchants, and manufacturers to a share of power, and distinction:—that a few popular representatives are somehow or another admitted there whose votes go for nothing but whose opinions are expressed there through the press more effectually than they would be in any other manner, and thus that salutary fear which we both like but which I would have more regularly and legitimately excited, is kept alive—these I think are all the advantages which flow from the present constitution of the House to the great body of the people. After all that I have said about the Honble House it is highly probable that I shall take my seat in it,—the business is not yet quite settled. No one is more sensible of the capabilities and resources of the Country than I am, but I wish to have security for their continuance, and above all I wish that door to be opened by which those reforms which you acknowledge

2 Nov. 1818 to be necessary might enter,—at present it is doubly and
trebly barred.—

Will you have patience to get to this line? I have severely
put it to the test, but you must forgive me. My brother is
getting better. Mrs. Ricardo unites with me in kind regards
to Mrs. Trower. Believe me ever

My dear Trower

Very truly Y^{rs}

DAVID RICARDO

Torrens I understand is to attack my doctrine of value in
the next number of the Edinburgh Magazine, and in the
number following MCulloch is to defend it. It is a friendly
contest. These gentlemen have lately met at Edinburgh.[1]

280. RICARDO TO MILL[2]

[Reply to 278.—Answered by 282]

Gatcomb Park
8 Novr 1818

My dear Sir

8 Nov. 1818   No sooner had Mr. Basevi left me than I went all round
South Wales with Mrs. Ricardo, and my two youngest girls.
The country is very beautiful, and the weather was very fine,
and I had only to regret that I was adding a fortnight more
to the idle time which I have been spending this year.
Mrs. Ricardo's health, and spirits, have been very bad, and
became worse when we lost all our visitors, and were
reduced to the small number of two; and therefore I readily
consented to accompany her in this little tour. My daughter
Fanny's health is no better, and she is on more accounts than
one the cause of much anxiety to us. We now think it neces-

---

[1] See above, p. 315.

[2] Addressed: 'James Mill Esqr / 1

Queen Square / Westminster'.

MS in Mill-Ricardo papers.

sary to consult some London medical man about her, and 8 Nov. 1818 for that purpose her mother is immediately going to town with her,—she will be the bearer of this letter. It will depend on this gentleman's opinion whether Mrs. Ricardo shall stay with Fanny a short time in London, and then return to me, or whether we shall commence our winter campaign now, and all that are left behind join Mrs. Ricardo in London. I do not think that there can be much danger in Fanny's case, but she certainly is become much thinner, and much weaker, than she was a month ago. You will be surprised to hear that she is going to be married to Edwd Austin,[1] a man 16 years older than herself, and you will still more wonder that no opposition that her mother and I could offer, have been of the least avail in deterring her from entering into a connection which we wholly disapprove. Nothing but the state of her health, and the fears of the consequences of the continued anxiety which this business caused her, could have induced us to yield, at least for the present, but she is so unwell that all her brothers and sisters were alarmed, and we could not help participating in their fears.

There is another marriage about to take place in our family in which I could have wished that the superiority of age had been on the gentleman's side instead of the lady's, but in other respects it is proper, and appears to be agreeable not only to the parties, but to all who are connected with them. My sister Esther will soon be the wife of William Wilkinson.[2] He is an excellent young man, a great favorite with all our family, and has a very fair prospect of succeeding in his business. Having dispatched these matters let me now speak of the contents of your last letter. I was very much

[1] Brother of Anthony Austin, who was married to Ricardo's daughter Priscilla.
[2] William Arthur Wilkinson

(1795–1865), a nephew of Mrs Ricardo, formerly Ricardo's clerk and now a member of the Stock Exchange.

interested, and very much pleased, at the account you give me of the result of the examination to which John was subjected by the gentlemen at the College. It must have been very gratifying to your feelings, and some little reward for your persevering exertions, to hear the just praises which were bestowed upon him. I hope it may lead to the formation of connections for John useful to his future settlement in life. At any rate it will be of great advantage to him if it introduces him into such society as you approve, for from the very retired and private manner in which he has been educated he stands in need of that collision which is obtained only in society, and by which a knowledge of the world and its manners is best acquired. With such knowledge John will probably become a shining character, and will convince the world that he has not degenerated from his sire.—

I hope that Mrs. Mill and you have now no traces of indisposition your complaint was happily of a nature not very difficult to remove.

Ralph is now here, he will leave me in a very few days, he is delighted with your country, and its inhabitants. From his account of them he has every reason to be so.

Torrens remarks on my doctrine of value will be in the Edin: Magazine, and not in Blackwoods, for I have seen it advertized in the table of contents of the former publication. I am glad that MCulloch feels confidence in being able to answer it. I wonder whether the article in Blackwood is from a friend or an enemy—I suspect the latter.

From the account which I have already given you of my late movements you will know that I have not had much time to devote to writing; I have nevertheless made a commencement in the way you recommended, but not with any result that can give me the least satisfaction. My first attempt was in an answer to a letter which I received from Trower,

of which I kept a copy, and without any hesitation I send
you that, and a subsequent paper which I have just written.[1]
It would be in vain to attempt to deceive you, I do not wish
it,—it is not my interest to do it. Know me for what I am,
and estimate me accordingly. I am disposed, as all men are,
to judge of myself favourably, but I cannot be blind to my
utter inability of putting my thoughts on paper, with any
degree of order, clearness, or precision. I am astonished at
my own deficiency, for it is a talent which every one about
me possesses in a superior degree to myself. You give me
hopes of acquiring it by practice, and I value it so highly, that
I shall not fail to persevere whilst I have a shadow of hope
that success will crown my efforts.—

I hear from various quarters that my book is selling very
fast, and that a new edition will soon be required. It will
perhaps be necessary that I should carefully go over the
whole subject again, and as I have not looked at it now for
more than a twelvemonth it will be in some measure new to
me, and I shall be better able to detect errors and inaccuracies.
I think in the last conversation we had together we agreed that
there would not be very great advantage in making any new
arrangement of the contents, as it appears to have made the
impression I could wish on those who have well considered it.

I heard from Mess.rs Bleasdale & Co, my solicitors, yesterday. They tell me that they have not yet received Lord
Portalington's abstract, but Mr. Humphrys informed them
that it was quite ready, and would be delivered to them in
the course of the week. He said that he had been waiting an
answer to a letter to Sir Hugh[2] Parnell which had prevented
its being delivered some days since. I wish this business was
settled.

[1] Letter 279 and, presumably, *Defence of the Plan of Voting by Ballot.*
[2] Should be Sir Henry.

8 Nov. 1818 You must as well as every other person who knew Sir Sam! and Lady Romilly, have been grieved and shocked at the melancholy events which have lately occurred in that family.¹ I hoped that Sir Samuel would for many years to come have contributed his efforts towards the amelioration of the condition of mankind. He had lately attained a situation which would have called for increased activity in his political career, and I confidently expected that his course would be marked by wisdom and honesty. What a sad termination to all our hopes!

Mrs. Osman Ricardo returns the books you were so kind as to lend her, with her best thanks. I believe she has sent a note with them to express these thanks herself. Pray give my kind regards to Mrs. Mill and your family and believe me

Ever Y^{rs}

DAVID RICARDO

My sister Rachel who is here has kept the Heloise, and engages to send it uninjured to Queen Square

281. RICARDO TO MURRAY²

> Gatcomb Park
> Minchinhampton
> 18 Novr 1818

Dear Sir

18 Nov. 1818 Your note dated the 10th was yesterday forwarded to me from Brook Street. I have not looked at my book³ since it was published and perhaps in reading it now I may discover some passages which I may wish to alter, but I am so bad a writer that I fear more to do harm than good by

¹ Sir Samuel Romilly had committed suicide on 2 November, a few days after the death of his wife.

² Addressed: 'John Murray Esqr/ Albermale Street / London'.
MS in the possession of Sir John Murray.
³ *Principles of Political Economy.*

attempting any different arrangement, therefore I believe 18 Nov. 1818
that I shall very soon be prepared for a second edition.

I am Dear Sir
Your obed. Serv.
DAVID RICARDO

If Mr. Malthus is going to publish[1] I submit to you
whether I should not wait to see his book, as I know that
I shall be attacked in it.

282. MILL TO RICARDO[2]

[Reply to 280.—Answered by 284]

Qu. Square West^r 18th Novr 1818
My Dear Sir

I can only write a few lines, for I am still hardly able to 18 Nov. 1818
write at all—and I am dunned excessively for two articles to
the Suppl. of Encyc. Brit.—But I think it necessary to tell
you, that I read your two discourses immediately when I
received them, and with the greatest satisfaction. I assure
you I speak nothing but the plain truth when I say that they
exceeded my expectation—the arguments are given neatly,
perspicuously, and strongly; and, delivered just as they are
written, would have a strong effect. I will give you a more
detailed criticism as soon as I am able. But I find it a very
difficult thing this time to get well. Nor do I well know
what is the matter with me. The seat of the malady is in the
intestinal canal; but I am weak, and languid, and disorganized,
to a degree that I hardly ever was before.

---

[1] The *Monthly Literary Advertiser* of 10 Nov. 1818 announced as 'in the Press,' to be published by Murray, Malthus's *Principles of Political Economy Considered, with a View to their Practical Applica-* tion, and the second edition of Ricardo's *Principles*. The former did not in fact go to press till a year later; cp. below, p. 370.
[2] MS in *R.P.*

I have not been able yet to see Mrs. Ricardo—but am happy to hear that Mr. Moses thinks Miss R. less ill than he expected—so that I fear we shall not see you before Xtmass. I am very sorry to hear that you have objections to her choice in a material affair, because I fear they must apply to the character, and not the circumstances of the party in question, which latter consideration would with you I am satisfied appear of no great weight. As to the disparity of years, in the second case, though as you say, they are on the wrong side, yet, if the parties are wise, that disparity, when it comes to be an inconvenience, can always be settled without the smallest disturbance to the mutual union. The young man will possess an invaluable friend, if he treats her as she will eminently deserve, and as from your character of him, there is every probability that he will.

I am very proud of my letter from Mrs. Osman Ricardo, which does her great credit, and shews that she reads with her own thoughts, not with thoughts borrowed from other people. What she says, that it is impossible to read Julie without wishing to be better, was the conclusion which struck me the first time I read the book. Please to present to her my very best compliments, and tell her I shall thank her very heartily for so generously accepting my bargain, as soon as I am in spirits enough to dare to attempt a letter to a young beauty.

By the bye, there is some mistake about the book—for both her letter and yours say that it was sent, but it has not come.

I really am not able to write news—and so adieu.

Most faithfully yours

J. MILL

283. RICARDO TO MURRAY[1]

Gatcomb Park
Minchinhampton
23 Nov.[r] 1818

Dear Sir

By the Stroudwater coach, which passes through this 23 Nov. 1818
place to-morrow, and stops at the Old White Horse Cellar
Piccadilly, you will receive one of the copies of my book,
which I have prepared for the press. You will observe that
there are a few very trifling alterations where I thought I
could make my ideas more clear. The first chapter was rather
complained of, as being long, and the subject complicated.
I have endeavoured to improve it, by dividing it into 4
sections.[2] Perhaps others may think this no improvement
at all, and therefore I should like to have the opinion of one
friend only on this point. For this purpose, I will inclose in
the parcel tomorrow, a letter to Mr. Mill, with a copy of the
Titles of the 4 sections, and I will ask him his opinion of
them. Your messenger can stop while he reads them, and
he will return them to him with any alteration he may suggest, which you will instruct the printer to adopt; or he will
advise their suppression altogether. I know that Mr. Mill is
very busy, and therefore I cannot trouble him to correct the
press; if such correction is absolutely necessary, with the
insignificant alterations I have made, the sheets must be sent
to me.

Perhaps you could get those few franked in which there
is any deviation from the old edition, and the others might
be left to the correction of the printer. I have another copy
of my book here, so that the old sheets need not be sent.—

[1] Addressed: 'John Murray Esq.[r] /
Albermale Street / London'.
MS in the possession of Sir
John Murray.

[2] In ed. 2 of the *Principles*, as
published, the chapter is divided
into five sections. Cp. below,
p. 333, n. 1.

23 Nov. 1818   The attack upon me in Blackwood's magazine[1] is I think very paltry—it finds fault with an opinion without examining the grounds which have been given for the opinion, and is really unworthy of notice.

I have some wish to see, and I desired Mrs. Ricardo to bring me, the last number of the New Edinburgh Magazine in which some part of my doctrine is disputed by Major Torrens.[2] Mrs. Ricardo sent me the wrong book, she has probably applied to you, and you have given her the right number. She will leave Brook Street for the country on wednesday morning (very early) next,[3] and if you have any thing to send she will bring it.

Y^{rs} truly

DAVID RICARDO

284. RICARDO TO MILL[4]

[*Reply to* 282.—*Answered by* 289]

Gatcomb Park
23 Novr 1818

My dear Sir

23 Nov. 1818   The few lines you wrote to me, were very encouraging, and will induce me to continue writing, in the hope of smoothing and overcoming the difficulties which now beset my path. I send you another of my wise discourses,[5] which I beg you to read at your leisure, and return it to me with the rest when we meet in London. Do not give yourself the trouble to write on the subject of my faults and omissions—

---

[1] See above, p. 316, n. 2.
[2] See above, p. 315.
[3] 25 November.
[4] Addressed: 'James Mill Esqr / 1 Queen Square / Westminster'. Not passed through the post: it was enclosed with letter 286 to

Murray, who sent it on by messenger.
MS in Mill-Ricardo papers.
[5] Probably *Observations on Parliamentary Reform.* See postscript to this letter and the opening of letter 298.

I know that your time is very valuable to you, and you will have plenty of opportunities when I am in London to talk over with me all these matters.—

Mr. Murray is in a great hurry to print a second edition of my book, and I have been busily at work in reading it over very attentively twice, within these few days. I am afraid to make many alterations in it. With such an unskilful hand, the risk would be great that I should not improve it.—I have however ventured to divide the first chapter, on value, into five[1] sections, the titles of which are inclosed, and I have to ask again of your friendship, to say to the bearer of this letter, or rather to write on a piece of paper, that he may shew it to Murray, whose messenger he is, whether you would suppress this plan of dividing the chapter into sections altogether,—if so the printer had better copy the old edition verbatim. But if you approve of the division into sections, then correct the Titles of them, or substitute any others which you may think more proper. At the end of each section I have concluded by a summary of the doctrine which I wished to prove, as for example "It appears then by this section that notwithstanding the accumulation of capital, commodities would not necessarily vary[2] in relative value from a rise in wages, unless it was accompanied by increased facility or difficulty in the production of one or more of them."—[3]

I have mentioned Torrens twice with approbation,[4] but on looking over his book I find so much that is wrong in it that I cannot bestow general praise on him, I commend him only for an able illustration of a particular principle, or for having maintained in a particular case a correct opinion.

[1] Replaces 'four'.
[2] First written 'vary', then replaced with 'rise', finally restored to 'vary'.
[3] Above, I, 56, n. 1.
[4] Above, I, 96–7, n. and 271, n.

23 Nov. 1818   I have been a little puzzled what to do respecting MCullock
I have not time to consult him respecting the passages he
would have modified or omitted, and on looking over the
book I see no opinion which I do not continue to hold. To
shew him however my wish of attending to his suggestions
I have altered the conclusion of page 329[1] and have said
"a minister is induced to have recourse to more direct taxes,
such as income and property taxes neglecting the golden
maxim of M. Say that "the very best of all plans of finance
is to spend little, and the best of all taxes is that which is least
in amount." Will this do? or should I write to MCullock?

I have been looking carefully at the passage which displeased Mr. Ensor,[2] and as I have doubts whether my opinion
was correct I have altered it, by referring the evils to which
some poor countries are subject to bad government, insecurity of property, and a want of education in all classes.
I have not mentioned Ireland, but have spoken generally.
I hope that I shall disarm him of any future censure.

On the whole I have, I hope, rather improved the book.
The examination to which I have again subjected it is so far
satisfactory in its result that I do not find any opinion which
I wish to retract—I am more and more confirmed in the
truth of the general doctrines.

The account you give me of your health gives me much
concern. After breathing such a variety of airs in the most
healthful parts of the country, you have no right to be ill,
and if your indisposition should be still unremoved I request
you to come to us. Our air is excellent and few invalids
come to us without deriving great benefit from it.—

Mrs. Ricardo returns in a day or two. The physician does
not speak doubtingly of Fanny's complaint but talks confidently of her recovery. My objection to her choice is not

_____
[1] Above, I, 242.   [2] Above, I, 100, n.

on account of the *circumstances* of the party, *they are* I
believe respectable, and are of inferior consideration, but
Mr. Edw.ᵈ Austin, whom you know, is 16 years older than
her,—he is moreover in very bad health and has been so for
2 or 3 years, the consequences in my opinion of a very
dissipated life, so that in constitution he is much older than
in years. Besides this, I abominate the companions with
whom he has constantly associated. He has long been the
friend of Col! Berkeley, and a very frequent inmate of
Berkeley Castle. In this part of the country the fame of this
latter gentleman is very notorious. He appears to delight in
ruining the peace of mind of young women, as well single
as married—he has very lately seduced a young woman
who was before much respected at Cheltenham, and who
is the mother of 2 children. Her husband has discovered
the affair and her happiness in all probability is blasted for
ever.

In this circle I have little fear that Fanny will be introduced,
but a man who can countenance such conduct by continuing
an intimacy with the perpetrator of it, and whose enjoyments
consist chiefly in hunting, is not the protector and companion
that I would select or approve for my child.—To do him
justice however his temper is good, and I know of no stain
on his own moral character. He may make a good husband,
and all may be well, but the place where his business will
require him to reside is not to my mind. There is scarcely
any society at Wotton which can be called desirable;—none
which can give any stimulus to the employment of the
mind.—

Mrs. Osman Ricardo was very much pleased with your
message. I have intimated to her that she must correspond
with you direct for I will not be made the vehicle to convey
your gallant speeches.

23 Nov. 1818 If I am not very much mistaken there was a postscript in my letter to inform you that my sister Rachel had taken possession of your books on the promise of conveying them safely to your house. I hope she has fulfilled this engagement.—

I have sent a message to Mr. Hicks by his son on the subject of the information which Mr. Hume would like to have. It will I apprehend be only necessary for him to particularize the Agricultural and the manufacturing parishes in Gloucestershire, and then by a reference to a thick book published by order of the House of Commons the information can be obtained. That book I have, and if Mr. Hume has it not I can lend it to him. I believe it is in the open closet in my dressing room in Brook Street and by sending any body who could select it from others may be got there.—

With respect to Mr. Koe I fear that I cannot be of service to him in the way you request first because I fear that my recommendation to my solicitors in favour of any conveyancer would not go far, and secondly that as far as it will go it must be exerted in favour of young Basevi [1] who begins business in the ensuing month on his own account. His father is naturally very anxious for his success, and he is the oldest and I believe one of the sincerest attached friends to me that I have. Adieu

Truly Y^{rs}

D Ricardo

On looking over the paper which I was going to send you, I am so discontented with it that I cannot send it.

[1] N. Basevi.

285. RICARDO TO MᶜCULLOCH[1]

[*Reply to* 271.—*Answered by* 290]

Gatcomb Park, Minchinhampton
Gloucestershire 24ᵗʰ Novʳ 1818

My dear Sir

I thank you much for the sheets of the Supplement to   24 Nov. 1818
the Encyclopedia which you were so good as to send me by
my brother. I have read with great satisfaction the two
articles which you have written, one on the Corn laws, the
other on the Cottage system. They appear to me to be correct
in principle, ably and clearly written, and to contain much
useful and important information. I would say more, because
I feel more, but you have disqualified me for the office of a
judge, by rendering my impartiality suspicious. The favourable manner in which you have noticed me has certainly been
very highly gratifying to me.

Mr. Murray has very suddenly applied to me for permission
to print a second edition of my book:—its sale it seems has
been much accelerated by the distinguished notice which you
took of it, and Mr. Murray is so much of a political economist
as to know that it is his interest to increase the supply with
the demand, and he seems also to be aware that the demand
for some articles is very much governed by caprice. For
these reasons he is very desirous to get the book out as soon
as possible. I have been busily employed these last few days
in reading it over with attention, chiefly with a view to find
out those passages which you think[2] hold out an apology to
ministers for taxation, but I fear I have not succeeded. In
page 329[3] there is something like it, and I propose altering
that passage by substituting the following words after

[1] MS in British Museum.—*Letters*   [2] See above, p. 280–1.
to MᶜCulloch, IV. Presumably   [3] Above, I, 242.
posted in London by Murray;
see letter 286.

24 Nov. 1818 "a minister" instead of those which now stand there. "a minister is induced to have recourse to more direct taxes, such as income and property taxes, neglecting the golden maxim of M Say "that the very best of all plans of finance is to spend little, and the best of all taxes is that which is the least in amount." Perhaps instead of this you would suggest something different, and would oblige by giving me your opinion freely on all those passages which you would like to see altered. I promise to use equal freedom with you, and to retain my own expression if I am not convinced by you. As the first few sheets will immediately be in the press, I hope you will excuse my requesting you to write to me immediately.

I understand that Major Torrens has written an article in the Edinburgh Magazine on my observations on value.[1] I have not yet seen it, but expect to have it here in a few days. Major Torrens and I had a long conversation on this question, without convincing each other.[2] I have distinctly stated in my book,[3] that value is not regulated solely by quantity of labour, when capitals are employed in production which are not equally durable. I mean to insert in Page 38[4] the following observation to be printed in the next edition and which I think more fully answers Major Torrens' objection. "The same result will take place if the circulating capitals be of unequal durability. If from the nature of two different trades, in which equal capitals are employed, one manufacturer could not bring the commodity he produced to market in less than one year, while the other could bring his there, in three months, the commodity of the first would fall in relative value to the second, with every rise of wages and fall of profits. It must be unnecessary to go into further

---

[1] See above, p. 315.
[2] Probably in February; see above, p. 253 and cp. p. 251. See also the 'Fragments on Torrens',

above, IV, 303.
[3] Above, I, 66.
[4] Above, I, 61, n.

calculations to prove this to be true, as it rests precisely on 24 Nov. 1818 the same principle as the case already considered, namely, the different degrees of durability of two equal capitals." Forgive me for troubling you so much at large with these matters. My brother only passed a few days with me in the country since his return from Scotland. He speaks with so much delight of the country he has been visiting, and of its inhabitants, that he has given me a great desire to visit it. When I shall be able to gratify this desire I am not at present able to tell. I trust however that either in Scotland or in England I shall ere long have the satisfaction of assuring you in person of the esteem with which I am

Most truly yours
DAVID RICARDO

286. RICARDO TO MURRAY[1]

Gatcomb Park, Minchinhampton
24 Novʳ 1818

Dear Sir

I send you the book, and two letters;[2] one for Mr. Mill 24 Nov. 1818 which you will be so good as to send to him, and let your messenger wait for an answer. The other, not directed, is for J. R. MᶜCulloch Esqʳ College Street Edinburgh; and I hope you will be able to get a frank for it and dispatch it immediately, as I should wish to have Mr. MᶜCulloch's answer before the printer arrives at page 321.[3]

Yʳˢ very truly
DAVID RICARDO

[1] Addressed: 'John Murray Esqʳ' —not passed through the post (cp. letter 283).
MS in the possession of Sir John Murray.
[2] Letters 284 and 285.

[3] Replaces '300'. Page 321 of ed. 1 (above, I, 237) is the first page of sheet Y, which includes p. 329 (above, I, 242) where the chief correction suggested by MᶜCulloch is made.

287. TROWER TO RICARDO[1]

[Reply to 279.—Answered by 295]

Unsted Wood—Godalming—
Nov.[r] 24. 1818

My Dear Ricardo—

24 Nov. 1818   In the sentiment with which you preface your Constitutional argument I most cordially agree, "that we may continue to esteem each other, and give each other credit for sincerity, whether our political opinions accord or not." I am convinced, that our friendship is too firmly fixed, and I trust our minds are both too liberal, for difference of opinion on any subjects to loosen the ties, that attach us to each other —Nor, do I even *dispair*, that our ideas will *approximate*, although they may not entirely *coincide*, upon this particular subject. You state your argument clearly and forcibly; and, if I agreed with you in the *premises*, I should find it difficult to deny the *conclusion*. Thus far, however, we do agree, that the only legitimate object of all Government is the happiness of the people, who live under it; and that a Government consisting of Kings, Lords and Commons, (mutually assisting and controlling each other) is the form best calculated to ensure that desireable object.—Now it follows, that whatever *reform* may be introduced into this Government should have a reference to the *principle* upon which it is established, and should not endanger the preservation of that *balance of power*, which is essential to its existence.— Previously to the adoption of any Reform two questions must, therefore, arise.—First, is the change desireable in *itself*; secondly, supposing it to be so, is it *consistent* with the *principle* of the established Government? Will it interfere

[1] Addressed: 'To / David Ricardo   directed by Ricardo 'For James
Esqr / Gatcomb Park / Minchin-   Mill Esq.[r] / Queen Square'.
hampton / Glocestershire'.   Re-   MS in *R.P.*

with, or derange, that distribution of this power, allotted to 24 Nov. 1818 each branch of the constitution, which is necessary to the preservation of the whole? This, then, I take to be the point at issue between us. *I* consider that a Reform (or Alteration as I call it) carried to the *extent*, that you wish to carry it, would endanger the safety of the Constitution; would give such additional force to the *popular* part of it, as would be inconsistent with the security of the other two branches— You are of a different opinion and your answer to my objection is "that all *reasonable persons*, having no *private interests* to serve, would select, as representatives, those only, who would engage to maintain the monarchical and aristocratical branches."—But, let me ask, whether this is the description, that can be fairly given of the Electors of great Britain—"Reasonable persons having no private interests to serve", "not disposed to give up a greater good for a smaller". That you admit such *must* be the character of the Electors to justify *your* view of the subject, I readily infer, from your saying; "shew me the *sinister interest*, or the *probability* of a *bad choise*, and I will consent to deprive the individual, to whom they attach, of the right of electing Members." No doubt if the electors *were* all reasonable persons, having no *private interests* to serve, not disposed to give up a greater good for a smaller, and qualified by habit and education to form correct notions upon the nice and delicate question of constitutional policy, they might safely be entrusted with the uncontrolled power of electing the whole of their Representatives. But, that they are *not* thus qualified, at present, I presume to imagine; and that they *will not* readily become so, I am very apprehensive. To *approximate* to such a desireable state of things, which indeed *would satisfy me*, (for it is foolish to aim at impossibilities, or even at great improbabilities,) you must carry your scheme of

24 Nov. 1818 reform *further* than you propose; and by so doing I should feel much more disposed *to go along with you*. Limit the right of voting at Elections to such persons, who by their education have the ability to decide correctly; and who by their situation have the power of acting independently.—Upon what *other* subject of importance are we disposed to defer to the opinions of those, whose situation and circumstances render them incompetent to arrive at a just conclusion, or even to enter upon a consideration of the question? Yet, upon the momentous question of choosing those, who are to govern us, we are content to be guided, for the most part, by men whose ignorance, sordidness, and passion, render them fit instruments, for the mischievous designs of desperate and dangerous demagogues!—If, therefore, you are to *alter* the Constitution, with a view to its supposed primitive theoretical perfection, you should take care, whilst you extend the elective franchise to those from whom it certainly *ought not* to be withheld, that you withdraw it from those in whose hands it was not *originally* intended to be vested. But, even admitting the electors should become as qualified for the discharge of their important duty, as could reasonably be expected, under any circumstances, still, I contend, that if you were to let loose into the House of Commons the full force of the popular part of our constitution, that it would be *impossible* for the *other branches* to preserve, for a continuance, anything beyond a mere *nominal authority*.—The uncontrolled power over the purse, which is vested in the Commons, gives them, necessarily, such a superiority over the *other* branches, that, unless the influence of *these* was suffered silently to operate, to a certain extent, in that House, the whole form of the constitution would speedily be changed. If *no* such influence existed in what way could the other branches express their own opinions, when in opposition to

the Commons; but by *open dissent* on the part of the Lords, or by *veto* on the part of the Crown.—And, surely, it were much better for the safety of the *whole* that these conflicting sentiments should be *quietly* arranged by means of influences *moderately operating*; than by constant recourse to those means provided by the theory of the Constitution, but, which could not be frequently indulged in without producing the most mischievous effects upon the body politick. If you say, that these sentiments ought *not* to be expressed, when in opposition to the declared sentiments of the Commons, then it is obvious, that you are contending for the *supremacy* of that House, and that you would have our Constitution a *mixed* Government merely in *form*, but a *Republic* in *substance*—If, on the other hand, you admit, as you must do, whilst *approving* of our mixed Government, that the opinions of the other branches *should be felt*, and that the ultimate result of the deliberations of the Legislature, should be the *mixed and mellowed opinions of the three branches*, then, I say, there is *no way*, in which those opinions can be so *safely* expressed, with a view to the general interests, as by the influence of these two branches, operating *quietly and moderately*, in the House of Commons. You will observe, that by this means the *original principle* of the Constitution is *preserved*; but that experiment and experience, the perfection of all things, have suggested a mode by which the principle should operate in a manner more conducive to the health and safety of the Commonwealth.—I admit, that it is a question, and an important one too, to *what extent* this influence ought to be suffered to operate. But it is obvious, that no general rule can be laid down upon this subject. It is a matter of *feeling* and *observation*, and one in which the public is too much interested to fear, that it will be overlooked—And sure I am, that this is not the danger to be

24 Nov. 1818 apprehended in the present times; my apprehensions run in an opposite direction. No doubt, the last long war threw great additional influence into the hands of the Crown, and it is well, that it did so, for in perilous times the safety of a Country mainly depends upon the strength of the Government—But, it seems to be forgotten, that these times are speedily passing away, and with them, that additional power and influence in the Crown, which they necessarily created. Yet, the cry of dissatisfaction continues, although the disease (if such it be) is rapidly disappearing.—And, it is important to remark, that, with a view to preserving the just balance of the Constitution, it is *no less necessary* to watch the degree of influence, which is possessed by the *popular part*, than it is that of the other two. And, that *that* influence should be measured and regulated to prevent its undue preponderance. —And herein, appears to me, to consist the important duty of the Statesman—To bear constantly in mind, that the Government, over which he presides, is a complicated piece of machinery, consisting of various parts, endowed with different principles, and[1] curiously harmonising, assisting, and controlling each other, for the benefit of the whole—But the perfection of this machine, and the powerful and beneficial effects of which it is capable, depends upon the *due degree* of power being preserved by *each* of the principles of which it is composed; and that, as the balance of the *whole* must equally be destroyed by the undue preponderance of *any one* of the *Members*, it is his imperious duty to endeavor, at all times, to *preserve the balance*, by throwing into the scales of that which is *lightest*, the degree of influence necessary to preserve the just equilibrium.—

If this be a just view of the subject it follows, that a *sufficient* security for the preservation of the Constitution is

[1] In MS this 'and' is ins. after 'curiously' instead of here.

not to be found in the honesty of the electors, or in the virtue of our representatives, for if the machine be constituted with a tendency to lean too much to the popular side, it becomes necessary that means should be adopted to counteract this defect and to preserve the just equilibrium.—That such is the natural tendency of our Constitution is the declared opinion of our ablest constitutional writers; and if this truth were felt formerly how much more forcibly must it now impress itself upon our minds when we witness the rapid growth of the power of popular opinion.—To that opinion legitimately expressed, and prudently tempered by the wisdom of Parliament, I look, with confidence, to those reforms and improvements in Government, which are suggested by the evidence of experience and required by the progress of events.--

I fear I have, thus, run my observations, to what you may conceive, an unwarrantable length, and certainly much beyond what I intended. Yet in looking over your letter I observe there is still much remaining upon which I am tempted to remark.—But I believe I have embraced the substance of your opinions, and have considered the main points upon which we are at variance; and as I do not feel myself prepared or qualified to send you an essay on the subject, I will not fatigue you with any more desultory remarks. At all events I am happy to find you are likely to take your seat in that Assembly, where your sentiments may be advantageously expressed, and where you may join in that conflict of opinions by which truth is elicited, and wisdom established.

Report says I am to congratulate upon the approaching marriage of another daughter—I hope it will add to your happiness as well as hers—Poor Sr S. Romilly! I honour[ed][1]

[1] MS torn.

24 Nov. 1818 him much and I hoped great things from the devotion of his enlarged mind to our criminal code, although in many of his political opinions I saw much to condemn.—

Mrs. Trower begs to join in kind remembrances to Mrs. Ricardo and family and believe me

Yrs very sincerely

HUTCHES TROWER

288. WAKEFIELD TO RICARDO[1]

Private

Pall Mall December 4ᵗʰ 1818

Dear Sir

4 Dec. 1818   My friend Vizard was telling me that he had heard that you had arranged to be returned for Portalington—and as I think it probable it may be by the means of a loan to Lord Portalington—I think it may be important to you to be aware of every thing which I know about it—at least it is only the trouble of my writing this letter and taking the chance of its being of any use.

The gentleman with whom I was in negociation for about it—is Mr. Kirkland—who is military agent to the Duke of Kent and I suspect agent to Lord Portalington—I mean army agent—as I understood him Lord Portalington has borrowed a considerable sum of money on annuity—for which purpose his Estates including the borough of Portalington was assigned to Trustees one of whom is Sir Henry Parnell[2]—who is brother in law to Lord Portalington—and has long acted as agent for his Estates. Mr. Kirkland proposed the Trustees borrowing money on mortgage to pay

[1] Addressed: 'for/David Ricardo Esquire/Gatcomb Park/Minching Hampton' and marked 'Private'.
[2] Sir Henry Brooke Parnell (1776–1842), M.P. for Queen's County, had been a member of the Bullion Committee and Chairman of the Committee on the Corn Trade, 1813; he was created Baron Congleton in 1841.

off the annuities—he first asked for £50000 and subsequently for £20.000 upon Irish Interest. viz 6 p^r C^t the legal
interest of that country—the Interest to be paid half yearly
at Puget and Bainbridge's[1]—

I proposed to lend the first sum—if he would return any
person I nominated for the borough—this after some hesitation was refused I then as you will recollect my writing to
you[2] offered the £20000—and to pay such a price for the seat
as Mr. Pascoe Grenfell should determine was a fair one—
Mr. Kirkland is cousin to Mr. Arbuthnot the Secretary to
the Treasury and he asked—if you would vote with ministers
—and when I told him that politics must not be named—
but perfect freedom he said—Lord Portalington found there
was nothing to be got by returning an opposition man—he
would have a ministerial one—after this our negociation
ended—

If you are lending your money—I think you ought to
have 6 p^r Cent. Ireland is all a registered country—your
security should be instantly registered. If you push Sir
Henry Parnell—he will join in the security—which will
insure punctual payment of the Interest—

I have known a great deal of Sir Henry Parnell who is a
remarkably pleasing man—he is nephew to the Right Hon^e
John Foster[3]—and was once his public secretary—and was
brought up under him—but he deserted him in a very sudden
way to join the whigs—when they came into power. and
has been opposed to his Uncle ever since—When I was with
Mr. Foster—which was immediately afterwards—I joined

---

[1] London agents to the Bank of
Ireland.
[2] Letter 238.
[3] John Foster, afterwards Lord
Oriel, the last Speaker of the
Irish House of Commons. It

was at his suggestion that Edward
Wakefield had written *An Account
of Ireland, Statistical and Political,*
2 vols. in 4to, London, Long-
mans, 1812.

4 Dec. 1818 with all those who were about him—in thinking that he had
treated his Uncle with ingratitude—I am still not without
a strong feeling—that he was ready to join the winning party
for his own purposes—notwithstanding which I should
confide in him—in a negociation of this sort—He coincides
with you—in your opinions as to Bank restriction—indeed so did Mr. Foster—and his nephew John Leslie
Foster.[1]—

I have been on Lord Portalingtons Estate and speaking in
a general way—I have an idea that it is good security.—

If any thing else strikes you—which you may think that
I know about it—I shall be very happy in rendering you
every information in my power—and by writing "*private*"
on your letter, it will reach me unopened. I am

> Your most faithful humble servant
>
> EDWARD WAKEFIELD

David Ricardo Esq

289. MILL TO RICARDO[2]

[*Reply to* 284]

My Dear Sir   Qu. Sq. Dec.ʳ 4ᵗʰ 1818

4 Dec. 1818   I must scribble to you a few lines, though I am too
languid to get up, to get a bit of decent paper to write to you
upon. But I fear you may wait for my opinion, on any of the
printing points you were pleased to submit to me.

The division of the first chapter into sections I approved
of entirely and sent it to Murray, with a slight alteration, in

[1] M.P. for Armagh, author of *An Essay on the Principle of Commercial Exchanges, and more particularly of the Exchange between Great Britain and Ireland; with an Inquiry into the Practical Effects of the Bank Restrictions,* London, 1804.
[2] Addressed: 'David Ricardo Esq / Gatcomb Park / Minchinhampton / Glo'stershire'. MS in *R.P.*

two (I think) of the expressions. The note I also thought
very proper.

I think you will have very fully discharged all your obligations to Torrens, by praising him as far as you say.

And with regard to Mr. McCulloch, as you have certainly not said any thing which goes to encourage the depriving of the people by taxes of one farthing beyond the lowest possible, it is not necessary for you to say more than you propose to obviate any such misconstruction. I think therefore any communication with him on the subject is needless. What he would like to have is the authority of your name against excessive taxation: and so should I: but it is for you to judge whether this work is the place for the peculiar incalcation of that doctrine. I fear, not.

Ensor's objection being to the facts of your instance, you, by leaving out the instance, of course avoid the objection.

Upon the whole too, I cannot but approve of your resolution to publish the book anew, with only these alterations. For though I do not agree with you, that you could not have made it better; that is, more easy to the learner—for I am sure you could; yet I know that your time can be better employed. For as you had nothing on that subject to learn, your time would have been lost in regard to your own improvement. And then the world have your ideas—other people will employ themselves in preparing them for the digestion of different classes of feeders. What now concerns you, is, to collect evidence, on all the other great questions in which the interests of human beings are involved. And in this I have no doubt you are proceeding with great success. The only thing I am anxious about is your adopting resolution enough to repel all causes (that ought to be repelled) of interruption and delay. I am very angry with you for not sending me the Discourse you mentioned, after

4 Dec. 1818 it was prepared. I hope another at least is ready by this time; and I ordain and command that both be sent to me, by the very first opportunity. I shall most probably follow your kind permission of postponing my particular remarks till we meet, when they will form the subject of interesting conversations. By the bye, I hope you do not mean to keep away longer than Xtmass.

I sympathize with you most sincerely in your difficulties about Miss Ricardo. Your objections are but too good. And if there were no hope of breaking such connections as you mention, I should not think any exertion of authority on your part too much. You ought at any rate to have an explanation with the gentleman, of the most solemn kind; to exact from him a solemn obligation to that effect, as the only condition on which you will ever be prevailed upon to give your consent. This done, as you would do it, in the tone of friendship, and with the clear exposure of all the reasons for it, as regards his own happiness, would very possibly have a great effect. Your wisdom, your talents, the respect which is borne to you by all the world, and the great things which you and you alone have inabled yourself to do for your family, entitle you to assume a tone of authority with all of them, which it would be much for their good that you assumed more frequently and more decidedly than you do.

I am still labouring with but imperfect success to get well. But I have had advice from your brother Moses, which I prefer to all I have yet received; and which I am endeavouring to follow. I am, too, certainly better. Many thanks for your kind invitation. I should have abundant pleasure in accepting it; and I have no doubt that it would do me good. But I have too many cogent motives for remaining at home; and postponing the pleasure of intercourse with you till the renewal of our walks.

I had nearly forgotten to say about Koe, that of course 4 Dec. 1818
whatever you are able to do for Mr. Basevi, is doubtless a
matter of peculiar obligation on your part. But I believe
that the lines of Mr. B. and Mr. K. are totally distinct. Koe
is not a Conveyancer, but a Chancery Barrister—if I am
correct in my distinction. Basevi himself might be of use to
Koe. I will not allow you to say that your application to your
Solicitors is not entitled to respect, and will not command
it.

Most faithfully yours
J. Mill

290. MᶜCULLOCH TO RICARDO[1]
[Reply to 285.—Answered by 300]

My Dear Sir   Edinburgh 6 Decr 1818
    It was only yesterday that I had the honour to receive 6 Dec. 1818
yours of the 24ᵗʰ ulto—Considering the difficulty and
abstract nature of the subject, and the prejudices generally
entertained against the founder of any new theory, your
work has I think been eminently successful—I feel very
much gratified by the intelligence that a second edition is
about to be sent to the press; both because it shews that your
work has met with that attention from the public which it so
well deserves, but which is not always given to unassuming
merit, and because it augurs most favourably for the improvement of the science—
    The statement in your work of the accuracy of which I am
most disposed to doubt, is that in Chapter 15 p 336[2] regarding the impossibility of improving the condition of a
country by diminishing its public debt—In one point of view

[1] MS in *R.P.*   [2] Above, I, 246.

6 Dec. 1818 your statement is certainly correct—But the contracting of a large public debt has other consequences besides the mere loss of the capital borrowed and spent unproductively by the government—By laying the foundation of a pernicious system of gambling and agiotage it enables a few individuals dexterously to avail themselves of the fluctuations in the price of the funds, and to acquire immense fortunes not by the exertion of a steady and persevering industry, but chiefly by dint of superior sagacity in taking advantage of the errors of less fortunate speculators—These fluctuations too, inasmuch as they flatter the confidence which every person has in his own good fortune, combined with the facility of immediately selling out stock, attach an inordinate proportion of the national capital to the trade in the funds,—a trade which cannot possibly be of any great public advantage— A reduction of the national debt would not therefore fall entirely on the bona fide holders of stock, and in so far as it only affected the other individuals to whom I have alluded it could not be reckoned very disadvantageous—

Besides a national bankruptcy would at the worst only cause a *bouleversement* or overturn of the private fortunes of individuals,—an overturn, I admit, which as it would be productive of very great and general distress, ought, if possible, to be avoided,—but as it would leave the productive capital of the country *entire*, and as it would also enable almost all those taxes which reduce the profits of stock and check the accumulation of capital to be dispensed with, it cannot I think be disputed that it would, after the first frottement had been got over, be attended by an increasing demand for labour, and by an increase of national wealth—

These hasty remarks will explain my meaning; and if you think there is any force in them, you will perhaps qualify

some of the expressions on p 336[1]—I think the alteration you   6 Dec. 1818
propose making on p 329 will be a great improvement—
Instead of "There are no taxes" etc at the head of p 189,[2]
I would beg leave to suggest the adoption of the following
paragraph—"Still however it is certain that but for taxation
this increase of capital would have been much greater—
There are no taxes which have not a tendency to lessen the
power to accumulate—All taxes must either fall on capital
or revenue—If they encroach on capital, they must propor-
tionably diminish that fund by whose extent the extent of
the productive industry of the country must always be
regulated; and if they fall on revenue they must either lessen
accumulation, or force the contributors to save the amount
of the tax by making a corresponding diminution of their
former consumption of the necessaries and luxuries of life—
Some taxes will produce these effects in a much greater
degree than others; but the great evil of taxation is to be
found etc"

It occurs to me that you might with advantage limit
the number of your references to Mr Buchanan[3]—His
work never attracted the smallest attention, neither, in
my humble opinion, did it deserve more than it has met
with—

I think you ought to extend the preliminary part of your
Chapter on Currency and banks—You might in the space
of three or four pages engross into it the substance of the
first part of your most excellent pamphlet on "an economical
currency"[4]—I think you might also enlarge a little on the
principle of *limitation*[5]—I may mention that I have given
Mr Jeffrey a review of your pamphlet on Currency, and I

[1] The passage was reprinted without alterations; see above, I, 246.
[2] Above, I, 152; McCulloch's suggestion was adopted verbatim.

[3] This suggestion was not adopted. Cp. below, VIII, 4.
[4] Adopted, see above, I, 356–61.
[5] See above, I, 354, n.

6 Dec. 1818 presume, though I am not quite certain, it will appear in next number of the Review[1]—

I met with Major Torrens when he was here, and had several conversations with him regarding your theory of value; but as was the case with yourself and the Major, neither of us could make any impression on the other— I have written a short paper in reply to his observations on your theory in the *last* number of the Edinburgh Magazine,[2] which had it not been for uselessly increasing the cost of this lengthened epistle I would have sent you—I do not think the Major will be inclined to carry on the controversy—He says that the comparative value of commodities is regulated entirely by the quantity[3] of capital expended in their production; but as capital itself consists only of accumulated labour, he is even on his own hypothesis fighting about a straw—

As the Supplement to the Encyclopædia will be published in the course of a week, perhaps you could contrive to make a reference to my article on corn—This would stamp it with an authority to which it cannot otherwise have any pretensions, and might in other respects be of considerable service to me[4]—

Nothing could afford me greater pleasure than to see you in Edinburgh, and I am sure I may say the same thing of all my friends—In the meantime however I hope to have the honour and gratification of occasionally hearing from you— And

I remain with the greatest respect
Yours most faithfully
J. R. McCulloch

David Ricardo Esqre

---

[1] *Edinburgh Review*, Dec. 1818, Art. III.
[2] See above, p. 315.
[3] In MS 'quatity' or 'quality', reading uncertain.
[4] See the notes added in ed. 2, above, I, 267 and 318.

291. MILL TO RICARDO[1]

[Answered by 292]

West.[r] Dec.[r] 7–1818

My Dear Sir

I dined on Saturday[2] at Benthams with Brougham and 7 Dec. 1818
Whishaw, on which occasion Brougham begged that I would
write to you, on two subjects.

The first is that of your seat. He took me aside to tell me
that the matter is finally settled, and that you will be seated
the very first day that the forms of parliament will admit. He
stated, however, that in order to secure the advantage of
having your interest paid at a Bankers in London, on security
of the most perfect regularity, he had been obliged to give up
the Irish interest[3]; and that the security for the seat would
extend to four years. Yesterday, also, Wakefield called upon
me, and said he had learned from Vizard, that it was P—t—n
for which you expected to come in; and then he gave me a
history of what had occurred to himself in regard to it, and
said he had written so and so to you.[4] I told him I was very
glad he had so written, as, if the account he had of the place
was right, these were all matters for you to have before you.
I then, without explaining to him any thing, asked him, if you
had the payment at 5 pc.[t] of the interest on a loan of from
£20,000 to £36,000, secured regularly at a Bankers in
London, and paid £4,000 for a seat secured for four years, he
should think you paid too dear, according to the actual state
of the market? He replied, certainly not.

The other subject is one about which Brougham is very

---

[1] Addressed: 'David Ricardo Esq.
/ Gatcomb Park / Minchinhap-
ton / Glo'stershire'. Received by
Ricardo on 12 December; see
his reply.
MS in *R.P.*

[2] 5 December.
[3] The maximum rate of interest
under the Usury Laws was 6 per
cent. in Ireland, 5 per cent. in
England.
[4] See letter 288.

7 Dec. 1818 hot; and about which he has been very eager to consult with
me a great many times, since I returned to town. It is part
of his schemes on the education subject, which seems to be
engrossing his whole mind. In consequence of his conversations with Owen, who spent ten days here in his transit from
the continent, Brougham has become strongly impressed
with an idea of the importance of Owen's *infant* school; or
an institution for taking the children from the parents during
the day, after three years of age—when they can be trained
in good habits, and under the exercise of reason, instead of
being trained in bad habits, under gusts of passion, irascible
and sympathetic, in the hands of their poor parents. The
great relief to the parents by exemption from the obligation
of superintendance during their hours of work ensures their
concurrence. In our conversations it was agreed, that the
public mind was not yet ripe for proposing such a thing in
parliament. It was also agreed that a pattern-school, for
people to go and see, a shew-school in short, was one of the
best means for ripening that mind. It was computed that
£500 would be fully sufficient to hire rooms, and accomplish
the business for a year. And Brougham undertook immediately to set about getting names for the money and the
management. He told me on Saturday at Benthams, his
progress—that Lord Lansdowne was to be one, he himself
another, John Smith Lord Carringtons brother[1] another,
Babington[2] another, and that now the question was not
about who could be got, but whom it would be best to chuse,
because people were eager to concur in it: that in order to
keep the thing select, his wish was, to confine the management to *ten* persons, of important names, and that they

---

[1] John Smith (1767–1842), M.P.
for Midhurst.

[2] Thomas Babington (1758–
1837), M.P. for Leicester from
1800 to 1818.

themselves should contribute the money, viz. £50, a piece—
he then added, that he wished much that *you* would be one of
them—and entreated (as he was exceedingly hurried) that
I would write to you an account of his wishes and views. And
I do not think that I have omitted any thing.[1]

Whishaw told me, that you have some expectation of
Malthus at Xtmass, and had invited *him*, but said as I understood him, that it would be out of his power to go. I wish
you all happiness, and should like to partake of it, but must
think of other things.

I have had another visit from Mr. Moses, who takes a
most *kind* interest in my recovery. I had good news for
him—for by following his directions, I am sure I am better.
The theory of my disease, which he substituted for that with
which I had been bothered, convinced me at once—and so,
Dr. Ricardo, for ever!

I can give you hardly any news of the Westminster
canvas[2]—for my health, and occupations have hindered me
from going near them—and Place has been too busy among
them, almost ever to come near me. I understand however
that the reform party are in full activity for Hobhouse[3]; that
their organization is far more perfect than it has ever been;
that the Maxwell committee is doing very little; and that the
prospect for Hobhouse is very fair. I think it not very likely
that the Whigs will start any body, though they are averse to

---

[1] As a result of Brougham's
initiative the Westminster Infant
School was opened early in 1819.
The list of founders includes Mill
and the others mentioned above,
but not Ricardo. (See S. Wilder-
spin, *On the Importance of Educating the Infant Poor, from the Age
of Eighteen Months to Seven Years*,
2nd ed., London, Simpkin &
Marshall, 1824, p. 23.)

[2] The election of a member for
Westminster to fill the vacancy
caused by the death of Romilly.
Place was chairman of the Reform
Committee. (See Wallas, *Life of
Francis Place*, pp. 132–9.)
[3] John Cam Hobhouse (1786–
1869), although unsuccessful on
this occasion, was elected as M.P.
for Westminster in 1820; afterwards created Lord Broughton.

7 Dec. 1818   Hobhouse. And in that case I conclude the reformers will beat the ministry, though with a man too little known to excite any enthusiasm I am doubtful if the people can be got to crowd to the hustings. The sanguine actors say they will: That the people are now sufficiently up, to be animated, and that to enthusiasm, for the *cause*; and that the excitement of a *favourite individual* is no longer required. This would be very good news, if one were sure it were true.

How goes printing on?[1] And how goes speech-making on?[2] Let me see some fruits of the last without delay. I cannot tell you how delighted I am about the speedy prospect of your being in your seat, and the specimens you have given me of what you can do it.

Adieu,

J. MILL

292. RICARDO TO MILL[3]
[*Reply to 291.—Answered by 294*]

Gatcomb Park
12 Decr 1818

My dear Sir

12 Dec. 1818   You will have been surprised that your last letter should have remained so long unanswered, but you will acquit me of blame when I tell you that I have been on a visit to Mrs. Ricardo at Cheltenham since monday, and have only reached home this afternoon.

With respect to Mr. Brougham's messages, you will not think me wrong for making such observations on them as

---

[1] Ed. 2 of the *Principles* was now in the press.
[2] See above, p. 302.
[3] Addressed: 'James Mill Esqr / Queen Square / Westminster'. On back of cover, in Hume's handwriting: 'I could not get your length as I promised but tomorrow at 3 oClock if I can. J. H.' (cp. the end of the letter). MS in Mill-Ricardo papers.

occur to me. The agreement that Mr. Brougham made with Lord P., or his agent, was in August last, and it was then stipulated that I should receive 6 pc.ᵗ inᵗ, payable half yearly, at Messʳˢ Pugets in London.* Now why should any alteration be made in these terms? If any thing had occurred to make the bargain advantageous to the other party I should not have complained, but should have scrupulously fulfilled the conditions. Why should not they do the same? Why after nearly 4 months should a new condition be thought of —a fall in the interest from 6 to 5 pc.ᵗ? It is not meant I presume that the interest will be guaranteed by any London banker—that indeed would be a stipulation to compensate for the more disadvantageous terms to which I am expected to acquiesce—but I apprehend that nothing more is now proposed than what was proposed before, that the interest should be *payable* at a Banker's in London. If this be as I suppose I can see no reason why the original terms should be altered, nevertheless if you and Mr. Brougham think otherwise I must yield my opinion, but why £250– pʳ Annᵐ more than before should now all at once be demanded when an express agreement has been made it is for Lord P. or Sir H. Parnell to explain. I am quite sure that you will think I am doing no more than right in expressing my candid opinion on this or on any other matter on which you may write to me.—

Now for the other message with which Mr. Brougham charged you. If it is part of the plan of the establishment which he proposes, to feed as well as to take care of and educate the children of three years of age, and upwards, belonging to the poor, I see the most serious objections to

* You left with me Brougham's letter to you which is now before me.

12 Dec. 1818 the plan, and I should be exceedingly inconsistent if I gave my countenance to it. I have invariably objected to the poor laws, and to every system which should give encouragement to an excess of population. If you are to feed, clothe, and educate all the children of the poor, you will be giving a great stimulus to a principle already too active. To such a scheme I cannot be friendly. But if it is proposed to take care of, or only to educate the children that are to be admitted into this institution, my objection is of no value, and in that case I will willingly contribute my £50–. Here again I have need of your indulgence for the honest declaration of my opinion.

I hope that my brother Moses may be right in his opinion of your case. I shall be very angry with both of you if I do not find you strong and hearty on my return to London.

I cannot join so heartily as I would wish to do in sympathy with Hobhouse, on occasion of the Westminster canvas, because he advocates the cause of Universal Suffrage. I really believe that the reformers have done injury by going so far in their demands. If their views had been more moderate they would have had great additional support, and would equally have secured the substance for which they are contending.—

I have written very little lately. You are so encouraging that I have every motive for persevering in my endeavours to overcome the obstacles which frighten me. I have written an answer to Torrens paper in the Edinburgh Magazine[1] in defence of my doctrine of value. I will send it to you when I have an opportunity, as also another letter which I have written to Trower[2] in defence of the opinions I gave in my former letter, in reply to his observations.

[1] See above, p. 315, n. 1.
[2] Letter 295.

Malthus will be here in a day or two, I wish you could have met him. He will be here I fear quite alone for War-burton who was to have come at the same time has written to say that he is prevented coming, and Mrs. Ricardo, and every one of my family, are from home. Even Osman and his wife are absent.

Murray writes to me that he has received a copy of a translation of my book into French, with copious notes[1]—he would have sent it to me, but he thought I should receive a copy through the means of Say. I fear that Say is not quite friendly towards me, but I am sure that he is not just if he is otherwise.

I told you that I only got home from Cheltenham this afternoon—it is well that I have got home without a broken limb, for my gig horse, after coming 15 out of 18 miles as quiet as possible, commenced kicking without any apparent cause, and so violently, that I thought it prudent to jump out of the gig, which I did without receiving the slightest injury; but my poor horse after kicking the shafts from the gig, and wounding himself very severely with the iron, or the frag-ment of the shaft attached to it, fell, and before we could disengage him from his harness, we were obliged to let him go. He soon disengaged himself from his incumbrances, and galloped away. He was so much hurt that I feared that he would never be fit for work again. The farrier however thinks he will come about. I shall never drive him again.

As you requested I shall enclose this letter to Mr. Hume.

Very truly Y^{rs}

DAVID RICARDO

---

[1] *Des principes de l'économie politi-que et de l'impôt*, 'par M. David Ricardo; traduit de l'anglais par F. S. Constancio, D.M., etc.; avec des notes explicatives et critiques, par M. Jean-Baptiste Say', Paris, Aillaud, 1819, 2 vols.

293. RICARDO TO MURRAY[1]

Gatcomb Park
Minchinhampton
13 Decr 1818

Dear Sir

13 Dec. 1818   On my arrival at home I found your letter dated the 7th in which you inform me of a piece of news of which I was not before aware, that my work was translated into French and that you were in possession of a copy. You will oblige me by procuring a copy for me, but should that be difficult, you will probably be good enough to let me look over yours.—

I find too a copy of the 2[d] Edinburgh Magazine, and the last number of Blackwood's here.[2]—

In a few days I may probably trouble you with a note which I shall wish to be inserted at about the 375th page.[3] I will take care that you shall have it in time.

I am Dear Sir
Faithfully Yours
DAVID RICARDO

294. MILL TO RICARDO[4]
[Reply to 292.—Answered by 296]

West.[r] Dec.[r] 18   1818

My dear Sir

18 Dec. 1818   I immediately transcribed that part of your letter which it was requisite to communicate to Brougham, and sent it to him; telling him, at the same time, that I coincided in all your

---

[1] Addressed: 'John Murray Esq.[r] / Albermale Street / London'.
 MS in the possession of Sir John Murray.
[2] Cp. above, pp. 332 and 354.

[3] The footnote on Torrens, above, I, 271.
[4] Addressed: 'David Ricardo Esq. / Gatcomb Park / Minchinhampton / Glo'stershire'.—MS in *R.P.*

remarks. And I had a conversation with him on the subject 18 Dec. 1818
yesterday. He says you are perfectly right in the remarks on
the interest, provided the paying at Pugets was in the original
proposal, as well as the 6 pc^t, the first of which circumstances
he had forgot, and is not now sure that the 6 pc^t was not an
inference of his own, rather than mentioned by them at first.
However, he thinks under all the circumstances you ought
either to have the Irish interest, or what you express yourself as if you would deem a compensation, the guarantee of
a London Banker; and says you *must* have one or t' other.
But as Sir H. P.[1] will very soon be in town, he thinks it better
to wait for him, as the subject can be gone through better
in conversation than by writing.

With regard to the feeding of the children, or doing any
thing whatsoever toward their maintenance, as I should have
condemned it, in the same terms as you do, I should have
been satisfied there was no use in your being applied to on
the subject—but there was never any idea of the kind: so
that your money and your endeavour may be freely bestowed. The question as to the utility, is the same as the
question, whether the thing can be made general, and of this
I have some doubts—but at any rate the experiment is not
a costly one.

With regard to the Westminster election, about which I
feel but little interest, I am by no means sure that *your* objection to Hobhouse will in the end be that of going too far
in parliamentary reform. I wish I were sure that he would
continue to go as far as you.[2] Of you, as soon as your
understanding is convinced, there is perfect certainty; because

[1] Sir Henry Parnell.
[2] A few weeks later Hobhouse
had so far watered down the statement of his opinions on Reform
that the Whig candidate, George
Lamb, claimed that he was prepared to go further; Lamb was
elected. (See Wallas, *Life of Francis
Place*, pp. 137–8.)

you are governed by a sense of duty. But, if he acts the shuffler, there is one comfort, he will be treated as such. But, the man whose grand ambition is to be well received in fashionable society, who has not elevation of mind to hold him up above that wretched atmosphere, cannot in the present state of our country have political virtue—the one is absolutely incompatible with the other. If ever you begin to aim at that bright reward of your virtues, I shall give up even *you*.

You excited my concupiscence by mentioning the translation with copious notes, of your book. I immediately sent to Murray, begging him to lend it me. He wrote word back, that he had sent to the French booksellers, but found there was not another copy in town, and that he had sent the first to you. Now therefore as soon as you are satisfied with your sight of it, I pray that you will lose no time in sending it to me. It may come with those M.S.S. you keep me longing for, to your great disgrace. By the bye, I am very happy that you are to send an answer to Torrens—for I am not satisfied with that of MacCulloch. I long to see what you are to send. I am glad to hear of another letter to Trower; these discussions which lead you to analyse the common place objections which have always been, and always may be, advanced against every step that is to be taken in favouring the progression of human nature, give you skill in the exercise, by practice, a little of which is all that you want. A very little time will make you more astonished at your own superiority over the set you will have got among, than you are now intimidated by the idea of your inferiority.—Mind, I do not dispense with the discourse you had ready for me, and did not send. You may, by Humes *volunteered* offer, send any thing under cover to him, that will not exceed two or three covers in one day; but you may at any rate send him two a

day for any n.º of days running. I have been able to work him   18 Dec. 1818
into an approximation to a knowledge of your book—he is
a convert to all the doctrines; but he does not yet always apply
them correctly—however he is always open to instruction.

I congratulate you on your escape from your gig. Your
horse has been too well fed, and too little worked, which is
apt to be the case with your horses. I hope Miss Ricardo is
recovering, whose complaint I understand is near a-kin to
my own, and that you are enjoying yourself with Mr.
Malthus. I should have enjoyed being with you. Say when
I may expect you here. By the bye, have you ever read
Turgots works? I have been at them lately. They will
interest you highly. Did you ever read his life by Condorcet?[1]

Adieu

J. M.

295. RICARDO TO TROWER[2]

[*Reply to 287.—Answered by 304*]

Gatcomb Park
20th Dec.ʳ 1818

My dear Trower

I was sure that I was not mistaken in judging of your   20 Dec. 1818
sentiments by my own. I was sure that you would not have
a worse opinion of me because I differed in opinion with you
on a subject on which we had neither of us any interest to
come to a wrong decision, and yet I am glad that I stated this
conviction in my last letter, because it has drawn from you

[1] Both the *Œuvres de M. Tur-
got*, 9 vols., Paris, 1807 and *The
Life of M. Turgot…written by the
Marquis of Condorcet and trans-
lated from the French*, London,
Johnson, 1787 are in the library at
Gatcombe.

[2] Addressed: 'Hutches Trower
Esqʳ/Unsted Wood/Godalming/
Surry'. London postmarks, 'Tot-
hill Street' and '24 Dec. 1818'.
(The letter was first sent to Mill,
see opening of letter 296.)
MS at University College, Lon-
don.—*Letters to Trower*, XXIII.

20 Dec. 1818 an assurance of your regard and friendship, which has given me great satisfaction. I shall proceed now without fear to consider the different arguments contained in your last letter, and first I must observe that in an enquiry into measures which are likely to produce good government, we must not confine ourselves to the question whether parliamentary reform would or would not endanger the establishment of King, Lords, and Commons. We must look steadily to the end of all government, which we agree, is the happiness of the people. As we both think that the establishment above mentioned is best calculated to secure the object which we have in view, we should if we were legislators, acting under the proper influence, make it our endeavor to establish it; but still it must be considered only as means to an end, and those regulations are the best which give us the greatest security that the end will be obtained. It is surely unwise to make the means the end, and thereby limit our enquiry to whether we may chance to strengthen or weaken one of the branches of our constitution.

I want to get all the wisdom and virtue of the country to act in the Government. Whether that end can be attained by a parliamentary reform is a different question, and remains for discussion, but your argument is that even if it could be attained you would not make use of it. Why? because it would endanger the independence of the monarchical and aristocratical branches of the constitution. Is not this saying "I think a certain form of government the best, and on this point I will not admit the wisdom and virtue of the country to decide." Now I am a more warm admirer of our constitution than you are, for I am so persuaded of its excellence that I have no fear of putting it in the power of the wise and good to overturn it. Instead of so using this power they would more firmly establish it. Without being aware of it you are guilty of a species of intolerance, and on the same principles, you might insist on any particular system of religious belief —any particular doctrines in political economy, or any other opinions that you may have justly or unjustly imbibed. You might say these opinions appear to me essential to the people's happiness and I will not admit even wisdom and virtue to decide upon them. I think that you will agree I am justified in these remarks when I call to your recollection the following passage in your letter. "But even admitting the electors should become as qualified for the discharge of their important duty, as could reasonably be expected, under any circumstances, still I contend that if you were to let loose in the House of Commons the full force of the popular part of our constitution it would be impossible for the other branches to preserve for a continuance, any thing beyond a mere nominal authority...unless the influence of the other branches was silently suffered to operate, to a certain extent in that House the whole form of the constitution would be changed ...it would be merely a mixed government in form, but a Republic in substance." You appear to me to have changed the subject in discussion—it is no longer an enquiry into the best means of making the people happy, but into the best means of preserving the monarchical and aristocratical branches of the constitution, for you admit that if the practice of the constitution conformed to its theory—if the people were really represented in their house of parliament and were free from the influence of the other branches, irregularly and corruptly applied, they would be the only real and efficient power in the state. Is not this admission at variance with another part of your letter, where you speak of this government being formed on a principle of the due balance of powers, the preservation of which you say is essential to its existence? If influence is necessary to the preservation of this

20 Dec. 1818 balance—influence too not defined, nor capable of being either defined or[1] controlled,—which you yourself say "should be measured and regulated to prevent its undue preponderance," how can there be in the constitution itself a due balance of powers? No;—depend upon it there is no check in the constitution against this influence—it will be used at all times for the benefit of those who happen to be in possession of it, and will be under no other controul than that of their own views of advantage. The check is not in the constitution—it is as I said before in public opinion, expressed through the medium of the press—in the trial by jury—in the published speeches of a few popular members of parliament, who have no influence by their votes, but by their tongues, and in the right of convening public meetings and thereby organizing opposition—these are the checks to which we owe all the happiness and liberty we enjoy. You may think that this is the most eligible mode for the people to control their government,—I should differ with you, but this is the real question to be discussed with those who are friends to a reform of parliament, and who wish to extend the elective franchise to such of the people as would make a good use of it. It is to this point I want to conduct our argument. I want those who oppose me to acknowledge candidly that the people are not represented, and that they do not think it expedient that they should be; instead of which I meet daily with people who avow themselves friendly to moderate reform, but when they explain their views it becomes manifest that they wish for no reform at all, for they say that it would be impossible for government to proceed to any good purpose, if the people had even a majority in the House of Commons, whatever precautions you might take in bestowing the elective franchise. This is Malthus's argu-

[1] regulated' is del. here.

ment, who has been staying with me for a few days, and has just left me. I could not however bring him to confess that he really wished for no reform at all.

It must I think be admitted without qualification that there is no such thing as a balance of the three powers in our government. If it could for a moment exist it would disappear immediately that either of two out of the three powers should combine their interests against the third. In our government the mutual interest of the monarchy, and the aristocracy to combine cannot admit of a doubt, one possessing the privelege of bestowing every place of honour and emolument, and in a degree never possessed perhaps by any former government, —the other having an overwhelming influence in the legislature, which may be advantageously disposed of to the minister. No reform would be effectual to counteract this powerful combination but such a real representation of the people as should give them a majority in the house of commons.

In one part of your letter you were disposed to yield the substance of all that I am contending for, but you suddenly recollected that it might endanger the independence of the monarchy and aristocracy, and you withdrew your concession. You say that if my scheme of reform went further you would be more disposed to go along with me. You call upon me to "limit the right of voting at Elections to such persons who by their education have the ability to decide correctly" and then you would have fewer objections to reform. In other words you would require security for a good choice of representatives and this is precisely what I want. If I can not obtain it without limiting the elective franchise to the very narrowest bounds, I would so limit it; but I am persuaded that we should most securely get our object, and should be less exposed to hazards of a different kind, by extending the elective franchise,—not indeed uni-

20 Dec. 1818 versally to all the people, but to that part of them which cannot be supposed to have any interest in overturning the rights of property. Come back to this admission, and our difference will not be very difficult to settle, but do not mock us with the name of a representative government, denying us all the advantages which may be derived from that form.

The report that you have heard respecting my daughter's approaching marriage is true, but it is not a subject of congratulation to me.[1]

Every body joins in lamenting the untimely end of Sir S. Romilly, he was a very useful man, and would have laboured effectually in procuring for us an amelioration of the criminal law.

The second edition of my book is in the press. I have made very few alterations in it. Murray has just received a copy of a French translation of the first edition,—the only copy in London, with notes by M. Say.[2] I have looked over the notes—they may be considered as M. Say's defence of those opinions of his on which I have animadverted. It would not be becoming in me to decide which of us is nearest to the truth, I must leave impartial readers to do that. They are written in perfect good temper, and where his conscience will allow him to praise me, he does it in the most flattering manner. The French edition is in two volumes.

Malthus came over from Bath and stayed with me at Gatcomb for a very few days. We have neither of us lost our interest in the discussion of questions which we have so often debated before. His work[3] will not appear till the end of next year.

Mrs. Ricardo joins with me in kind regards to Mrs. Trower.

Ever truly Yours
DAVID RICARDO

[1] See above, p. 325.   [3] *Principles of Political Economy.*
[2] See above, p. 361, n.

296. RICARDO TO MILL[1]

[Reply to 294.—Answered by 297]

Cheltenham 22ᵈ Decʳ 1818

My dear Sir

I cannot send you more than half a sheet, least I may 22 Dec. 1818
make my packet too bulky for Mr. Hume's privelege. I yesterday sent you Trower's letter to me—to day I send you
my answer to him.[2]—After you have read it put a wafer or
seal to it, and dispatch it by the Post.

I received your letter at the post office on saturday on my
way hither. I am glad that you do not think me wrong in
remarking the altered terms which are now proposed for the
loan. In Mr. B.'s[3] note to you he does not mention 6 pcᵗ as
his inference, but as the condition on which the business was
settled.

With regard to the experiment of educating the young
children I have now no objection to offer to it,—though I
think that it will not answer as a general plan.

The French translation of my book with M. Say's notes
has been returned to Mr. Murray—I hope you will soon see
it. M Say does not appear to me to have clearly seen the
doctrine which I wish to establish,—but I would rather hear
your opinion than give mine. That both our views might
have been at once before the public I could have wished that
the notes were translated and published with the new edition.
So much of the edition is printed, however, that it could not be
done otherwise than by putting them altogether, as an appendix, with reference to the pages to which they are attached.

Mr. Malthus staid a very short time with me. We had our
usual discussions both on politics, and on political economy.

---

[1] Addressed: 'James Mill Esqʳ / 1   [2] Letters 287 and 295.
Queen Square / Westminster'.   [3] Brougham's.
MS in Mill-Ricardo papers.

22 Dec. 1818　He read to me some more of his intended publication.[1] He has altered his opinion you know about there being land in every country which pays no rent, and appears like M Say to think that when that is proved, my doctrine of rent not entering into price is overthrown—they neither of them advert to the other principle which cannot be touched, of capital being employed on land, already in cultivation, which pays no rent. I have entered my protest against his omitting the consideration of this important fact.

On politics we did not more nearly accord—he talks of a reform but when his plan is examined it is in fact no reform at all. I insisted on the propriety of calling things by their right names.

I hope Hobhouse will continue to be virtuous, and still more do I wish that I may never think the smiles of the great and powerful a sufficient inducement to turn aside from the straight path of honesty and the convictions of my own mind. Where so many fall I dare not boast of my superior integrity,—but I implore you to speak the truth to me if you see me beginning to swerve from my duty. I wish much to get the character with those with whom I associate, and who have many estimable qualities, of daring to differ from them.

I have not entered into a long dissertation in my answer to Torrens. I wrote it for my own satisfaction and with no idea of publishing it. I will send it to you when I get back to Gatcomb.—

To-morrow we are to have a county meeting at Gloucester, to consider of an address to the Prince Regent, on the death of the Queen, at which I must preside. From thence I shall return home, and hope that I may not be obliged to go to London before the time that my family go, to present it.—The marriage of my daughter will make us stay later in

[1] *Principles of Political Economy.*

the country than usual. This will not of course retard the 22 Dec. 1818 settlement of the business that Brougham has kindly undertaken for me, as I can give directions to my brother to pay the money as soon as my solicitor tells me that every thing is right.—It is probable that I may not finally leave Gatcomb till the very end of January.

I am glad that you are making such progress with Mr. Hume, I hope that you may succeed in making him a good political economist.—My daughter is I think better, and in a fair way of recovering.—I hope that you also are making progress in the same way.

Ever Y^{rs}
D RICARDO

297. MILL TO RICARDO[1]

[Reply to 296.—Answered by 298]

My Dear Sir   West^r 24th Decr 1818

I have just read and dispatched your letter to Trower,[2] 24 Dec. 1818 and as I shall not have it by me to refresh my memory hereafter, I will put down while I have them, the remarks which occurred to me. I think you have well selected the two points upon which the whole of his reasoning—or rather not his reasoning, but his loose talk—decidedly turns: 1st That any reform which shall be more than a name, would destroy the monarchy, and aristocracy; 2dly that this would destroy the balance. These are not only the two points upon which *his* letter exclusively hinges, but it is the only thing *specific* upon which the talk and writing of all the opponents of reform almost exclusively hinges. For, as you very justly observe: the whigs will come to nothing specific; they double and

---

[1] Addressed: 'David Ricardo Esq./ Gatcomb Park / Minchinhampton / Glo'stershire'.—MS in *R.P.*   [2] Letter 295.

24 Dec. 1818 wind, and run the course of mere hypocrites. They uniformly do, as you have found out, that your friend Malthus does; in *words* say they are for reform; but when you force them to explain themselves, very distinctly shew that they are for no reform at all. I like Trower's explicitness much better; and should sooner hope to make a convert of him, because he is sincere.

Your remarks upon these two cardinal points are excellent. On the first, it is just the proper answer to say, that it is substituting the means for the end; in fact, it is neither more, nor less than laying it down as proper to sacrifice the end to the means: than which a greater contradiction of reason, it is altogether impossible to conceive. This view of the question we must never weary in holding up. Monarchy, and aristocracy, they say, are good—Why? as means to good government. And then they add—dread to seek for the means of good government because you will destroy monarchy and aristocracy! You see the good government is only pretext! the monarchy and aristocracy are the *end*; because they reckon themselves either partners in the variegated despot, or allied to him, and likely to share in his favours.

As for the second of these points, the *balance*; the utter nothingness of that you see through so completely, that you are always able by a few words, to make it transparent to every body. But the odd thing is, that though refuted, they never fail to repeat. You will find, in as many letters as Mr. Trower writes to you, and in as many discourses as any of the rest of them holds with you, when you shew them undeniably that nothing less than a reform to such and such an extent can afford any security for good government, can prevent the many from being the slaves of the few; they only turn round upon you, and tell you that you will destroy the balance, or that you will destroy the monarchy and aristocracy.

Still these discussions of ours do a great deal of good. The men with whom we hold them are men of influence. If we do not convert, we stagger them, and make them much less audacious, and by consequence much less successful preachers of bad doctrines. I could tell you several curious, and upon the whole satisfactory discussions, I have had, since I came to town, if I had room for it.

I am full of contempt for these notes of Say. Murray sent me the book immediately; and you may say to him, when you write, that I am much obliged to him. There is not one of your doctrines, that he has seized, or perceives the force of in any degree. Think of his saying, in, I believe, the very first of his notes, that you have assuredly in the text committed a great error, because in talking of exchangeable value, you have not included profits of stock and rent, as constituent parts.[1] This is to declare, as plainly as words can speak, that the man knows not in the smallest degree what your book is about. As far as I have yet gone (for I dare say I shall be tempted to read the whole of the translation) all his notes appear to be of the same stamp. They sink the man in my estimation to a very inferior level. Do you mean to print them at the end? Or do you think them worthy of any notice?

I am sorry you are to be so long in coming to town—and I am sorry the wedding is to be so soon. A little delay might have been salutary. But I am strongly inclined to hope the best. I have formed a good opinion of both the brothers[2]— and think that good sense, and reverence for *you* may work a *radical reform*, even where you are most apprehensive.— Your long delay in the country renders it more imperative

[1] *Des principes de l'économie politique*, par M. David Ricardo, Paris, 1819, vol. I, pp. 28–9, note by Say on the paragraph 'If we look to a state of society', above, I, 24–5.

[2] Anthony and Edward Austin; see above, p. 325.

24 Dec. 1818 upon you to send me papers—papers: written, and to be written. I long to see your answer to Torrens. It ought to be in next months magazine. I think I said to you, that Macculloch's answer did not please me.[1]—Your stay in the country will be favourable, I hope, to writing.

I only intended to *begin* my letter to you—and lo ! I have gone on, till it is almost completed. I had as well finish now —and when I have finished, it had as well go. Yes—I am getting better, though slowly—but I am sure your brother[2] is the doctor for me, and I am going to dine with him by way of fee—is not that handsome in me? I had a call from Mr. Ralph to day, but unluckily was out, walking. You say, in your letter to Trower, that Malthus's book will not be out till the end of next year. What is the meaning of that? Why, it is advertized as now in the press.[3]—I was affected almost to tears upon reading poor Romilly's will in the Morn. Chron. of today.

Truly yours
J. Mill

298. RICARDO TO MILL[4]

[*Reply to 297.—Answered by 303*]

Gatcomb Park
28 Decr 1818

My dear Sir

28 Dec. 1818   On friday, I sent you the observations which I had written on Torrens paper in the Edinb. Mag., and yesterday I dispatched to you the paper on reform which I was before going to send you, but of which I was ashamed at the moment that I was about to enclose it.[5] You have asked for it, and now

---

[1] Above, p. 364.
[2] Moses Ricardo.
[3] See above, p. 329, n. 1.

[4] Addressed: 'James Mill Esqr / 1 Queen Square / Westminster'.
    MS in Mill-Ricardo papers.
[5] See letter 284.

you will see that I ought to have put it in the fire, instead of consenting that your valuable time should be taken up in reading such miserable effusions.—My reply to Torrens was never meant for publication—you recommend me to write, and I thought that I might as well employ an hour on that subject as on any other. I have perhaps said too much on my agreement with Dr. Smith in the passage that I have quoted from Torrens. The fact is that Torrens does not represent Smith's opinion fairly he makes it appear that Smith says that after capital accumulates and industrious people are set to work the quantity of labour employed is not the only circumstance that determines the value of commodities, and that I oppose this opinion. Now I want to shew that I do not oppose this opinion in the way that he represents me to do so, but Adam Smith thought, that as in the early stages of society, all the produce of labour belonged to the labourer, and as after stock was accumulated, a part went to profits, that accumulation, necessarily, without any regard to the different degrees of durability of capital, or any other circumstance whatever, raised the prices or exchangeable value of commodities, and consequently that their value was no longer regulated by the quantity of labour necessary to their production. In opposition to him, I maintain that it is not because of this division into profits and wages,— it is not because capital accumulates, that exchangeable value varies, but it is in all stages of society, owing only to 2 causes: one the more or less quantity of labour required, the other the greater or less durability of capital:—that the former is never superseded by the latter, but is only modified by it. But, say my opposers, Torrens, and Malthus, capital is always of unequal durability in different trades, and therefore of what practical use is your enquiry? Of none, I answer, if I pretended to shew that cloth should be at such a price,—

28 Dec. 1818 shoes at such another—muslins at such another and so on—this I have never attempted to do,—but I contend it is of essential use to determine what the causes are which regulate exchangeable value, although they may be so complicated, and intricate, that practically, the knowledge may be very little useful. Malthus thinks it monstrous that I should say labour had fallen in value, when perhaps the quantity of necessaries allotted to the labourer may be really increased. I attempted to use the Socratic method of arguing with him, and had nearly succeeded in shewing him that he really admitted my proposition, when he became as cautious, and wary, as the man whom Franklin had often refuted by that method. I asked him whether if corn could be produced with a great deal less labour, it would not fall in value as well as in price:—he answered yes, it would so fall. I then asked him whether with such a fall in the price of corn, labour would continue to be permanently at the same money price, and to this question he would not give me any positive answer. Now if corn fell 50 pc.ᵗ, and labour only fell 5, my proposition would be made out, because in all those mediums which had not varied in value, according to his own admission, labour would have fallen in value, although the labourer would enjoy a greater abundance of commodities. But you will be sick of all this, and will wish that I had forgot that I might address you at any length I pleased, since I could make use of Mr. Hume's privelege.—

I did not expect that you would be satisfied with Say's notes.—Some of them are ingenious, but he does not grapple with the real question in dispute,—he makes a shew of answering it, but he completely evades it. In his note on gross and net revenue[1]—he begs the question;—he first supposes that a part of the revenue received by the labourers

[1] In the French ed. of Ricardo's *Principles*, vol. II, pp. 222–4.

is more than their wants require—that is to say is net
revenue, and then he says that there is an advantage in
increasing the gross revenue altho' you do not thereby
increase the net revenue. In what I said on that subject I
expressly guarded myself, by saying, that Adam Smith had
not argued this question on a supposition that by increasing
the number of labourers you were increasing the number of
human beings susceptible of and enjoying happiness,—but
as it regarded the increase of the disposable wealth and power
of the country; and yet M Say answers my observations by
saying that there would be a greater number of human beings
enjoying happiness.[1] I have left it to Murray to do as he
pleases respecting translating the notes, and adding them to
the end of the work. If they were much more able I should
both from my wish to have the subject well discussed, and
from a feeling of pride in having a distinguished and able
adversary have liked to have made them as public as I could,
although it might have been thought that I had the worst of
the argument,—but now it is quite indifferent to me. I think
of making no other answer to M Say's observations but that
of remarking that he has left my main position respecting
the regulator of rent unanswered.[2] Is it not wonderful that
after Malthus publication on rent, after acknowledging the
same principles as I contend for, he should now agree with
Say, and contend that there is no corn grown in any country
which does not pay a rent?—he says that he committed an
error in saying otherwise, and that I have followed him in it,
and by the conclusions which I draw from it, have proved
the incorrectness of the principle. His book is delayed, I
believe, partly at Murray's suggestion of the time of year
now fixed upon being the most favourable time for publication, and partly, I think, from doubts which he cannot help

[1] Cp. above, I, 348-9, nn.   [2] Above, I, 413, n.

28 Dec. 1818 entertaining of the correctness of his opinions. So much for
Polit. Econ.

On the question of Reform I shall not have much more to
say, and therefore you will be relieved from the distasteful
employment of looking over my meagre performances.
Malthus used one or two arguments here which I think I
successfully answered at the time, but I shall be more satisfied
to see his objection, and my endeavor at refutation, on paper.
I wish too to consider, and on that point I must have the
advantage of some conversation with you, whether, if reform
was obtained in such a degree as to make the House of
Commons the real and efficient representatives of the people,
the monarchical part of our constitution would be in any
danger of being overthrown. Are there not great and manifest advantages attending a monarchical executive, which
would secure the preference of that form, if we had to
establish for the first time the Government of this country?
Being established, would not the evil of change—the known
sentiments of the people—the powers which the monarch
has of appointing to all places of honour and profit—of
dissolving parliament and some other of his prerogatives,
which he would not be disposed to yield without a struggle,
make it almost certain that the only change which would
result from a reform would be a change in the administration
of the Government, and not in its essential forms? At the
time that Magna Charta was obtained—when the star
chamber was abolished, and other priveleges obtained for
the people, in the reign of Charles Ist —when the executive
Government was more strictly restrained at the revolution,
no attempt was made to alter the form of the Government,
but in the progress of knowledge the people became more
sensible of the fences necessary for their security. Is it not
the same now? Do we not see that we want additional

securities—that some which we thought would prove effectual have not proved so—that we have new dangers to guard against, and perhaps also that we have improved in knowledge and in the science of Government, which enable us not only to discover the causes to which we may attribute misgovernment, but also suggest to us the remedy? Are not all these improvements perfectly compatible with the preservation of the monarchy? and not only compatible, but is there any one symptom of the reformers generally being republicans in disguise, who call out indeed for reform, but mean revolution? If they really were so, I should not abate my wish for reform, because I should be sure that if we had a good and wise legislature, no countenance would be given to any project which had revolution for its object. I should be sure that any end which they would pursue, would be that of the happiness of the community, and with the accomplishment of that end I should be satisfied.

It would be of great use if our adversaries could be convinced not only that good men would pursue good ends, but that those good ends were precisely the same as they deem good. They cannot believe that if power be given to overturn, it will not be used for that purpose. They might as consistently argue that a man's hands should be tied because if they were loose, he would have the power of doing mischief to himself and others.—I must have your opinion not only on the best means by which we may be finally enabled to obtain a good government, but also supposing the means obtained what measures a conscientious legislator would recommend as constituting the good government sought.—

I am glad that you approved of my answer to Trower,— my strength lay in his weakness. I do not find that I manage my arguments with any improved skill; and at our County meeting when I heard the Duke of Beaufort falter and pause,

28 Dec. 1818 so painfully, that no one thought he could proceed, in proposing the Address to the Prince Regent, I thought of the
probability of my being placed in a similar awkward predicament, if I ventured to listen to the sound of my own voice.

I am glad to hear that your health is improving, and my
pleasure is increased in finding that you attribute it to my
brother's advice. When we admit the principle that different
professions should be represented in parliament, we will use
our interest to have him returned as representative of the
medical profession.—

I have received a letter from Mess. Bleasdale my attornies
—they have at last received the Abstract of Lord P.'s title
but not in a perfect state,—they are promised to have the
deficiency supplied immediately. To shew you that the 6 pc^t
interest could not be Mr. Brougham's inference only, I will
copy a passage from their letter. "We understand from
Lord Portalington's solicitor that it had been agreed in case
the interest was regularly paid in London by a day to be
fixed it was to be only 5 pc^t, but otherwise it was to be 6." [1]
Unless guaranteed by bankers here I would rather receive
6 pc^t in Ireland, but the original agreement was 6 pc^t payable
in England.—

About 3 years ago I was very much pleased by reading
Turgot's life and works.[2] He was a reformer,—but although
the abuses which he wished to remove were most con-
vincingly demonstrated by him to be such, what difficulties
had he not to encounter and for how short a time was he
entrusted with the power of being useful! At least this is the
impression that remains with me. He was a very able
political economist, considering the prejudices of his time.—
I have read Millar with great pleasure.[3] I have been reading

---

[1] This letter, dated 22 Dec. 1818,   [2] See above, p. 365, n. 1.
is in R.P.   [3] Cp. above, p. 197, n. 1.

Montesquieu's Spirit of Laws, I expect to see something 28 Dec. 1818
better on that subject bye and bye. His views are liberal but
he speaks too much in favour of Glory and of pure monarchy,
—and the virtue which he makes the active principle in
Republics is represented too much as a disinterested principle
of action.   Yʳˢ truly
                              DAVID RICARDO

We were all very much affected here by the perusal of
poor Romilly's will. Every thing tends to shew that he was
an upright, excellent man. His kindness and attention to his
relations were amiable features in his character.—

299. McCULLOCH TO RICARDO[1]
[Answered by 300]

My Dear Sir   Edinburgh 27ᵗʰ Decr 1818

    I herewith send you the sheets of the article [2] to which 27 Dec. 1818
I alluded in my last letter to you. I hope they will meet with
your approbation—

    I am very glad to perceive from Murrays advertisement
that you do not intend bringing out the new edition of your
great work in two volumes[3]—It is infinitely better as it is—
In my opinion every new edition of Malthus Essay has been
decidedly inferior to that which preceded it; and this I think
chiefly from his manifest decision to increase the bulk of the
book in order (for there can be no other reason) to make it
sell for a greater sum[4]—

[1] MS in *R.P.*
[2] The review of *Economical and Secure Currency*. See above, p. 354, n. 1.
[3] 'Mr. Murray, Albemarle-street, will publish the following Works in the course of December: ... The Principles of Political Economy and Taxation. By David Ricardo, Esq. A New Edition 8vo.' (*Monthly Literary Advertiser*, 10 Dec. 1818.)
[4] *Essay on Population*, 1798, 1 vol. 8vo; 1803, 1 vol. 4to; 1806 and 1807, 2 vols. 8vo; 1817, 3 vols. 8vo; but 1826, 2 vols. 8vo.

27 Dec. 1818   I have promised to write the article *Exchange* for the Supplement to the Encyclopaedia Brittanica, and, if it is not presuming too much on your kindness, I will submit the proof sheets for your correction—Could you inform me whether Mr Mushet in any subsequent edition of his pamphlet, corrected his table of the exchange between London and Hamburgh in the manner pointed out in your reply to Mr Bosanquet?[1]—As Encyclopaedias ought to be rendered as complete as possible for reference it would be of great importance to give a correct table of the course of exchange between London and Hamburgh or Paris, for forty or fifty years back—

I am afraid you will be thinking that I am becoming a very troublesome correspondent, but the subject must plead my excuse—

Have the goodness to remember me to your brother and believe to be

My Dear Sir
Yours faithfully
J. R. McCulloch

David Ricardo Esqre

[1] See above, III, 168–9.

INDEX OF CORRESPONDENTS
1816–1818

denotes letters not previously published